SILENT COUNT

Jim Overmier

Cover and interior design by:
Rob Wood / wrh-illustration.com
Printed in the United States of America
First Printing, 2013

ISBN-10: 0-9912947-1-8
ISBN-13: 978-0-9912947-1-8

www.silentcount-thebook.com

To my wife, Mary-Ellen, and our two sons, Mark and Tyler, whose own personal sacrifices helped make it possible for me to, not only coach football for so many years, but to also write this book. I love you.

Contents

Preface

Shortly after accepting the position of quarterback coach at Gallaudet University, I telephoned one of my best friends, Gary Morrow, to share my decision with him. Gary had always been an incredible source of creative ideas for me, and during that conversation he came up with yet another. He suggested that I maintain a daily journal so that I could one day write about what he felt was going to be a really interesting experience. And so I've done just that.

But why write a book? Some will think I chose to write this book to chronicle the episodic nature of coaching college football. Not true. Some may conclude that I'm attempting to bring to light the social adversities faced by the deaf community. Not so. And others may, in their hearts, believe that I've penned this story just to demonstrate how God works through His faithful servants. Again, that wouldn't be the case. While I'd consider it a blessing if God were to use my literary skills for His own glory, it wasn't the motivating factor in me telling this particular story. Although I wouldn't argue the point that perhaps it should have been.

The primary reason that I've written this book isn't so complex. I simply want to share the story of my unique and wonderfully entertaining experience as a football coach at Gallaudet University. There are but a handful of men with such experience on their coaching resumes, even fewer who were neither deaf nor hearing impaired. I'm one of those men. Helping deaf young athletes to achieve their dream of playing college football was quite a rewarding journey, and one that I believe you will enjoy reading about.

*

The transition from high school football coach to college football coach probably happens quite frequently throughout the country, though usually for men much younger than I. But it rarely happens in the way I'll describe. Gallaudet University is a school for the advanced education of the deaf and hard of hearing, and it's the only such school in the world. That itself would be enough to make this story interesting. However, what makes my tale particularly unique is that I'm not deaf or hard of hearing.

One spring morning in 2007, while sitting in front of a computer at my office, I was perusing an internet website dedicated to local high school football. I was a high school football coach, and had been for more than a decade. Like lots of local high school coaches, I checked the site, and its message boards, on a regular basis. It was a great way to see what was being said about your football program by other coaches and fans from around the state. It was also a convenient place to check on game scores and prognostications as well. Anyway, I came upon a help wanted ad placed in one of the message boards by Gallaudet University's new head coach, Ed Hottle. He was looking to hire a quarterback coach. Now, you've often heard that God works in mysterious ways? Well, I guess sometimes He uses the Internet.

You see, I wasn't looking for another coaching position that day. My current coaching job at Severna Park High School in Maryland was perfect for me. We had great kids from solid families and communities, a good coaching staff, and a supportive administration. Plus, it was only a fifteen-minute drive from my home. But coaching quarterbacks was my specialty and, naturally, the ad piqued my interest. I was very intrigued by the possibility of me coaching college football, especially at my advanced age. Many, if not most, high school coaches, aspire to one day coach at the collegiate level. I was no different. And so mostly out of curiosity, I called Coach Hottle and spoke with him at some length about football, and specifically, the job. At the conclusion of our conversation, he offered me an invitation to meet with him on campus for an interview. I accepted his offer.

Prologue

A
S I drove up to the small gatehouse at the main entrance of Gallaudet University, the world's only university specifically designed to educate deaf students, a security guard emerged from within the house to greet me. He was a small, black man with a big smile. He didn't appear to have a gun, or a nightstick, or even a small can of mace anywhere on his person. I'd thought again that it was odd that the Gallaudet University security guards didn't carry a weapon. After all, the campus was situated in a very tough part of Washington, D.C. where crime was a daily occurrence.

Although he carried no weapon, there were two noticeable hearing aids, one behind each ear. From each hearing aid came a tubular extension that curled from the back of the ear forward, connecting to a flat, disc-like part of the device that sat inside the opening of the ear. He greeted me with the same flashy smile that he'd given me each day for the past week, and waved me through with a hearty "good morning" in sign language. I say hearty because deaf people generally show a good deal of expression when they sign. It's a huge part of their communication process. Usually, I'd return the greeting in the same manner which meant extending the back of my right hand from my mouth toward the ground, like blowing a kiss, and then raising it back up with my left hand resting in my right elbow. It's a little tough to do while driving and you have to look at the person to whom you're signing. Not a good idea to sign and drive, though most of the deaf people that I know do it frequently.

On this particular morning, I'd planned to demonstrate my developing ASL (American Sign Language) skills by signing to the guard that I was an assistant football coach headed to the field house. ASL is a system of standardized hand gestures and movements used by the deaf to communicate quickly and easily. After a week of coaching football at Gallaudet, I'd learned most of my signing skills from the players, a little from the staff, and some from the Internet. I was eager to try it out on someone other than a football player, coach, or trainer.

"Good morning," I signed and smiled. "I'm an assistant football coach and I'm going to the field house." I communicated via several gesticulations of my hands and was feeling pretty good about the effort and my ability to now communicate in a different language. My smile broadened.

The guard began to laugh.

"What?" I signed by drawing my right index finger across the palm of my left hand as I also mouthed the word.

He laughed a bit harder, the palms of his hands extended outward, his head nodded back and forth as he leaned toward me. "Coach," he exclaimed in a strong, but noticeably untrained, voice that originated from deep in his throat. "You said that you're a shitty football coach going to the field house."

I'd screwed it up.

"Don't worry," he said, "I know that you're not a shitty football coach." He smiled and waved me through the gate, toward the field house.

When you sign the word "assistant" you make a fist with both of your hands, extend the thumb of your right hand and place it into the bottom of the fist on your left, right into the bend of your left 'pinky'. Leave it there, at least for a second, and gently push your fist upward. It gets a little tricky when you separate your hands, though. If you pull the thumb down and away from your left fist too quickly, you're actually signing a certain four letter word meaning "excrement," though I still don't know what the correlation is that would render the signs so similar. I guess it's similar to speech. Sometimes, it's all about how things are said.

The guard was still chuckling when I looked back in my rear view mirror.

1

The Drive to Gallaudet

I t's pretty much a straight shot to Washington, D.C. on U.S. Route 50 West from the quiet community of Crofton, Maryland where my family and I reside. Crofton is also where I own and operate a small passenger transportation service called Coach & Courier, a business that I began in 1995. With the business, I had made the trip into the District hundreds of times, a drive that would normally take about 30 minutes without traffic. When you cross over the Anacostia River and into Washington, D.C. from Maryland, the change in scenery is sudden and dramatic. The air even smells different. Within just a few minutes you're travelling along litter strewn streets lined with dilapidated businesses and abandoned vehicles. There are homeless beggars and street peddlers at most intersections. There is some urban renewal as you enter Washington, D.C. through its northeast corridor, but for the most part it's a sad pictorial of what was a vibrant part of the city.

The scenic backdrop of the U.S. Capitol Building, the Washington Monument, and other federal architecture just a few blocks away, reminds you that you're in our nation's capital. Some of those structures are indeed awe inspiring. But as you cautiously drive along the aged railroad tracks that run adjacent to New

York Avenue, it's hard not to consider the dismay that a first-time tourist might experience when unexpectedly surrounded by such blight. Gallaudet University is located in that same part of northeast Washington, D.C. If the area surrounding the campus isn't the worst in the city, then it's certainly right next to it.

The condition of the roadways and thoroughfares throughout, however, are uniformly horrid. In fact, it only took a few visits to the campus early that summer before the front end of my car began to "chatter" terribly. Was it the struts? Was it the brakes? Was it a motor mount? I didn't know for sure. But, if I was to have a flat tire, I knew that I was committed to an exit plan of rimming my way out of town. Before I'd even arrived at the campus of Gallaudet to interview for the job of quarterbacks coach, I'd begun to debate which of my cars I'd drive into and out of the city: my 1993 Chrysler mini-van or my 1997 Lexus sedan? Was the van in good enough shape to get me to and from the school safely? It was a tough decision.

Should your car break down in northeast D.C., it could easily become a matter of life and death, literally. About a year earlier, a close friend of mine had been shot in the back while refueling his car at a gas station just a mile or so from Gallaudet. A former Secret Service Agent, and still an armed employee for another federal agency, he was attacked in the light of day and in full sight of all nearby. Several years later, he has yet to recover completely from his wounds and ensuing infections. The culprit was never arrested. I figured if that could happen to Steve, armed with a powerful hand gun himself, it could certainly happen to me, armed only with a whistle.

My first opportunity to visit Gallaudet University occurred in May of 2007. On that particular spring morning, I had an eleven o'clock interview scheduled with Head Football Coach, Ed Hottle. Although I thought that I had left myself plenty of drive time for the trip, a few wrong turns had left me with little time to spare by the time I finally came upon the school. The campus was surrounded by a black, steel picket fence about eight feet high and finding a way in proved to be a bit challenging. The first gate that I approached was closed off with long, concrete barriers. So was the second.

I continued to navigate my way around the perimeter of the university. I eventually made it all the way around to the opposite side of the campus where I approached yet another set of gates. Beyond them I could see goal posts, a scoreboard, and several athletic fields. I felt for sure that I was now getting close to where I needed to be. However, those gates had been barricaded as well. And so I continued down the street until I reached the intersection of West Virginia Avenue and Florida Avenue, the western boundary of the school's campus.

There were a few cars in front of me as I waited for the traffic light to change and I had a moment to survey the general area. The streets immediately surrounding the campus were congested with row homes of varying architectural styles, but nearly all constructed of either brick or mortar. Most of them had steel bars across the windows and doors. Some of them had been recently renovated and were quite attractive, but most were pretty run down. In a strange sort of way, it was the nice homes that seemed to look out of place, as if they didn't belong in that neighborhood. Interestingly enough, it turned out that many of the students at Gallaudet actually lived in those homes, renting out a room or sharing the unit with their friends and roommates. Mostly Caucasian and toting backpacks and book bags, the students who walked along the street appeared to be out of place as well, just like the nicer homes.

The traffic light turned green and I proceeded right onto Florida Avenue where I quickly came upon an entrance into the school that was open. It turned out to be the main entrance to Gallaudet University. I drove up to the right of a small gate house beside which stood a security guard.

I stopped my car as I neared the guard. I could tell by his face that he was preparing to "speak" with someone who wasn't deaf. I guess that he could tell by my own face that I wasn't sure if he was deaf. I noticed the radio on his shoulder and a hearing aid over each of his ears. I assumed that he could indeed hear.

"Good morning," he said to me.

"Good morning," I replied. "I'm looking for the field house."

"It's the second building on your right, sir," he said as he smiled and pointed down the road just a bit. "You can park in the garage behind it." Though he seemed to struggle with his voice, he otherwise spoke pretty clearly.

"Thank you," I said as I drove off. He nodded.

I found the field house after just a few moments. In front of the doors to the field house was a large, brown sculpture of a bison. It seemed to me like that was a pretty good landmark to look for when trying to find the building. He could have told me about the sculpture, I thought, since the building itself didn't resemble a typical field house. In reality, it didn't appear to be much different from any of the other nearby buildings.

I drove into the lower level of the garage, parked, and glanced around the garage for a second. There were steel bars across the openings between the floors that led to the streets off campus. There was an emergency contact point a few parking spaces away toward the stairwell leading to the upper level. I locked the doors to my car and headed up the steps. Walking from the coolness of the lower level below and out onto the bright sunny sidewalk above, the warmth on my face felt good. Although it was my first time interviewing for a college coaching job, I was very confident in my ability to coach the game at any level. I just hoped to be able to convey that confidence to Coach Hottle. And so, as I walked along the side of the field house and approached the bison sculpture out front, I asked the Lord for a little additional support that day.

2

The Interview

The walk through the doors of the field house and into the main lobby was like entering a portal from one world to another. Without the sound of traffic on the streets outside, the helicopters in the skies above, or the construction work going on around the campus, there was nearly complete silence.

It began to sink in that I wasn't likely to hear music coming from a desk radio or the broadcast of news, weather, and traffic updates from local radio stations. There would be little, if any, idle office chatter, and most conspicuously absent would be the sound of telephones ringing or being answered. And there wasn't. From an office off of the lobby I heard the sound of paper being stapled and that was about it. Unable to quickly locate a building directory, and short on time, I walked toward that office doorway to ask for directions to Coach Hottle's office. I wasn't sure just how I was going to ask for those directions though.

I smiled as I poked my head inside to find a young, blonde -haired woman working feverishly at her desktop computer. I began instinctively to ask for directions, but stopped quickly as I noticed her slight smile fade quickly to an expression of concern. She held her left index finger up toward me, then turned and motioned for the assistance of another woman seated at a desk across the room. Looking back at me, she smiled again and shrugged her shoulders slightly. The other lady, a well-dressed, middle-aged black woman, walked over to me to offer her assistance.

"Hi. May I help you?" she asked.

"Yes," I said, "I'm sorry to bother you, but I have an appointment with Coach Hottle of the football team. Where might I find his office?"

"Well, it's downstairs. Are you familiar at all with the building?"

"No, ma'am," I shook my head and frowned. "It's my first time here."

"No worries," she said. "I'll take you there. It's a somewhat difficult office to locate."

And off we went. I waved back at the young woman in the office as we began our walk across the lobby. She smiled, waved back, and returned to typing on her keyboard. I followed the lady across the lobby to a stairwell where I held the door open for her.

"Thank you," she said as she led me down the stairs. "Are you a football coach or a sales rep, or both?"

"Coach," I replied.

"Well good for you. Will you be coaching here at Gallaudet?"

"Perhaps," I said as she looked back over her shoulder at me. "I mean it depends on the interview, of course."

"Of course," she smiled. "We can sure use all the good football coaches we can get."

At the bottom of the stairwell, we walked through a large wooden door and into a long, plain corridor of white, cinder block walls. She led me through what seemed like a maze of corridors, in fact, each scarcely decorated, if decorated at all, and somewhat dimly lit. We passed what appeared to be a few empty classrooms and several storage rooms along the way.

"Here we go," she said as we approached a double set of wooden doors on our left. "Good luck, Coach." She rapped firmly on one of the doors and then turned the door knob, opening it slightly.

"Yeah, c'mon in," called out a man's strong voice.

"Coach Hottle? I have a gentleman here to see you," she said.

"Thank you," I heard him say as she stepped away from the door and back into the hallway, allowing me entrance into the office.

"Thanks again," I said to her softly.

She smiled at me one more time and went back the way we'd come.

"C'mon in," Coach Hottle said as I entered the room. He was seated behind a large desk with his feet propped upon it, a white visor on backward, and leaning back into a black, leather chair. He held his cell phone against his right ear and waved to me with his left.

"You Jim?" he said, peering over his eyeglasses. He stood to shake my hand. Coach Hottle wasn't a tall man, maybe about five feet eight inches, but pretty stocky in build.

"I am," I said as I extended my own hand to shake his. His grip was firm, which didn't surprise me.

"I'll be right with you," he said as he nodded and motioned for me to close the door. He sat back down, lightly tapping upon a few of the keys on his computer keyboard.

"Take your time, Coach," I said as I turned and closed the door. I took a seat in one of the two chairs in front of his desk and glanced around the room. It wasn't the office one would expect of a head college football coach. It was more of a storage room converted into an office. The high ceiling some ten to fifteen feet overhead was actually the floor of the basketball court in the gym above. There were two additional doors behind his desk, which led into the equipment manager's office and maintenance facilities. This was a makeshift office for Coach Hottle and his football program. He was fairly new on the scene at Gallaudet himself; this was just his third season at the helm. He'd been the main inspiration and driving force behind turning the university's football program around and preparing it to play in its inaugural season as a NCAA Division III team. Up until now, they'd competed solely as a football club against other clubs, community colleges, and junior varsities. In fact, I'd played against Gallaudet a few times myself, as quarterback at Anne Arundel Community College back in 1979.

Like the hallways outside, there wasn't anything fancy on the walls. There was a white dry-erase board to my right and a set of crude depth charts on the back of the twin doors behind me, one for the offense and one for the defense. A few tall bookshelves behind his desk looked to be of surplus quality and, as one might expect, stocked with books about football drills, strategies, and coaching philosophies. A bunch of binders and notebooks also lined the shelves, as well as a few small cans of chewing tobacco. Along the top shelf were several framed team photographs of schools where he'd previously coached, including his alma mater, Frostburg State University, which is located in Western Maryland. There were also documents and team photographs from Dennison University in Ohio, Delaware Wesley, and his most recent coaching position, Calvert High School in Maryland.

One picture in particular managed to catch my attention. It was a framed photograph of a bald-headed man posing in a football uniform, but I didn't recognize the uniform, or the player. The man was striking a defensive posture, leaning slightly forward and flexing his arms before him like a gorilla. But, instead of a mean, tough-guy look, the man was flashing his pearly whites in grand fashion. I thought at first that it might be a joke photograph because the man in the photo looked to be a little too old to play football. And he had bulging eyeballs like the late actor, Marty Feldman. I squinted to get a better look at the photograph, somewhat curious and genuinely amused.

"Okay," Ed said, wrapping up his call. "Thanks. I'll get back to you. Uh-huh."

Ed hung up and saw me looking at the photograph on the wall. He turned the visor around on his head so that the bill was now above his brow.

"Is he a former Gallaudet player?" I asked, pointing my index finger toward the photograph.

"Nah," Ed chuckled, "He's just a guy I know. We used to coach together." Ed sat up in his seat and leaned forward, interlocking his fingers, and resting his hands upon his desk.

"Hmm," I smiled, "pretty interesting picture."

"Pretty interesting guy," Ed grinned as he looked back at the photograph. "So thanks for coming down. Did you have any problems finding the place?"

"Not much," I lied, "I've been down this way a few times."

"Good, 'cause it can be a real bitch getting down here." Ed then nodded toward the doors behind me. "When we're behind closed doors we can talk to each other normally, but outside those doors we have to sign while we talk, okay? The people around here are pretty sensitive about these things."

"Okay," I nodded.

"Really," he continued, "most of the administrative people on campus don't even like it when we speak and sign at the same time. So, unless you know how to sign…"

I shook my head that I did not.

"We'll just keep the doors closed for now," he said as he gestured toward the closed doors behind me. "But, don't worry. You'll pick it up pretty quick." He slid his chair back away from his desk, "If you want to coach here, you'll pick it up pretty fast. Let me put it that way."

Ed rose to his feet and took a few steps toward the bookshelf, looking for something. The back of his neck was sunburned. His shoulders were fairly broad and his back long and square. The bottom of his baggy, navy blue, mesh shorts dropped to just below his knees, making his legs appear to be disproportionately shorter than they actually were. He reached up onto the shelf, pulled down a DVD, and inserted it into the combination DVD/television set which sat on a small table next to my chair.

"Check this out and I'll be right back, ok?"

"Sure," I said. I adjusted my chair to gain a better viewing angle of the small television.

"I'll be right back," he repeated as he opened the door. He paused for a moment and looked at the two depth charts on the back of the doors. After looking to the left, and then to the right, he slid one of the names on the offensive depth over to the defensive chart.

"You won't have him. I need that guy this year," he said and then left the room, closing the door behind him.

The DVD started. It was a short, sports documentary produced by ESPN about the resurgence of the Gallaudet Football Program. There were highlight clips from the last few seasons, including Ed's first in 2005. The clips featured dark, ominous clouds over the school's small football stadium, Hotchkiss Field. On it played two football teams, battling one another on a sloppy, wet, and muddy field. The narrator's voice was deep; he spoke without inflection.

"The sound of football at Gallaudet University," said the narrator. Silence fell upon the screen as the highlights rolled on, players running, tackling, and diving upon one another. You could hear the sounds of the crowd, the grunting of the players, and the screaming of the sideline coaches, but then suddenly, you couldn't. It was very effective.

The DVD continued and I watched with interest. It detailed the 2005 season of the Bison and focused on the adversity its players and coaches faced. Several players were interviewed individually in a darkened room before a dimly lit backdrop. As they signed, their words appeared at the bottom of the screen and a man's voice spoke on the player's behalf. They offered their goals and expectations and their desire to compete and play the game of football at the collegiate level. Several of those players were still on the team, and I'd come to know them well, including our star quarterback, Jason Coleman.

Of course Coach Hottle was interviewed, too. Neatly groomed and without his spectacles, Ed spoke of the anxiety in the locker room and on the campus as they prepared to expand the program beyond what it had been. He explained how the main difference between Gallaudet's athletes and those of other universities was that the other schools had more athletes who could hear. No news there. What one could derive from the documentary was that the heart of the athlete at Gallaudet was no different than anywhere else. In fact, as I'd learn, these kids may have had just a little bit more.

While football had initially begun at Gallaudet in 1894, the school had had only one winning season in its history. In 2005, Coach Hottle's first year at the school, the team would go undefeated, winning all nine of its games. They started the 2006 season with three straight victories and finished the year with six wins and just two losses. They actually played a few teams with NCAA Division III credentials, too, including Becker College of Worcester, Massachusetts, and SUNY Maritime from just outside of New York City. And now, here they were about to earn those very same credentials for themselves. The 2007 season that would begin in just a few months included games against eight legitimate college football programs.

The DVD presentation lasted about ten or twelve minutes and it wasn't long after it concluded that Ed walked back in holding a few papers in his hand. He laid the papers on his desk and sat down behind it.

"What did you think?" he asked.

"Well done," I said. "It was very interesting."

"Do you remember the part where they filmed me from behind, walking down the darkened hallway?"

"Uh huh."

"Looks like I'm headed for the locker room or someplace important, right?" he smiled.

"Yeah."

"I was actually looking for the bathroom so I could take a fucking piss," he laughed.

I chuckled, although I was a little taken aback by Ed's choice of words. But I'd been around enough football coaches to know that certain words, like the "F" word, were quite common in many coaches' everyday vocabulary, as was a general lack of eloquence. I seldom used the word, myself, except maybe as an angry exclamation here and there. As a high school coach, foul language was something you had to be very careful about and refrain from using. We didn't tolerate it from our players, the team managers, or even our cheerleaders for that matter. Nevertheless, it didn't bother me too much when another adult used it in a private conversation, although it always generated some level of personal discomfort. Maybe Ed just used it a little more freely at Gallaudet because no one ever heard him, I don't know. I also didn't know ASL for the "F" word, not yet anyway, but I was pretty sure that it existed and that Ed probably already knew it himself.

We then talked for several minutes about our past coaching experiences and a little bit about how coaching affected our families. While I explained that I had a twenty-three year old daughter in Rhode Island and two young sons still in the house, Ed mentioned that he'd met his wife when he was a graduate assistant coaching at Frostburg. She'd been a student. Now she was at home in their house near Annapolis and several months pregnant with their third child. She was due to give birth during the season.

"I told her she better have the fucking kid during our bye week," he joked. A bye week was a week when the team was not scheduled to play a game.

I forced a small smile and looked down.

"Hey, I'm a football coach. It's football season. They understand that now," he said, meaning his family.

Ed continued to fill me in on the difficulties of coaching in a deaf environment and the many challenges I'd face as a quarterbacks coach at Gallaudet. I wasn't quite sure if we had actually begun the interview or not, or if our discussion was part of the interview process. So I just went right on along with the conversation. He talked about several of the returning players and the expectations he had for them that season. Although he spoke directly about the team's undefeated season a few years back, he was noticeably vague about his goal for the team this season, their first as an NCAA Division III team. When I asked him how many games he thought they'd win this year, he responded with a question of his own.

"How many games do I *expect* to win this season?" he asked.

"Yes," I said.

"All of them," he looked me in the eye. "I expect to win all of them."

Ed stood up from behind his desk and invited me to join him on a tour of the facilities. I followed him back out into the hallway. Our first stop was just around the corner, the equipment room window where all of the athletes picked up their gear, uniforms, towels, and such. This is also where they'd turn in their dirty uniforms for cleaning and where I'd eventually retrieve our game balls and a scrub brush to rub them down with. Kris Gould, the university's equipment and facilities manager, stood on the other side of the chest-high window.

"Kris? This is Coach Overmier," Ed said out loud as he signed. "He's a quarterback coach, might be coaching with us this fall."

Kris was about the same height as Ed, but with a much slighter build. His short, wavy, light-brown hair framed a long face and a broad smile. He approached the window and offered me his hand.

"Nice to meet you, Coach," he said with a little drawl in his voice.

"Nice to meet you, too," I said. As it turned out, Kris was hard of hearing and relied heavily on the hearing aid above his ear. His voice was strong and clear, though, and a little sterner than I'd expected. He was about my age, maybe a little younger, in his mid-forties.

"Kris is the main guy around here. He takes care of all of us, the building, and all of our equipment," Ed said. "We couldn't get anything done around here without him."

Kris smiled.

My first impression was that Kris was probably a great equipment manager. His office was tidy and organized. Football uniforms were neatly stacked on a long table, towels and laundry bags folded on the shelves, and various types of athletic equipment stored in their proper places.

We shared a bit of small talk; Ed signed to Kris on my behalf a few times here and there, just in case anyone was in the area who might be offended. Kris didn't seem to mind that I didn't know sign language, and after a short time he didn't bother to sign when speaking to me. I guess he figured that I didn't understand it anyway. Throughout the season, as we got to know one another, I'd attempt to sign as I spoke to him. Kris signed along with me to help me.

"You from the area?" he asked.

"My family and I live in Crofton," I said. "My folks live on the Eastern Shore."

"Oh, mine, too."

Kris's parents lived on Maryland's Eastern Shore, about an hour and a half drive across the Chesapeake Bay Bridge. He visited them frequently. Single, he spent a lot of time working at the field house, partly due to his great work ethic and partly because he lived on campus. In addition to his salary, the university provided Kris with living quarters just a stone's throw away from the field house. He also had dining privileges at the dining hall.

"All right, sir," Ed said as he casually saluted Kris with a two finger, Boy Scout salute, "I've got to run across campus shortly and I wanted to show Jim around before I did that." Again, Ed signed as he spoke.

"Well, I hope you come on board, brother," Kris smiled and again shook my hand.

"Thanks, Kris," I returned the smile. "Hope to see you again soon."

"Me, too." he said.

As we walked away, Ed patted his right thigh with the palm of his right hand. Some change jingled in his pocket. Suddenly, I was very aware of sounds that I'd always taken for granted.

"Kris is a good man," Ed said in a low voice, "a pain in the ass sometimes, but a good man."

I followed Ed out of the building, through a nearby set of glass double doors. Just below street level, we walked up a concrete ramp that wound up and around the field house to the stadium. At the top of the ramp, Ed stopped, put his hands on his hips, and peered out across the football field.

"This is it. Hotchkiss Field," he said. "It's kind of cool." He looked over the top of his glasses at me. "We come out of the building, walk up the ramp, and run right out onto the field."

The field was a little ragged, worn out pretty well down the middle. It wasn't the quality playing surface that one would expect at the college level, but then again, until now, Gallaudet had only been a club football program. Ed sensed that I might not be too impressed.

"We're working on it. It is what it is. I hope to get an artificial surface one day, but for now it's what we've got." Ed signed as he spoke, but I gathered that he wasn't signing everything that he said out loud. "We practice on the small field over there as well as in the stadium." He pointed beyond the football field to a small grassy area on the other side of the running track. The practice area lay between the backstop of the baseball diamond and the fencing around some tennis courts.

"If that's what you've got, that's what you've got," I said. I looked back toward the stadium. It wasn't so much a stadium as it was an elaborate set of aluminum grandstands set in tiered levels of concrete. There were no press boxes or anything, no concessions area, no big screen televisions, and obviously no public address or loudspeaker systems. It was simply grandstand seating with a single entry portal, and maybe twenty rows of aluminum bleachers that extended the length of the field. Above the portal jetted a concrete cantilever that provided an overhead covering, but for only a few spectators.

"How many people will the stadium hold?"

"About twenty-five hundred," Ed said, looking up at me from under his visor, "which is about twenty-one hundred more than we usually need." He tilted his head toward the roadway that passed by both the field house and stadium. We began to walk along the walkway toward the front of the field house. "Hopefully we can get some lights next year as well," he said.

I looked back at the stadium. There were no overhead field lights.

"You're working on it?" I said.

"I'm working on it," he said as he bumped his fisted hands on top of one another. "Like everything else around here, I'm working on it." Again, he made the gesture. The fist bumping was ASL for 'working on it'.

I got the impression that Ed wasn't terribly happy with the current facilities at Gallaudet. I also began to wonder if he'd jumped in over his head or if he just wasn't satisfied with the school's level of commitment to supporting a Division III football program. Either way, I was sensing some frustration on his part with the way some things were going on campus and with the Athletic Department in particular. And that's where we ended up, in the Athletic Director's office at the far corner of the field house's main level.

Inside the AD's office, Ed signed briefly to the secretary there and then introduced me to her. Although Ed had signed his introduction, she wasn't deaf and spoke very clearly, signing as she spoke.

"Hi," she said as she signed. "It's nice to meet you." She pointed at me.

It would be the first phrase I actually learned to sign. I smiled as I watched her hands. She signed it again, slowly, for me.

"Nice," she said as she slid the palm of her right hand across the open palm of her left hand.

"Nice," I repeated and mimicked her gesture.

"To meet," she said as she touched her pointing index fingers together. Again, I did the same. She then pointed toward me directly, "you."

"Ah," I said as I repeated the hand gestures. "Nice to meet you," I finished by pointing at her, which felt funny because I'd always been taught that it wasn't polite to point at other people.

She smiled.

Ed explained to her that I was interviewing for the position of assistant football coach, quarterbacks coach to be specific, and that he was showing me around the campus. Well, at that point I knew for sure that I was well into the actual job interview. He asked her if the Athletic Director was in his office. She nodded and motioned for Ed to poke his head inside the door of the interior office. Ed peeked inside and then stepped into the office. Still standing in front of the secretary's desk, I could see Ed signing to someone away from the door. He signed for a few moments more and then a man joined Ed in the doorway.

The man was Ed's boss, Athletic Director, Jim DeStefano. DeStefano had hired Ed to get the football program up to speed so that it could be considered for NCAA participation.

"This is Jim DeStefano, our Athletic Director," Ed signed to me.

DeStefano wasn't a big man, though he stood well above Ed; he was a pleasant fellow with a rather genuine smile.

"Hello," he signed to me with a slight wave. He was deaf. I waved back and smiled. He slid his palms together, connected the tips of his index fingers, and pointed at me. I knew what he was saying and returned the gesture.

"Nice to meet you," I signed. He smiled broadly and nodded his head affirmatively as he signed to Ed. I glanced over at the secretary to see if she'd noticed my signing. She raised her eyebrows and flashed a small smile. Ed and Jim signed for a few more moments before Jim signed in my direction while Ed interpreted.

"He said that he wishes you well and hopes to see you on the field coaching the team," Ed said as Jim looked on.

"Oh," I nodded. "How do you say 'thank you?'"

Jim placed the fingers of his right hand against his lips and then brought them forward as if blowing a kiss. He'd read my lips and was demonstrating how to say 'thank you'.

I looked at Ed. He nodded and made the same gesture. I turned toward Jim and signed, "Thank you." Jim repeated the gesture. "Why is he saying 'thank you' in response to my 'thank you'?" I asked Ed.

"You're welcome," Ed said in a low, but clear voice as he passed by me on the way to the door, "it's the same sign. He's saying 'you're welcome.'"

"Oh," I said as I waved to both Jim and his secretary and followed Ed out the door. As I looked back through the glass windows of the office, I could see them smile and wave goodbye.

"Seem like nice people," I said.

"Yeah, they are," said Ed as we made our way toward the front of the field house. "They're real nice people."

As we walked, Ed spoke of how it could be frustrating to coach at Gallaudet and the need for patience when working with the deaf athletes. Oddly enough, when I called him a few weeks earlier to discuss my qualifications and availability for an interview, Ed told me that he'd left coaching high school football because he didn't have the patience to deal with the kids at that level. So I was curious to know what motivated him to cope with the frustration now. Perhaps it was a nice paycheck, or an impressive job title? But, as I'd find out along the way, Ed was in no way a patient man by nature.

We continued to talk about coaching football and how different it was to coach at Gallaudet. We exited the field house and walked into a building just across the street, the I. King Jordan

Student Academic Center. The building housed the student union, the school bookstore, a post office, and a small eatery. It was, named after the university's first deaf president. Jordan had been appointed president in 1988, the first deaf person to hold the position since the school was established in 1864. The building was a central meeting place on campus and popular with the students.

"I've got a short meeting over at College Hall and instead of leaving you in the waiting room there, why don't you hang around here and get a feel for the place?" Ed suggested.

As we walked down a few steps and into a seating area outside of the Market Place eatery, he pointed out the cafe just to our right and the school bookstore, which was at the top of the stairs in the center of the building.

"That'll work," I said.

"I'll give you a call on your cell in about fifteen minutes when I'm done, and you can meet me back at my office so we can discuss a few more things," he said and walked toward the rear exit of the building. "Otherwise, just give me a call if you need me during that time."

"Okay," I said, watching him strut out the doors. I don't know if he really had a meeting or not, or if it was his way to test my mettle, but fifteen minutes came and went and he never called back.

Meanwhile, while waiting for him to call, I walked over to a nearby table and grabbed a seat. I felt a little awkward at first, sort of like being in another country where the people around you don't speak English. Except here the language wasn't spoken, it was expressed. And, of course, everyone around the room was expressing themselves using ASL. They were very adept at it; their hands moved very fast. It was fascinating to watch people using their hands and fingers to communicate.

Most of the people in the building appeared to be students. They all seemed to be very young, as one might expect on a college campus, but there were quite a few older students as well. They were from all races and seemed to be of nationalities from all over the world. There were people milling about, reading, writing, and sitting along the walls, or at the tables outside the eatery. Some were dressed quite neatly and some, of course, were not. Some walked with backpacks and others with their hands in their pockets. While some carried on in small groups, there were others who chose to sit alone, or with a girlfriend or boyfriend, snuggling in the corner. It was a typical college atmosphere, except for one thing--there were no voices.

There was plenty of sound, of course, like shuffling feet, books being dropped, food trays, and sliding chairs. But there were no voices, no conversations to be overheard, no music, and no laughter. Occasionally, someone giggled or laughed, but it was often more like a screech, or a grunting. There were plenty of conversations going on, don't get me wrong. Usually, you only overhear conversations of those sitting somewhere nearby or those who might be speaking a little more loudly than necessary. Here, though, every conversation could be "heard," including those completely across the room, if you knew how to interpret sign language. I don't know what the rules of etiquette are regarding this, but I imagine eavesdropping is eavesdropping. And if I'd known how to sign, I could've eavesdropped on every one of those conversations, including the guy and his girlfriend fighting at the top of the stairs. I assumed that they were fighting because they seemed very angry with one another and I recognized at least one of her signs as an international sign of displeasure.

Watching the frustrated young woman, I noticed that everyone seemed to use a great deal of facial expression when signing. It was part of their communication process, and it allowed them to emphasize whatever it was they were trying to communicate with their hands. There were those who signed with a great deal of expression and animation, and others who were much more subdued. And it occurred to me that their signing styles were just a part of their personalities, similar to those of us that speak loudly, or softly, or fast, or slow.

One of the students was a rather interesting fellow who seemed to be very popular. He was a good bit older than the rest of the students, maybe in his late twenties. I guessed that he was either a graduate assistant or a professional student, someone who'd been around a while.

This guy really seemed to enjoy being the center of attention, too. He laughed and smiled, and he played around with just about everyone. They all seemed to know and like him. He was a stocky white guy with a dark complexion, possibly of Italian descent, and stood about five-foot eight inches tall. He wore a white t-shirt, blue jeans, sandals, and toted a navy blue backpack over his shoulder. What was unusual about this particular guy was his 1970's afro-style hair. He had the same hair as the television character known as Epstein in the sitcom "Welcome Back Kotter." One difference, though, was that right down the middle of his dark brown afro was a patch of white hair, which reminded me of the movie *Gremlins,* and the character, Stripe.

"There goes Stripe," I'd later chuckle to myself whenever I saw him out and about on campus, identifying the guy with the little, mischievous gremlin known by the same name.

After a few minutes of watching Stripe, the room darkened quite a bit as the sun was momentarily obscured by cloud cover. In fact, it darkened so much that I found it odd that a school building would get so dim simply because the sun went behind a few clouds. And then I noticed there weren't any lights on in the building. There were no light fixtures on anywhere in the room, in fact, not down the hallways, not in the eatery, and not in the small study lounge across the way. I thought, perhaps, that maybe the school was saving energy during the mid-day heat. When the sun reappeared the room was again awash in light.

A few moments later, a young woman descended the stairway with a small crate in her arms. Smiling broadly, she made her way to the center of the seating area and sat the crate on a table in the middle of the room, about twenty feet from where I sat. She signed to everyone in general, all around the room, smiling the entire time. I didn't know what she was signing, of course, but I recognized that she used one particular sign several times and that each time she used that sign, several of the students seemed to repeat it, including Stripe.

Stripe looked at her and placed the index fingers of his hands against his thumbs with the other three fingers extended outward, sort of like "the itsy bitsy spider," or how we might use our hands to indicate that everything was "okay." Then, he extended his arms and the "okay" signs upward and away from his body. As she walked back toward the stairs, she repeated the same gesture several more times. I watched as the students came from all around the room and began to assemble around the table with the box.

Curious, I stood and walked over toward the group. Stripe, of course, took the lead and began distributing whatever was in the box to everyone around. As I drew near, he smiled at me and offered me an ice cream sandwich. I pointed to myself, as if to ask, "for me?" He made the "okay" sign again and handed me the ice cream. I nodded in the affirmative, to say thanks, and took the ice cream. I remembered that Jim DeStefano had taught me just a few minutes ago how to sign, "thank you," and I turned back toward Stripe. I placed the fingers of my right hand near my lips and extended my hand out toward him. He smiled and nodded, offering me another ice cream. I smiled, shook my head 'no,' and returned to my seat at the table several feet away.

The young girl who had brought the ice cream downstairs worked in the school bookstore on the upper level. Apparently, the electricity was out in the building and was expected to remain off for some time. The ice cream was from the freezers in the store's frozen food section. It would soon melt. The "okay" sign is ASL for the letter "F" and when extended away from the body using both hands means "free." Well, that was a tasty way to learn a little more ASL.

After finishing off the ice cream, I meandered about the student union for a short time. As I walked, I generally kept to myself, although I did nod occasionally to some of the people that I passed by. I climbed the stairs to the second level and window shopped outside of the school bookstore for a few moments then moved down the hall into what appeared to be an instructional academic area.

For some reason, I felt a little nervous about being near the classrooms, like maybe I was in an area where only students and faculty should be. So, I did an about face and strolled back toward the commons area and out the doors to the courtyard behind the building. I checked my watch and realized that Ed's meeting was going a lot longer than he'd anticipated. About forty-five minutes had passed.

I thought about whether or not I should call him as he'd instructed me to do. But if he was still in his meeting, maybe I shouldn't. But, then again, maybe he was waiting for me to call. And so I dialed his cell phone number. It rang once.

"Ed Hottle, Head Coach, Gallaudet Football," he answered.

"Hey, Coach, it's Jim Overmier. I'm just checking in as per your instructions."

"Yeah, c'mon over, I'm back in my office."

"See you in a few minutes," I said as I hung up with a rather strange feeling about the situation. Was this part of the interview process, my ability to acclimate to the environment, or was Ed just that forgetful?

I followed the walkway around to the front of the building and across the street toward the field house. It didn't take very long to get back to the basement below the gym, but it did take a few extra minutes to follow the maze correctly to the doors of his office. I knocked.

"C'mon in," I heard Ed call out.

As I entered the office, he gestured with his head toward two chairs that sat facing his desk. I sat down.

"Did everything go alright?" he asked.

"Not a problem," I said. "I even got a free ice cream for my time."

I explained the free ice cream deal to him. He tugged down on his visor, nodded his head, and tapped with his fingers on what looked like a cell phone. Ed had a small electronic device resembling a cell phone that allowed him to communicate with his players. He could send text messages to players on campus as well as all around the country.

"I just told JC that he now has a quarterback coach," Ed smiled.

Well, I guess that was Ed's way of telling me that I had the job. While flattered to have impressed him enough that he wanted to hire me right then and there, it was a little presumptive on his part and again, I was taken aback a little. I mean, was it my qualifications? Was it my ability to procure free ice cream? Or the fact that I was on a short list of candidates that included just me? After all, how many quarterback coaches were there in the Washington, D.C. area willing to learn sign language, take leave from work every afternoon, and travel into the District seven days a week? And work for just a few thousand dollars? Not many, I thought. But, all coaches have a little ego and I was no different. Being a collegiate football coach sounded pretty cool and having the opportunity to work with college athletes was appealing. But while I wanted to accept the position, I really didn't want to confer that decision to Ed. So I let the moment pass without acknowledgment.

"JC?" I asked.

"Jason Coleman, our starting quarterback," Ed said as he pointed to the depth charts on the back of the doors behind me. "He's a fucking stud. The boy is an incredible athlete."

I looked at the two white depth charts with names scribbled in black, green, and blue Sharpie on small magnetic strips. The one on the right was the offensive depth chart and on it were names lined up by position, about 28 names or so. There were three names in the quarterback column: Coleman, Fletcher, and Gardner. Coleman was on top.

"What's he think about having a position coach?" I asked, remembering that I'd seen Jason on the ESPN DVD that Ed had played for me.

"He loves the idea. He's never had a position coach. He just makes things happen."

"That's good. It's always easier to work with someone who wants to learn."

"Just don't fuck with his mechanics and shit," Ed said, "I don't want him all fucked up. This will be his fifth year playing quarterback here. He'll graduate in December. And you better learn to sign quickly because Jason is old school."

"What do you mean, he's old school?" I said.

"Jason is a part of the deaf community that wants to keep the deaf culture private, no changes, even for the better. And that includes medical advances, too. He was one of the leaders when the students protested the appointment of Dr. Fernandez a few years back. Remember that?"

I nodded that I did, and remembered seeing on the news a few years back that the students had protested the newly appointed University President, Dr. Jane Fernandez. They basically shut the campus down for several days until she gave in and resigned.

"She wore a hearing aid and therefore wasn't deaf enough," he said. "So learn how to sign because you're fucking in his world now. Got it?"

Again, I nodded my understanding, and sat back into the chair as if to contemplate whether or not I was indeed ready to step into Jason's world. Remember, I hadn't yet accepted the position, nor had Ed formally offered it. I then began to wonder just how proficient I'd have to become for Jason Coleman to accept me as a coach. I thought the same about the rest of the players as well. I looked back at the depth charts.

"Fletcher?" I asked.

Ed stood up and walked toward the depth charts. "Fletch is a stud, too, but he'll run at two back while JC is the quarterback.

He's the one you need to work with because he'll take over after JC graduates." The two back is a flexible player who can either line up at running back or in the slot as a receiver.

"How about Gardner?"

"Jimmy Gardner is never going to play fucking quarterback here," Ed grimaced. "He thinks he's a quarterback, but he's not. He fucking sucks."

Ed then slid the name 'Gardner' down to the bottom of the depth chart, well below the entire formation and list of names. It was clear that, for whatever reason, Jimmy Gardner wasn't one of Ed's favorite players. I raised my eyebrows and turned back toward the desk as Ed rolled the sleeves of his white, long-sleeve t-shirt up over his forearms and took his seat.

We talked a good bit longer, mostly about the style of offense that he expected his new coordinator to employ. Ed mentioned several times that he hadn't yet hired an offensive coordinator, seemingly trying to gauge my interest in applying for that position. I said that I wasn't prepared to even consider the opportunity; not because I couldn't handle the job, but because I wasn't at a time in my family life where I wanted to close down our transportation business and spend 24 hours a day, seven days a week working with the football team. When I was younger I'd have loved the idea, but not now, not at 47 years of age with two kids still in school.

At Severna Park High School where I was currently coaching, we'd transitioned to using the triple-option offense since our players, though good athletes, were a usually a little under-sized. The triple-option offense relied on good decision-making and execution to overcome defensive teams with considerable advantages in size and strength. And we had the perfect model to work with, too, just about ten miles away at the United States Naval Academy. The Navy coaches were usually very accommodating when we requested assistance or advice and our team flourished within that system. We implemented a short passing game to compliment the triple-option attack and within a few years won the county championship. Our quarterback that year, Greg Zingler, actually went on to play quarterback for the Naval Academy football team.

But Ed wanted no part of "that fucking Navy bullshit" and dismissed any suggestions that I made to perhaps bring the same sort of offensive package to Gallaudet. I thought that since it had worked for us there that it might work at Gallaudet as well since the athletes were relatively similar. Coach Paul Johnson, a very experienced head football coach at the collegiate level, had been very successful with it at the college level, using it at Georgia Southern and Navy. He would later have a lot of success with it at Georgia Tech as well.

So it was a good thing, I thought, that I didn't make myself available as a candidate for the offensive coordinator job. Ed and I were already on two different paths of thought regarding the offense, and he didn't seem to be the kind of guy who considered anyone else's path to be one worth travelling. Now, don't get me wrong, I can be the good soldier, or company man, if you will, and as an assistant coach, I'd do what the head coach wanted me to do. It's just always a lot more comfortable if you know that your head coach won't throw you under the bus should his system fail. Ed seemed a bit too impulsive and stubborn for me to have been comfortable in that working relationship. I could be wrong about him, but I didn't see anything throughout the season that would lead me to believe that I hadn't hit the nail on the head regarding Ed's personality. He had his sensitive moments, but for the most part, Ed Hottle was a pretty intense guy.

"So?" Ed said as he peered at me across the top of his eyeglasses. "Are you fucking ready to coach college football or not?"

Not only was I going to have to learn how to communicate with the players using sign language, I was apparently going to have to add some color to my vocabulary in order to communicate with college football coaches. But I was ready.

"When do I start?" I said.

And with that, I was a college football coach.

The next day, I notified Coach Hines at Severna Park High School that I was leaving to coach college football. At first he didn't believe me because it seemed a little implausible that I would jump from coaching his junior varsity team to coaching college football. But having taken advantage of a similar opportunity himself to coach college football many years ago, he quickly came to understand my decision. And we came to the mutual agreement that if I ever wanted to return to coaching high school football that I'd be welcomed back at the school and to his staff. Truth be told, if I was going to return to coaching at the high school level, there was no question that I'd have wanted to go back to Severna Park.

3

Meeting the Coaching Staff

Though not yet officially under contract, things began to happen almost immediately. There was a lot of work to do in preparation for the inaugural season ahead. Although Ed had apparently pared down his list of job candidates to one coach in particular, the team didn't yet have an offensive coordinator just two months before the players were due to arrive on campus. So not only was I unfamiliar with the quality of the athletes that I'd be working with, I didn't even know what kind of offense I'd be preparing the quarterbacks to run.

An even more pressing issue was the fact that I didn't know how to sign in the least. During my years as an Air Force aviator, a simple mantra had been drilled into my brain, "Aviate, navigate, communicate." In other words, keep the plane airborne, figure out where you are and how to get to where you want to be, and then tell someone what you're doing. If what you were doing wasn't something that you ought to be doing, someone would let you know in fairly short order. In this case, it was the complete opposite. My college coaching career wasn't about to take off until I'd learned to communicate.

Just a few weeks after my interview, we had our first staff meeting and Ed dictated that the meeting, and each staff meeting thereafter throughout the summer, would also serve as a sign language class. For me, this was a very practical measure since I had absolutely no contact with the deaf community on a daily basis, either at home or at work. Up until that point, my experience with ASL had been solely via the internet on my home computer. I'd taught myself how to sign the letters of the alphabet through an ASL website. I was also able to learn how to sign several simple, but common, phrases.

The meetings would be very helpful to me, as well as just being on the campus. In the meetings, we were required to sign everything that we spoke simultaneously, even if we had to slow to a snail's pace to do so. At first, and probably throughout my time at Gallaudet, most of my signing consisted of meaningless gesticulations, but I gave it a shot anyway. It must have been somewhat painful for the deaf coaches in the room, but they were very patient with us new signers.

The first meeting took place in one of the main level classrooms of the field house. It was an early evening meeting in order to accommodate part-time, assistant coaches, like myself, who had regular jobs elsewhere during the normal work day. Upon entering the field house, I immediately saw Ed walking through the foyer of the building toward the hallway on my right. He had an intense scowl upon his face, so I avoided asking him any questions. Walking with him was a young white man, several inches taller than Ed, with a large, hulking build. Just behind his ear, but below his short, brown hair, was a hearing aid. They were peering into classrooms. The young man was Brian Tingley, a former offensive lineman at Gallaudet who now worked on campus. Although he hadn't officially graduated yet, he was the team's graduate assistant for the 2007 season. It would be the first season that Brian wasn't one of the players. Brian's first assignment as a Graduate Assistant (GA) was teaching sign language to the coaching staff that summer.

Ed caught sight of me standing just inside of the entrance and pointed down the hallway for me to follow him. He was looking for a place to hold the staff meeting and eventually found a suitable classroom. Once inside, we turned on the lights and arranged several chairs in front of a white dry-erase board. Ed began to leave the room in search of the other coaches, but before doing so stopped and introduced Brian and I to one another. I nodded to Brian and extended my hand to him in order to shake his.

"Nice to meet you," he said as he smiled broadly. His voice was strong and clear, with only a slight hesitation, something that I'd quickly get used to.

"Same here," I smiled back. I slid my right hand across my left palm, touched fingertips, and pointed toward him, signing that I'd learned from the secretary in the AD's office.

"Hey, good," he said as he returned the sign.

Brian Tingley, though many years my junior, would become my closest confidant on the coaching staff. Relatively quiet and reserved, Brian was a gentle, sensitive young man. He resided in an apartment just north of the city with his girlfriend, Mari, who worked with deaf students herself. For such a young guy, though, he seemed inordinately preoccupied with how his daily decision-making impacted his direction in life. And while he enjoyed living in the area and working at Gallaudet, Brian struggled daily with his decision to do so while his mother was in failing health back in upstate New York.

Recently diagnosed with cancer, Brian's mother had embraced Christianity as a means of dealing with her illness, which in turn had given him a new perspective on life as well. As a result, he'd recently developed a relationship with The Lord, which was somewhat of a radical change of direction for him since, as I'd eventually learn, faith wasn't something openly embraced within the deaf community.

Brian was noticeably nervous about teaching ASL to the staff, and more directly, meeting the demanding needs of his new boss. As a GA on the football staff, his life was about to become very difficult, much more so than he'd even imagined, and far more than

I, myself, would have anticipated. From that night on I felt compelled to be as supportive of him as I could, something I'd never been very good at in the past. You see, there are very few people in my life who would tell you that one of my finest character traits is being an emotionally supportive man, not even my wife. And she wouldn't be wrong to say so. As my friendship with Brian developed, I'd encounter a number of opportunities to work on that flaw, and I was okay with that. In fact, I learned to embrace them.

One by one, and two by two, the other coaches on the staff found their way into the classroom and we greeted them as they arrived. Several knew one another from coaching the year before, working on campus, or being former football players themselves. But only a few seemed to be proficient in sign language.

The first person that I met was Kerry Phalen, our offensive line coach. He had coached on Ed's Gallaudet staff the year before, as well as with Ed at a high school in Calvert County, Maryland for several years. Kerry was a physical education teacher and had quite a commute from his school to Gallaudet, at least an hour. Bald and a good bit over weight, Kerry was a jovial fellow and flashed a smile almost as big as his waistline. He knew he was a little on the heavy side, too, and he made no bones about it. He wasn't very tall and I think that made him appear to be a bit more rotund than he actually was. He was also quite a talker. While I had never met him before, Kerry looked oddly familiar to me, though, right from the moment he walked into the room. It soon struck me that he resembled the funny looking, old guy in the picture behind the desk in Ed's office.

Two more coaches arrived, speaking to one another as they entered the classroom. One was a short, thin, black man in his late forties. The other was a tall, young, white man with broad shoulders and ruggedly good looks. Neither was deaf.

The black man was Ron Cheek, a campus groundskeeper who was coming on board as a new defensive backs coach. A native of the district, Ron was a local guy, very friendly, but quiet. He would be my roommate on road trips throughout the season.

The white man was also named Ron, Ron Luczak. He was the defensive line coach and had been on the staff the year before. He was dressed in business attire, but holding a motorcycle helmet. Ron had come from across town where he worked at Freddie Mac as a Risk Management Consultant. Like Ed, Ron had played his college football at Frostburg State University. While I didn't maintain a relationship with Ron after my season at Gallaudet, I often wondered what had become of him amid the turmoil of the financial meltdown at Freddie Mac and Fannie Mae in the year that followed. We were friendly with one another throughout the season, but Ron wasn't as caught up in the daily grind of coaching as the rest of the staff was. He was maybe in his late twenties and coaching was clearly not his career choice.

When Chris Burke came into the classroom, I'd no idea that he was deaf. He was talking, though not entirely clearly, and laughing and smiling. He worked across the street in the campus' main offices. Like Brian, Chris was a former Gallaudet football player as well. He was about 5'10" or so and had a stocky build, though not a physically impressive physique. He appeared to have a few years on him and I'd later learn that he was indeed in his thirties, and had also played more years of football at Gallaudet than anyone else. The team had been sanctioned differently several times and Chris' eligibility continually changed, so he just kept playing until eventually they either told him that he wasn't eligible to play anymore, for whatever reason, or the physical nature of the game simply caught up to his aging body. Now, he was the team's Assistant Head Coach and responsible for coaching linebackers.

Chris had long, dark hair that dropped down onto his shoulders. He was a bit of a rough looking guy, like maybe he'd seen some tough times in the alleys off campus. But, it turned out that he was just an old party dude and the effects of the good times long ago were beginning to show. Although Chris was very firm with the players, he was a very friendly and funny guy, around me anyway. He'd lost his hearing as a child, but was able to speak surprisingly well. Though I'd try to sign when speaking with him, I think he usually just read my lips.

Since everyone in the room at the time was able to either hear or read lips, there was little or no signing going on among the group, but rather lots of small talk. The guys were catching up on things that had happened since last season, like how their full-time jobs were going, and that both Kerry and Ed's wives were each expecting another child during the football season. And so I partook in the usual small talk myself with the general sharing of fairly meaningless personal interests and travel experiences. Outside of the classroom, we heard Ed's voice and then saw him pass by the doorway, walking just slightly ahead of a tall and slender, dark haired man. They continued past the classroom down the hallway toward the front of the field house. Moments later, a powerfully built, young black man walked in.

"Harold!" cried Chris Burke in a deep, straining voice. The greeting reminded me of the old television sitcom, Cheers, when the bar patrons would welcome the character, Norm, upon his entrance into the bar. The rest of the guys joined in to welcome Harold into the room. Harold was signing in a feverish manner, trying to say hello to each of them individually. He was quite obviously deaf.

"Harold Catron," Brian leaned toward me and said. "He's our running backs coach."

Brian signed to Harold that I was the new quarterback coach and motioned for Harold to move toward us. Harold signed in return and stepped up, grabbed our hands and gave us each a little chest bump as you see so many athletes do these days. Both he and Brian were large men, so I braced myself for the greeting.

Originally from Memphis, Tennessee, Harold now resided in the District and made his living as a personal trainer. Another former Gallaudet football player, he had graduated from Gallaudet in 2004 with a degree in Physical Education. For the past two years he'd coached football at the deaf high school co-located with the university on the north end of the campus. The school was a boarding school for deaf students from all around the country. Although it was officially known as The Model Secondary School for the Deaf, players and coaches simply referred to it as MSSD. Harold was a big man with a small, but pleasant smile. I'd later realize that while I certainly enjoyed Harold's presence on the sidelines, Ed had little confidence in Harold's commitment to coaching. But Ed needed bodies and Harold's was certainly a big one.

It wasn't long thereafter that Ed charged into the classroom, followed closely by the second man with whom I'd seen him walking several minutes earlier. As he walked past us, he removed his visor, tossed it onto the table along the wall, and stood with his hands on his hips, facing us. The second man took a seat a few chairs to my right.

"Everybody get a chance to meet one another?" Ed said to the room.

We all nodded while hesitantly glancing at the young man whom Ed had escorted into the room. Ed smiled, turned toward his guest, and said loudly, "Good. Now I want you all to meet Ryan Hite. Ryan will be our new offensive coordinator." We each offered varying forms of 'welcomes' and 'congratulations', both in sign language and speech, though Ryan did little to acknowledge any of us, other than the obligatory pursed lips and head nod.

"Ryan is from Ohio," Ed continued, "where he played wide receiver at Denison University. He'll be joining me as a full-time coach on the staff, handling most of the day to day responsibilities." The fact that we would have only two full-time coaches was not surprising. Very few schools the size of Gallaudet had the funding to support a full-time coaching staff. That's why head coaches, like Ed, reached out to the community for part-time assistant coaches, like me.

I looked over at Ryan, who had squeezed himself into the seat of a small desk chair. He was nearly as tall as me, maybe just an inch or so less at about six foot two inches, but much thinner. Ryan had short, dark hair and sported a light, scruffy beard on his chin. He sat with his mouth slightly agape, which I soon found out was because he usually had a wad of chew in his jaw, much like Ed did. It would be one of several character traits that Ryan either shared with Ed, or emulated. Another was the high degree of intensity with which he would conduct himself, perhaps the byproduct of impatience. It was often hard to tell if Ryan was nervous, confused, or annoyed, or all three at the same time. It's tough to get comfortable around a guy like that, and I'm not sure that any of us ever did.

And so our summer staff meetings began, with two-full-time coaches, a GA, and six part-time assistants. At Ed's direction, and periodic attendance, Brian did his best to teach us how to communicate with our players using sign language. Ed insisted that Brian teach us just as if we were attending one of the ASL classes offered by the university, without a spoken word. It was a little easier for the coaches who had been on the staff from the prior year, they were pretty much just taking a refresher course, though were in no way fluent. Working on campus, Ron Cheek had had a good bit of exposure to sign language, as one might expect, but again was far from proficient. That left just Ryan Hite and me as genuine sign language amateurs. Ryan would pick up the language much more rapidly than I since he would be working on campus and completely immersed in a deaf environment. Thus, I'd always be the coach asking others what was being signed in a team meeting or group environment where the signer signed so quickly that I couldn't keep up. And that happened a lot. I'm not sure that everyone else was able to keep up either, but they at least acted like they did.

The first few classes, or meetings, Brian taught us the ASL alphabet, though most of us already knew it. The alphabet was the first thing that I'd learned online and I felt pretty good about that. At least I could communicate, albeit very slowly, by spelling out the letters of each and every word. After demonstrating proficiency with the alphabet, we learned numbers and days of the week, in that order. Brian taught at a pace that was comfortable for all of us, including him. The deaf coaches were very patient and helpful as well. We eventually learned common phrases, then finally some basic football terminology, such as the words formation, player, line of scrimmage, and assignment.

Being the coach with the least amount of exposure to ASL, Brian would occasionally meet me off campus for lunch, or dinner, and teach me sign language while having a burger and a beer. While the classes were indeed helpful, it was mostly going to be an on-the-job learning process, and I was okay with that.

As the summer progressed, the classes evolved into staff meetings. Ryan rolled out his offensive playbook and Ed explained his defensive schemes. Ed had been an assistant defensive coach at several small colleges and by now was quite good at coordinating defenses. He was also very comfortable handling the entire defense on his own and wasn't shy about proclaiming it. He also took charge of the special teams units as well, those players who were on the field during kick-offs, punts, and field goal attempts. Personally, I believe that if Ed hadn't been somewhat insecure with the design and execution of an offense, he could have been a one man coaching staff. The only facet of coaching that Ed was less comfortable with than running an offense was delegation. He was a hands-on kind of guy.

Unlike Ed, who had a few years of signing under his belt by then, Ryan struggled to sign while explaining his offense. He was new to signing, like me, and we were very limited in our ASL vocabulary. It was such a slow process that he began to speak and sign at the same time. We didn't have all the time in the world to get our act together and doing so made things move along more quickly.

Much of Ryan's offensive design was new to the returning coaching staff since he had essentially brought it with him from Dennison. As a result, they were pretty skeptical of its complexity, at first. For example, they didn't think the wide receivers and quarterbacks would understand the short passing game with its complementary routes and single defender reads. In fact, the discussions would get a little heated at times. Ryan felt that the play design was basic, but Ed didn't think that it was compatible with the players' experience level. Frustrated by having to sign while defending his plays and offensive system, Ryan began to speak without the accompanying sign language. Ed would stop him, using sign language, and reminded him that he wasn't signing. And that, too, annoyed Ryan.

I was very comfortable with what Ryan was attempting to do with the short passing game. We had used it for several years at the high school level with a great deal of success and the kids had actually progressed far beyond what Ryan was hoping to implement. So I didn't think that our college football players would have a problem handling it. Then again I always seemed to have a lot more faith in player's abilities than most coaches that I knew did, including Ed. Time and time again, Ed would interject.

"You have to understand," he'd say. "These kids are deaf. They come from small schools for the deaf where sometimes the games were five players on five or seven on seven. You have to keep it simple."

"But it's simple," Ryan responded.

"If it's not simple to me," Ed would reply, "it's not going to be simple to them."

I agreed with Ryan that the short passing game was simple and that if we were going to play NCAA Division III football, the players ought to be able to handle it. I also thought that Ed and a few of the coaches were underestimating the ability of the players, especially our quarterbacks. With me teaching them something that I understood, and was very comfortable with, I thought that I could get them up to speed quickly. And so I finally jumped into the fray, coming to Ryan's defense. I figured that since we were going to be working together on the offense, that my support of his ideas might help get our working relationship off to a good start. Turned out that Ryan didn't figure the same and when I spoke up in support of his system, he shut me right down and said, "Ed's the head coach and we'll do things the way he wants."

It would not be the last time that Ryan left me hanging.

At that moment, I realized there was something about me that stuck in Ryan's craw. I figured that, as the offensive coordinator, he wanted to coach the quarterbacks, himself. It wouldn't be out of the ordinary at all for the coordinator to also be the quarterback coach, but it was what it was. Coaching quarterbacks is what I was best at and, after all was said and done, what Ed had hired me to do. Regardless, Ryan clearly harbored some resentment toward me. I guess that we just rubbed each other the wrong way. It happens.

In another meeting, I asked a question regarding quarterback reads in the five-step passing game, passing plays that took longer to develop and sought to advance the ball further down the field. His response to me was, "Don't worry about it. Stop being such a clinician." He was obviously referring to the fact that I'd worked as a coach at local quarterback clinics and frequently provided off-season, private instruction for high school quarterbacks. Brian looked at me and shrugged his shoulders. Thereafter, Brian jokingly referred to me as 'a clinician'.

The story of Ryan's past football related experience was definitely interesting. Although a wide receiver in college, he'd played quarterback while attending high school in his home town of Findlay, Ohio. When his high school team failed to meet expectations, many in the town felt that his performance as the quarterback had had a lot to do with it. His coach refused to play Ryan's backup, though, even when the local media called upon him to do so. But the head coach was Ryan's father, so how could he bench his own son? The backup quarterback would become the team's starter the following season, after which he went on to play quarterback in college at Miami University of Ohio. Later he'd win two Super Bowls as the quarterback of the Pittsburgh Steelers. That backup quarterback was Ben Roethlisberger.

Sometimes I missed a meeting here and there in order to attend my older son's baseball games. Mark was eleven years old and I tried to get to as many of his team's evening games as possible. My eight year old son, Tyler, usually played his games on Saturday mornings, which never posed a conflict with any of our staff meetings. I knew that I'd be missing their football games and didn't want my coaching football to be the reason that I missed their baseball games as well. I also missed a couple of meetings in mid-July when I typically ran my Quarterback Academy Clinic. I made up for it, in a way, by leaving my office in Crofton and driving down to the campus during the day to hang out in the football office or the training room. I used that time to work on my signing and get more familiar with the campus, the facilities, and of course, Ed and Ryan.

4

Meeting the Team

O ne day, after talking about the offense with Ryan in the football office, I decided to head across the street to the campus eatery for lunch. I was a little nervous about my ability to sign my food request to the short order cook there. Regardless, I grabbed a tray at the entrance and proceeded to the hot food area. When the woman behind the grill looked up at me, I pointed at the menu above her head, indicating that I wanted a cheese steak sub and fries.

"You want that with onions and peppers?" she said. She wasn't deaf.

"Oh," I said, a little caught off guard since I'd assumed that she might be deaf. "Onions only, please."

While in line and holding my food tray with both hands, an attractive young woman walked from the soda machine to the counter just in front of me and placed her drink on a tray. She looked up at me and smiled.

"You get the cheese steak?" she said in a slightly muffled, but very feminine voice, "They're really good here."

"Yes, I did," I said. What was going on? It's a deaf university isn't it? What was it about me that let these people know that I could hear?

"Haven't seen you here before," she said. "Are you visiting?"

"No, actually," I said, "I'm a football coach, new to the staff this year."

"Oh. That's great," she smiled again. "What's your name?"

"Coach Overmier," I said. "But it's easier to just call me Coach O."

The young woman's name was Vanessa and she was a student at Gallaudet, attending summer classes. She was from Chicago and although she could hear sparingly, she was by legal definition, deaf. I don't know why, or if it had anything to do with her being from a speaking family, but she spoke quite well. I also don't know if Vanessa wore a hearing aid or not. If she did, I never saw it. She told me she knew several of the boys on the football team and was looking forward to watching a few of our games later that fall. At the end of our short conversation, she wished me well in my new job. Just as the server handed us our sandwiches, three young men walked into the eatery, signing to one another in a friendly conversation.

"There are a few of your players now," Vanessa said.

Before picking up her tray, she began signing to them as they approached. All three watched her intently. She must have told them that I was a new football coach, because when she stopped signing, they all looked up at me, smiled, and signed that it was nice to meet me. I quickly realized that I couldn't return the nicety while holding my tray of food. I set it down.   "Nice   to   meet you," I signed, thinking that that little phrase was a great one to have learned so early on. Why I could walk all over campus just saying "nice to meet you, nice to meet you" and get along pretty well. One of the young men smiled and signed to me very quickly, but, I didn't have any idea what he was signing. I looked at Vanessa.

"He asked you what your name was," she said.

"Oh, thank you," I said to her. I looked at the boys and signed my name, "Coach Overmier." I signed the word 'coach' with ease, but had to spell out my name.

One of the players, the biggest of the three, managed to speak out the letters as I signed them, "Coach O...ver...mier?" An easier last name like Green or Quick would have been simpler. I had an idea.

"Hold on," I said, with my index finger pointed up in front of them. "Coach O," I signed.

"Coach O," they mouthed in unison and smiled.

The big fellow who'd spelled out my name, was a tall, barrel-chested offensive lineman named Phil Endicott, from Philadelphia. Throughout the brief introduction and ensuing conversation, both Vanessa and Phil helped me to sign with the other two players, Dima Rossoshansky and Justin Lathus. Like Vanessa, they were both from Chicago. I think they might have known her from their high school, The Illinois School for the Deaf. The three seemed to be very friendly as if they had known one another for some time. The conversation was very pleasant and when Vanessa left us, I thanked her for her help.

"No problem, Coach," she said as she took her tray to the dining area. "It was a pleasure to meet you. Good luck."

I shook hands with the players, exchanged smiles, and watched them sign to me as I picked up my tray and headed to the cashier. I'd absolutely no idea what they were signing. So I just smiled.

As it turned out, all three of the boys were really good guys. Dima was a bit short for a football player, but stocky and athletic. A sophomore running back, he had short, curly, brown hair, the shadow of a beard, and a pretty full mustache. I'd have loved to talk with Dima more often because he was always smiling and genuinely seemed to want to talk with me at length no matter what the subject. But I was embarrassed by my inability to sign more proficiently and felt that my laboring to do so would have made the conversation grueling for him. And so our chats were often somewhat shallow as a result.

Justin, a junior, was the team's center, although he didn't appear to be as physically fit as the other two. His curly, brown hair was much longer than Dima's, and more kinky than curly. His very noticeable limp made me wonder if he might be hobbled due to an injury. Later found out that he had a permanent hip problem. Both players were deaf and while Dima never spoke a word, Justin was able to "squeak" out utterances as he signed, especially when he became emotional.

Phil, the bigger and stronger of the three, had a strong serious air. I believe he was pursuing an engineering career. He was a senior and planning on getting married not long after graduation.

As I sat in the dining area and ate my cheese steak sandwich, I thought to myself that these guys didn't look like college football players. Phil did, somewhat, since it appeared that he'd spent some time in the weight room, but not Dima and Justin. Dima seemed a little small and Justin not only seemed small, but was physically impaired. But then it occurred to me that these guys had faced adversity and challenges all of their lives, and playing football was mostly about meeting physical challenges. So their lack of physicality might not have been that big of a deal to them on the football field. And after all, we weren't out to win a national championship, were we? If that was the goal, then there was a good chance that we might fall a little short of it. But it wasn't. No, these guys just wanted to enjoy the rewarding experience of playing college football, and our job was to help them be as successful as they had the potential to be, just like coaching anywhere else.

The rest of the summer the schedule was mostly the same. A couple of evening staff meetings with a day or two of milling about the campus in between. For the most part, the extra hours that I spent at Gallaudet that summer just became part of my daily routine, and my family came to understand that my workdays had just been extended somewhat. There wasn't much of a conflict with our schedules. It wasn't until our family vacation during the final week of July that football actually began to collide with family time.

While in the Shenandoah Valley of Virginia, our annual vacation spot, the resort's front office called our mountainside condo to tell me that a package had arrived for me. We were on our way to the swimming pool. So, in my swim trunks, I hopped into our car and drove down the mountain to the office. At the main desk, I showed the clerk my driver's license and she handed me a rather heavy, 11 x 14 document box. I took the box over to a wooden bench just outside the front doors where I sat and opened it. Inside was a three inch binder that contained the Gallaudet Bison Offensive Playbook. On the front of the book was a sticky note from Ryan with a request that I be familiar with the offense upon my return from vacation.

I spent some time by the pool reading the playbook that day, while my boys practiced their cannon balls and can openers off of the one meter diving board. I reviewed it again that night after the family had gone to sleep. It wasn't entirely unfamiliar to me. In fact it was a little simpler than I'd expected. But the receiver numbering system, or the way that we identified each receiver in a formation, was a little different than I'd seen. I didn't think it would cause the team any trouble, though, once we got used to it. However, the way that Ryan was planning on implementing his receiver packages seemed like it might cause a lot of confusion among the players. In other words, which receivers should be on the field, and where? But being the stranger to coaching college football, I figured that his plan was the norm for this level of football, so I didn't worry too much about it. Then I remembered Ed's concern that if it was confusing to him, it would be confusing to the players. I didn't know about Ed, yet, but I was a little confused. Nonetheless, I was confident that I'd pick it up. After all, I was a clinician.

The evening meetings continued regularly all the way up until Wednesday, August 8. On that night, we each received a coaching manual and the coaching attire that Ed expected us to wear at practice. Ed had it laid out and waiting for us: two pairs of navy blue, mesh shorts, two gray tee shirts, a navy blue, mesh baseball style cap with the letter "G" embroidered upon it in gold, and two blue, moisture wicking tee shirts. We also received a pair of New

Balance training shoes. The team was sponsored by New Balance so everything was emblazoned with "NB", their corporate logo. It was required that we wear the New Balance gear whenever we performed team duties.

Two sets of practice gear were not going to be enough, though, not for me. I didn't want to have to wash my practice clothes every night, or ask my wife to do it. And one pair of shoes wasn't going to suffice, either, especially if I had to wear them during a rainy practice or game day. And so I put up another $125 of my own money and requested another pair of training shoes, and two more shirts, one white and the other navy blue, and an additional hat. I'd keep one hat and a pair of shoes specifically for practice and the other set for games. That's the way I rolled. I always kept a fresh set of practice gear and underwear in my locker, too.

Ed briefed us on the itinerary for Friday, August 10, the day that the players arrived on campus and also at the field house for the distribution of equipment. Each of us would have a specific responsibility throughout the day that included checking in players, handing out gear, and speaking at our first team meeting that afternoon. I was a little nervous about finally meeting the team in an official capacity. I wasn't nervous about meeting the players, quite the contrary. I was excited to meet the players. I was just a little nervous that my usually excellent communication skills wouldn't translate well into ASL or that my knowledge of the game would seem somewhat elementary as a result. Even so, I was eager for Friday to come.

After a day off on Thursday, I arrived on campus Friday morning just after 9:00 a.m. and made my way into the field house. Ed and Ryan were already inside preparing a couple of tables for checking players in. Ed was barking loud orders at Brian, who seemed to be headed in two completely different directions at the same time. I asked Brian if there was something that I could help him with, but he just frowned and walked away. I heard the door to the field house open behind me and as I turned around to see who had come in, I felt a heavy hand on my shoulder.

"Good morning," said a man's brawny voice. His weathered face and husky frame looked familiar, but it didn't immediately register with me who he was until he smiled.

"Hey," I said instinctively, "good morning."

"You ready?" he said. And then I realized that he was Chris Burke. I hadn't recognized him because he'd had all of his long hair cut off. It was now nearly as short as my own. He looked good.

"Wow! Good morning," I signed to him. "I didn't recognize you. And yes, I'm ready." I didn't know how to sign all of that so I just said it, gave him two thumbs up and smiled. He read my lips anyway.

"Chris? I need you to get over to the dorm and make sure that those guys know to have their asses over here by ten o'clock." Ed bellowed out as he approached us, with Ryan following him. "Jimmy? Follow me downstairs to the equipment room. You'll work down there with Kris, handing out gear as players file through."

"Okay," I said.

I waited until Ryan had passed by me before falling into line behind him and Ed. I followed them down the stairwell and into the hallways below the gym. We passed classroom G40 on our left, where we'd eventually hold our team meetings before both practices and games. Just down the hall on the right, in the large storage room, we found Kris Gould, the team's equipment manager. He'd set up an equipment distribution area inside the room and prepared all the equipment for issue.

"Kris?" Ed called out.

"Yep," we heard Kris's voice respond from somewhere on the far side of the room. He emerged from behind a partition, where he had a desk. He had a smile on his face, as usual.

"Jimmy is going to help you get the boys into their gear. Ryan and I'll get everyone checked in upstairs, make sure that they are signed in on campus, and then join you in a little while, okay? Brian will be here momentarily to help you get the process moving."

"Okay," Kris said. "Good morning," he smiled as he grabbed my hand with both of his. "It's good to see you. Thanks for helping us out today."

"My pleasure, Kris," I said.

I really did want to help, but I also wanted the opportunity to practice my signing by getting to meet and actually "speak" with each player as they filed by to receive their equipment. Kris led me through a maze of assembled football gear including pants, shoulder pads, helmets, etc. About three-quarters of the way through the distribution line, he stopped in front of several cardboard boxes of leg and hip pads for the players' pants.

"If you could make sure that each player gets a set of pads that would be great," he said. "Just make sure that they get the right size, ok?"

"Not a problem," I assured him.

It was an easy job. As I looked into the boxes, a tall, thin young man walked out from behind a set of shelves, carrying two additional boxes. He placed them next to the boxes of pads and walked back behind the shelves. When he returned again, just a second or two later, Kris introduced him to me.

"Damian? This is Coach Overmier," he signed. I reached out and shook Damian's hand. He smiled and nodded.

"Coach, this is Damian Forkner, my student-helper this semester. He's going to give you a hand with these t-shirts," Kris told me.

"Nice to meet you," I signed.

Damian was tall and thin, and very quiet, too, even for a deaf guy. But, he was always very cordial and accommodating. His job was to use a Sharpie marker to write a particular player's jersey number into the rear collar of that player's two issued t-shirts. That way, Kris and his team of assistant managers would know which player the shirts belonged to after washing and drying them en masse following each practice or game.

And so, as the players passed by our station, Damian would check the roster and write that player's jersey number on the t-shirts and then hand them to me. After assessing what size pads a player required, and we quickly got down to just large and small, I'd set two plastic bags atop the shirts and hand it all to the player. One plastic bag contained hip pads and the other, knee and thigh pads. The player would then place them all into his equipment bag and proceed toward to the helmet fitting area where Kris and the representative from Riddell Helmets would fit them for their head gear. The assignment was perfect for me because it gave me ample opportunity to start to get to know each player while we waited for Damian to write the numbers on their shirts.

The players began to arrive at the doorway to the room around 10:30 a.m., and assembled in the hallway outside. Brian allowed one player at a time to enter, checked him in, issued him a belt, girdle, and pants and then sent him our way. They processed through fairly quickly, with the only bottleneck being just beyond us at the shoulder pads. Kerry had shown up and was helping there while Kris bounced between shoulder pads and helmets. I was a little surprised by just how average in size and stature the players seemed to be, if not relatively small. While most of the boys were completely deaf, others could hear with the aid of a hearing device. But they all signed fluently, as one might expect.

As they processed through I introduced myself. By the time they arrived at my station, though, most of them seemed to already know who I was. If they didn't, they at least knew that I was the other new coach, with the other being Ryan. In either case, they all figured out quickly that I was an amateur at signing. But, that didn't stop me from engaging in small talk, a habit of mine. I made it a point to ask each one of them where they were from while we waited for Damian. Slowly and often times very deliberately, they signed out the two letter abbreviation of their home state and occasionally, if time permitted their home town. They were from all over the country: Texas, Iowa, Florida, New York, Oregon, Arizona, California, Alaska, Hawaii, and the Virgin Islands. Most, but not all of them, had graduated from a high school for the deaf or deaf and blind. In fact, of the 55 players on the 2007 roster, 38 had attended such schools.

During the course of the process, I also met our quarterbacks, the veterans, and those who planned on trying out for the position. I met our starter, Jason Coleman, whom we simply called "JC." Although he was originally from the state of California, JC had most recently lived in Middletown, Maryland, not too far away. And then there was Fletcher Kuehn, who we called "Fletch." He was from Austin, Texas. And then I met Jimmy Gardner. He was from St. Augustine, Florida. And finally, I met two boys who wanted to try out for the position of quarterback, but whose names I hadn't seen on the depth charts. They were both freshmen. Joe Scroggins was from Little Rock, Arkansas and A.J. Williams from Albuquerque, New Mexico. A.J. was the only black kid of the five. They looked like a decent group of athletes, as athletic as any other position on the team, anyway, and they all seemed to have great attitudes. I was excited to begin working them.

After several hours, I'd met all of the players, including my three buddies from the eatery earlier that summer, Dima, Phil, and Justin. And do you know there wasn't one kid that I didn't like or wasn't able to elicit a smile from, not one. There was one player in particular that day, though, who seemed to be just a little more balanced, if you will, than most. . There was just something about him. His name was Roman Nawrocki and he'd graduated from the same school as Jimmy Gardner in St. Augustine, Florida. His nickname was "Rusty" and he had short, blond hair. At first glance, Rusty appeared to be tall and thin, but he was about six-foot two inches tall and 185 pounds, and had a very solid build. Like all the others, he was very friendly, but carried himself extremely well and walked with a little extra confidence. It might have been because Rusty had Olympic class karate skills. Those were very impressive athletic credentials indeed. He was just one of the fascinating athletes that I'd come to know during the season.

Although time passed quickly from morning into afternoon,

when the clock struck three, I was famished. We hadn't taken a break for food or drink in nearly six hours. Ed arrived in the equipment room following the departure of the final group of players and brought with him a fellow named Mike Weinstock. Mike had just been hired as the university's Athletic Director, replacing Jim DeStefano, who'd stepped down from the position.

Mike Weinstock was a tall man, about my height, with thinning, blond hair and moustache. And, like Jim DeStefano, he was deaf. He signed to us as a group, introducing himself and telling us that he was looking forward to a great season. At least that's what Brian told me Mike had said. He signed very fast as most fluent signers did. I couldn't read slow signing, much less signing at warp speed. What I did understand, though, was that he and Ed had ordered pizzas for us and they arrived shortly thereafter, much to my delight.

A few hours later, the entire team assembled in the gym above. Weinstock wanted to address the team as their new Athletic Director, and Ed had planned on formally introducing the coaching staff. He also wanted to issue directions for the start of practice the following morning. While Mike and Ed spoke to the team, the coaching staff sat together in the bleachers to the right of the team. During Weinstock's speech I realized that, for the first time in my life, I could talk while a speaker addressed a group without me getting into trouble for distracting either that speaker or his audience. That was unless someone in the audience or the speaker himself could hear, of course. This was an epiphany of sorts, for someone like me, who always seemed to get into trouble for speaking aloud during a class or an assembly in high school. Now, I could just pretend to pay attention and chat away, which was good because I was bored to tears. I didn't understand a thing the guy was signing. All I needed was someone who could hear what I had to chat about, which luckily for me that night was a few of the other coaches.

When Mike concluded his Athletic Director's speech to the team, Ed's plan was to introduce us coaches individually and have us say a little something. I knew what I wanted to say, I just wasn't sure that I could remember how to sign it. So while Mike's speech rambled on and on, I practiced signing my short introductory speech to the team. Finally, after about thirty minutes, he wrapped things up and Ed took center stage.

One by one, Ed introduced the coaching staff and one by one, we each stood before the team and said a little something. I watched as Ryan surprisingly struggled through his introduction. His awkwardness wasn't the result of limited signing experience because Ryan had had several weeks of signing experience by then. He just wasn't comfortable speaking in front of large groups. Both Ron Luscak and Kerry Phalen were very brief with their addresses. When I saw Ed sign my name to the team I walked out onto the gym floor, and introduced myself as Coach Overmier, using sign language the best I knew how. Then, as I'd done with players that I had met over the summer, I told them that it was okay to simply refer to me as "Coach O," which was easy to sign.

After the players were dismissed, Ed called the coaches down to room G40 for another staff meeting. It was one last opportunity for him to issue guidance to his staff for the next morning's first practice session. Ed was disappointed with the low number of players who had registered to play, just fifty four. He cited the new, higher academic standards at the school, the result of players now having to comply with NCAA rules and regulations, as a contributing factor. He thought the requirements had frightened away many quality athletes. But one quality athlete, Josh Ofiu of Anchorage, Alaska, had yet to arrive on campus. He'd join the team in a few days and push the roster to fifty five players.

When I finally left the campus it was nearly 10:00 p.m. and by the time I got home, my kids were already in bed and my wife was asleep on the sofa. I went to the refrigerator and made myself a sandwich. Afterward, I leashed our little dog, Toto, a Cairn terrier, and took her for a short walk. While under the streetlight just outside our home, I watched her sniff around the lamp post and go about her business. She was blind in her old age, and dependent on me for guidance. And though she didn't know where she was going, she knew what to do when she got there. Well, as a football coach, I really wasn't quite sure where I was going, either, or how I'd arrived at this point. I was just relying on God to guide me along, I guess. But, I knew whenever I got to wherever it was that He wanted me to be, I'd know what to do. And at that moment, under the street light outside of my home, late at night, the thought occurred to me that I was about to become one of but a handful of men in this world to have ever coached a deaf college football team.

5

Beat the Drum: The First Day of Practice Arrives

The first day of practice finally arrived on Saturday, August 11, 2007. I reached the field house at 7:45 a.m. It was the beginning of a beautiful summer day with bright sunshine and unseasonably cool temperatures. En route from the parking lot to the field house, I noticed that fairly heavy dew still gleamed from the surface of the grass fields both in the stadium and on the small practice field adjacent to it. There were several sets of dark footprints on the wet practice field that led from the stadium track, which separated the game and practice fields, to a large bass drum at the head of the field. Two portable tables were set up, and on each sat table a pair of orange water coolers. Someone had already prepared the field for the practice.

Inside the building, the players, coaches, managers, and trainers all hustled about, into and out of locker rooms, the training room, and the equipment room. The familiar sound of cleats, clattering upon the surface, rang throughout the hallways and vestibule as the players began to make their way outside and onto the concrete walkway leading up to the stadium and the practice areas. After a brief visit to the coaches' locker room, I met up with both Ed and Brian inside the football office. The rest of the coaching staff was either already out and about, or late. After some last minute instructions from Ed, the three of us made our way out of the building. Kris had directed Damian to load my coaching equipment onto the back of their Gator and take it out to the practice field. A Gator was a small golf-cart-like vehicle with a flat storage bed behind the driver and passenger seats. If you watch a football game on television, you might sometimes see the medical staff sit an injured player in the back of a Gator and drive him out of the stadium to the locker room. It is a very practical piece of equipment to have around.

Walking behind Ed and Brian as we headed out to the practice field, I found myself surrounded by players of all sizes, shapes, races, and ethnic backgrounds. Some had facial hair, some didn't, some were smiling, and others were not. Each player, though, wore either a white football jersey with navy blue numbers or a navy blue jersey with white numbers, except a few who wore yellow jerseys. Defensive players wore blue and offensive players wore white. There were also a few players wearing yellow jerseys. They were the quarterbacks.

Putting the quarterbacks in a different colored jersey is standard procedure on most football practice fields at all levels of the game. Defensive players are instructed by the coaching staff to avoid contact with a player in a red or yellow jersey while scrimmaging. It's not that quarterbacks aren't durable athletes, either. In fact, that would be far from the truth. They are usually some of the best athletes on the team. But skilled and competent quarterbacks are hard to find, and yet so essential to the overall success of a program. Exposing such a player to the risk of injury without taking some precaution was foolish.

In addition to their jerseys, the players also sported navy blue shorts, white socks, and cleats. Most of them carried their gold helmet by their side, though a few had already donned their head gear. The helmets were painted solid gold with no decal upon them, much like Notre Dame or Navy. The face masks were navy blue.

The coaching staff wore gray t-shirts with "GU Football" across the chest, navy blue, mesh shorts, and our navy blue, mesh baseball caps. However, I was the only coach wearing a fanny pack, and it didn't go unnoticed. Players and coaches alike pointed at it as they passed by me. Most would shake their head and smile. It didn't faze me though, because I was used to the gentle ridicule by then. During my first year of coaching high school ball more than a decade earlier, I'd seen another experienced coach wearing one during our team's two-a-day practices. It seemed all too practical, and besides, I hated carrying a lot of stuff in the flimsy pockets of my mesh shorts. So I went out and bought one the next day. Inside of my fanny pack I kept my car keys and wallet. I also carried lip balm, a pen, a notepad, and a small knife. It was also much easier to fold up a practice plan and slide it into the fanny pack than walk around with it stuffed into the elastic waistband of my shorts, like other coaches. Sometimes I wore it across the front of my waist, and sometimes I wore it along my lower back.

Another benefit of the fanny pack was that it allowed me to carry a basic thermometer during hot, late-summer practices. We seldom had trainers available on the field during our high school practices. Thus, it was up to the coaches to identify and treat players who appeared to be at risk of heat-related stress. So I didn't mind any heckling that I received for wearing the fanny pack; the benefits far outweighed the short-lived hassling. Anyway, since making fun of my fanny pack might mean extra conditioning, or a few more push-ups, the players usually kept their comments pleasant.

As we approached the track surrounding the stadium field, I suddenly had the panicked feeling that comes upon you when you think you've forgotten something that you really need. I reached up to my chest with my right hand for a lanyard that usually hung from my neck. I felt that it wasn't there and turned to go back toward the locker room.

"Crap!" I said, "I'll be right back," I called out to Brian and Ed.

Brian nodded, but Ed just stood and watched me as I turned on my heels and began to jog back toward the field house. After just a few steps, I stopped, shook my head, and turned back to rejoin them. Ed began walking again toward the practice field.

"Forget your whistle?" he said without looking back over his shoulder at me. I could tell, though, that he was grinning.

"Uh-huh." I was a little embarrassed. "Obviously I won't need it."

"Obviously," said Ed. "I did the same thing when I started. Everyone does."

At the practice field there were a few sheets of four by eight foot plywood laid across the running track for the players to walk over as they crossed from the stadium turf to the practice field. The plywood protected the surface of the track from their hard, molded cleats.

The practice field itself was small, maybe fifty to sixty yards long by about forty yards wide, with the length of the field running parallel to the playing field inside the stadium. There were no goal posts, just an open area of grass between tennis courts to the right and a baseball diamond to the left. On the far side of the practice field was a steep, grassy hill that dropped about eight feet, down to a tree-lined West Virginia Avenue below. A seven-foot high, black metal fence separated the walkway along the street from the campus.

In the grass at the left end of the field sat a large, bass drum, about four feet in diameter. It was affixed to a wheeled, wooden cart with its hollow end facing the practice field and the players. The skin of the drum was white, with the exception of a small area in the middle of the skin that appeared to be so worn out that it was nearly clear. I wondered just how much more pounding it could withstand. Chris Burke stood to the right of the drum holding what appeared to be about a three-foot long gong mallet. The end of the mallet was wrapped in an abundance of white, athletic tape. Chris was smiling like the cat that had eaten the canary.

The players assembled on the field for pre-practice stretch and agility exercises. They lined up in six rows of eight or nine guys facing the drum. The first line, though, stood with their backs to the drum and facing the rest of the squad. They were usually team captains. Otherwise, players with the lower numbers were near the head of the formation, closer to the drum, while the higher-numbered players were at the rear. I made my way onto the practice field and walked among them, smiling at each player with whom I made eye contact. I wasn't the hard-ass coach on the first day of practice that a lot of coaches were, although I once was. But, over the years I'd mellowed out a good bit. I now found it much more productive to establish a good player-coach relationship than become someone who they despised. And I didn't feel the need to change that for college football, especially since I had the expectation that most of the players would be much more mature and disciplined than high school players.

The quarterbacks' yellow jerseys all had lower numbers upon them. Therefore, they were at or near the front of their lines and at the head of the formation. As their position coach, I slowly walked over and greeted each one of them with a good morning, and in doing so got to within a few short yards of the large, bass drum. On the right side of the drum, Ryan stood with his hands on his hips and peered out across the formation of players. He looked as if he was taking charge, while Ed observed patiently from the far end of the field behind us. After greeting the last of the quarterbacks, I changed direction and walked toward the side of the formation, away from both Chris and Ryan, and the drum.

"Coach?" Ryan said out loud.

Instinctively, I turned toward him to see if he meant me. I use the word instinctively because there were two factors in play. First, when someone calls out the word "coach" in the vicinity of a field, gym, or weight room, anyone and everyone who is a coach will turn to see if that person is calling for them. It's a funny thing to watch if you're ever at a coaching convention or clinic. Invariably, someone always shouts out "coach" and two hundred guys turn around in response. Secondly, on the practice field with only deaf players and coaches, there could have been but a few folks whose attention Ryan was trying to get, right? So, although it may have been a learned response, I'll just say that I turned around instinctively.

"Coach?" he repeated with a smirk on his face. "You're wearing a fanny pack? Really? What's up with that?"

"I always wear it on the field," I said. "I hate having stuff in my pockets."

He shook his head from side to side and looked back to the players with a smile. None of them knew what he'd said to me or what he was chuckling about. Later in the day, when we were working with the receivers and quarterbacks, he made mention of it again by signing to the players that he'd never seen a coach wear a fanny pack. But to his surprise, the players thought the idea of a coach wearing a fanny pack was pretty cool.

From the side of the formation, I noticed Ed give a signal to Chris Burke from afar, the signal to commence practice. Ryan didn't see the signal. Like I imagined an emperor's guard would do, Chris drew back the mallet and, gripping it like a baseball bat, slammed it with all of his might against the side of the drum.

KABOOM!

The drum sounded like a fighter jet breaking the sound barrier. Ryan was caught completely off guard and nearly jumped out of his New Balance coaching shoes. He covered his ears with his hands as he bolted toward the street and away from the drum, his face wretched with discomfort. I'm sure that I'd have had the same reaction had it been me, but I still thought, "How in the world did he not know that was coming?"

KABOOM!

Chris struck the drum a second time and all of the players dropped down to the ground to begin their stretches. Having witnessed Ryan's reaction to the drum, and probably anticipating it, most of the boys laughed and pointed toward Ryan as they stretched. I was pretty sure that Ed had definitely anticipated it, and had probably even planned it, because he was laughing so hard that I could see the whiteness of his smile from forty yards away. Either way, it was pretty funny, especially since it hadn't happened to me.

Chris beat on the drum every ten seconds and each time he did, the players changed either their position or their stretching exercise. They couldn't hear the sound of the bass drum, but they could easily feel its reverberation. And so while the captains on most football teams usually call out the stretch and cadence from the head of the formation, at Gallaudet, that big, old bass drum does the job.

To this day, whenever I tell someone that I coached football at Gallaudet, they ask me if we still used the big drum on the sideline during a game. That drum has become legendary and is usually the first topic of conversation when people talk about Gallaudet and its football team. Guys who played a little football in college especially love to talk about playing Gallaudet and how that drum was a huge distraction for them. And although their individual stories are quite unique, they all seem to start out by talking about the drum.

In years past, the team did use the drum along their sideline for the offense to simulate its cadence or snap count. The players on the field could feel the percussion of the drum and on a pre-determined "drum count," initiate the start of an offensive play. In other words, hike the ball. At the start of a game the sound of the drum was usually an advantage for the Gallaudet offensive players, because it startled the players on the opponent's defensive unit. I know, because I'm one of those guys who played against Gallaudet when I played junior college football. They pounded on the drum to start their first offensive play of the game and all of our defensive players immediately looked over toward the Gallaudet sideline. And when they did, the offensive players from Gallaudet pounced on us. Fortunately, it didn't take too long for us to grow accustomed to hearing the drum before each of their offensive plays.

Once Ed arrived on the scene, though, Gallaudet stopped using the drum on the sideline during games. Instead, he preferred that our offense initiate plays using a "silent count." In other words, there was no "hut one, hut two, hut three" called out by the quarterback as you might be accustomed to hearing. And consequently, since it was Gallaudet, there wasn't a "boom, boom" from the bass drum, either. Instead, the center now snapped the football to start a play when he either received a direct hand signal from the quarterback to do so or whenever he was ready to snap the ball after receiving that signal. No other player on the offense knew exactly when the center was going to snap the ball until they saw the movement of the ball. And so, my answer to those folks who ask me if we still used the drum is "no," which usually comes as a surprise to the person asking.

No longer using the drum during games was just one of a number of significant developments that the team underwent during its transition from a club team to a NCAA college football program. Another, by the way, involved our offensive "huddle."

A little known fact is that the football "huddle" was invented by the Gallaudet football team. During a game in 1892, the Gallaudet quarterback thought the opposing team could read his hand signals, so he began circling his players around him to sign the next play to them, and in doing so formed what has since been called "the huddle." Although many teams playing today have adopted a style of football called the "no-huddle" offense, most still use "the huddle" on a regular basis and at every level of the game. Ironically, to execute the "no-huddle" offense, it's essential that the players and coaches become adept at using hand signals to communicate plays.

But again, once Ed arrived on the scene, Gallaudet stopped using an offensive "huddle." Ed didn't think the opposing teams could interpret our sign language, determine the play call, and then get that information to their players on the field before the start of the play. If they could, they deserved whatever advantage they'd obtained. Thus, for expediency purposes, we used a "no-huddle" offense, and it worked quite well for us.

And so getting back to the drum, we did continue to utilize it for "Flex" every day. Flex was the term that Ed had assigned to the team's pre-practice and pre-game regimen of stretch and agility exercises. The task of beating on the drum during Flex usually rotated among the managers, and occasionally, like the first day of practice, coaches. Players didn't get the privilege of beating on the drum because Ed had come to frown upon that idea.

He told me the story of a player a few years back who'd had a bad experience with the drum and because of that incident hadn't allowed it since. The player experienced soreness in one of his legs after practice one day and told the trainer of his discomfort. His leg became much worse over the next several days, to the point that the player went beyond the training staff to seek medical attention. Oddly enough, it turned out not to be a football related injury at all, but rather a snake bite that had occurred while sleeping in his campus dormitory.

Well, the player was sidelined for a couple of weeks and during that time he was assigned administrative duties and light work assignments related to the football team. One of those assignments was beating the drum during Flex. On the first day of doing so, Ed said that he remembered giving the player the signal to begin the exercise, and then turned away after hearing him pound on the drum. When he didn't hear the drum pounded a second time, he turned back to see the player dazed and covered in blood. After the player had initially struck the side of the drum, the mallet had bounced back off of the drum skin and struck the player in the face. Of course, he now needed more medical attention and six stitches. Pounding on the drum could be hazardous duty. And that was the last player to pound on the drum.

Even though we didn't use it on the sideline any longer, the bass drum did remain part of our daily routine and a tradition of Gallaudet Football. And it still made road trips with the team, travelling with us to each of our away games. The team managers were responsible for ensuring that it was loaded in and out of the bus's cargo holding area, as well as on and off of the game field.

For the most part, I stood and observed the players during Flex. Sometimes, though, I'd confer with another coach regarding the practice schedule or work on my sign language skills by communicating with players as they stretched. Often times I would inquire of the players the traditions and customs within the deaf community. But for the most part, Flex offered me a brief opportunity for reflection, when the city streets cooperated, that is. If you've ever been to Washington, D.C., or any big city for that matter, then you know that the sound of sirens in the inner city can seem to be almost constant. Whether it was police cars, ambulances, or fire trucks, there always seemed to be a siren breaking the otherwise peaceful air of the campus.

It was during Flex one day that I first noticed that the players were not distracted by such things. There were a ton of sirens in response to an emergency somewhere in the vicinity of the university and I gazed about, curious as to what might be happening a block or two away. But the players went about their stretching without so much as a head turning to see what was going on because, of course, they couldn't hear the sirens. Unlike me, they weren't distracted by any of the noises around the campus, whether it was sirens, traffic, or even gunshots. It was, after all, Washington, D.C.

At the completion of Flex on that first day of practice, Ed brought the team together and assigned them to small groups of players, mostly of like size or position. In other words, linemen were grouped with linemen and skilled position players with skilled position players, and so on. Several coaches had broken away and set up conditioning stations. There, they'd each conduct one of a variety of drills with each group for three minutes. After three minutes, the coach would send them to the next station where they'd participate in a different drill. Another group would then transition to that coach's station for the next three minutes.

The station drills segment of practice was scheduled to last about thirty minutes and during that time, I assisted Chris Burke at his station, the pro agility drill. The drill measured a player's explosiveness and simply required that the player to run to his left about five yards, back to his right ten yards, and then return to his starting position. Well, the first player in line was a big kid from Wisconsin named Daniel Dosemagen. Dosemagen stood about six-foot one-inch tall and weighed 325 pounds. He didn't look particularly athletic, though, just big. Bent at the waist with his hands positioned in front of him, the big guy looked out from behind the cage of his facemask at Chris, who was kneeling on the ground just a few feet in front of the player. When Chris nodded his head toward Daniel to begin the drill, Dosemagen didn't move. He just stared at Chris. Chris's eyebrows drew together and he threw his hands out toward Dosemagen and yelled, "Get to it." Either Chris had signed those words to Dosemagen or Dosemagen had read Chris's lips because he immediately leapt into the drill.

Throughout the practice segment I watched Chris's signing, hoping to quickly learn some fundamental signing skills that I could use to communicate with the players. Between groups, I'd ask Chris about certain things that I'd seen him sign, and then ask him to show me again so I could practice. Chris would either affirm my signing or correct it so that I was signing properly. With his assistance, I was able to offer some encouragement, or direction, to a few of the players as they either prepared for or completed the drill. But my time alone with players would soon arrive.

During the next segment of practice I had my first opportunity to work with players independent of the other coaches. After a short water break, the team again broke into small groups to work on individual skills. This segment of practice is generally referred to as "Indy," short for individual. With the players still hydrating themselves at the watering station, I set up my agility ladder and a few other pieces of equipment that I used for fundamental quarterback training.

The quarterbacks departed from the rest of the team and approached me where I stood in the corner of the stadium end zone. As they arrived, I tossed them each a football from a large, mesh bag that I kept with the rest of my equipment. The group consisted of the five quarterbacks that I'd met at equipment issue the day before: Jason Coleman, or JC, Fletcher Kuehn, Jimmy Gardner, A.J. Williams, and Joe Scroggins. They knelt on the turf in front of me as I began to explain and demonstrate several quarterbacking drills. At first I was a little nervous about communicating with them privately. It was important to me that I earn their respect as a coach as quickly as possible. And I didn't want my ineptness at signing to translate into ineptness as a coach. Just a few moments after I first began to sign instructions to them I heard someone call out my name.

"Coach O?" said a faraway voice.

I looked over my shoulder, but saw no one calling my name or seeking my attention. So I looked back down at the players in front of me who obviously hadn't heard the voice. They must have been wondering, "What in the world is he looking at?"

"Coach O, the sun," I heard the voice call out again.

And once again I paused to look over my shoulder. This time, though, I saw Brian, about forty yards away, waving his right hand and calling out my name. He was working with Kerry and a group of offensive linemen halfway down the field from where we were.

"Coach O, the sun," he repeated. "Go around them and sign."

I looked back at my players and then again toward Brian. I shook my head and shrugged my shoulders, not understand his meaning.

"They can't see your signing," he said. "They're looking into the sun."

I looked down at my players and saw they were indeed squinting and using their hands to shield their eyes from the bright sun as they attempted to read my signing.

"Sorry," I signed to them. And from that point forward, I always made sure the players had their backs to the sun when I gave them instruction.

Our first workout as a group went surprisingly well as each of the quarterbacks seemed to be genuinely excited about the prospect of learning new techniques and drills. Individually, they had distinctly different sets of skills, yet all were athletic and very physically capable players. I was equally impressed by the fact that they routinely encouraged and complimented one another. They all quickly grasped the concepts of my drills and worked diligently to execute them.

JC was the most experienced player of the group and had a distinct air of confidence. There wasn't any question that he was "the man." In the video that I'd watched in Ed's office, JC had had curly, brown hair. Now he had a clean shaven head, which contrasted with his dark brown eyes and eyebrows. Very handsome, he stood at 6 feet 3 inches tall and weighed about 200 pounds. For a big guy, he had very quick feet, decent speed, and terrific body control.

Fletcher Kuehne, or "Fletch," was probably the most athletic of all of the quarterback prospects. A shade over 6 feet tall and also weighing about 200 pounds, Fletch was strong and fast, and he ran with more power than most of the running backs. He possessed the strongest arm of the group, but had terrible passing mechanics. Consequently, he struggled with accuracy when passing the football. His knowledge of the position was limited, too, and his skills the least refined, but he was hungry to learn and I always loved that about Fletch. He too was a very handsome young man, sporting bushy, light brown hair and a rugged, protruding chin below strong facial features.

A.J. Williams and Joe Scroggins were decent looking guys as well. A.J. was a thin, black kid with an athletic frame. He had played quarterback the year before for his high school team in

New Mexico. But because his school was so small, they'd only played five players on five, or something like that, and A.J.'s role was more like that of a running back than a quarterback. Joe was a stocky, country boy from right off on the farm in Arkansas. He was a strong kid, too, but not quite as athletic as the others. And he wasn't well equipped to play the position, not at the collegiate level anyway. Neither of the boys was deaf, but rather hearing impaired, A.J. more so than Joe, and both would soon find a position on the team other than quarterback.

And that brings us to Jimmy Gardner. Jimmy had short, un-ruly black hair that always looked like he'd just gotten out of bed. And he always had two fuzzy lines of hair that appeared to creep down along the nape of his neck. I kidded him a lot about needing to get a haircut, at which he would usually just smile. Jimmy had the slightest build of the three quarterbacks who would work with me regularly, including JC and Fletch. He was also the youngest. The program listed him at 6 feet tall, but I think that was a little bit of a stretch. He weighed about 170 pounds.

Like JC, he was very smart. Like Fletch, he was hungry to learn. Unlike either of the other two, Jimmy was left-handed and had the best passing mechanics of the three. A quick release, along with decent footwork, allowed Jimmy to regularly throw the ball with much more velocity that either JC or Fletch. He just wasn't nearly as athletic as those guys.

All five of the quarterback prospects were extraordinarily pa-tient with my painfully slow and elementary signing skills. They could have easily just blown me off and played the game the way they wanted to, or always had. But, they didn't. They were gen-uinely eager to learn and enjoyed the benefit of having a coach specifically assigned to their position. Aside from Brian Tingley, I probably learned most of my sign language skills from JC, Fletch, and Jimmy. As our primary quarterbacks, they spent a lot of time with me in the classroom, on the field, and on the team bus. For-tunately for me, we developed a good rapport and they all seemed just as happy to teach me how to sign as I was to teach them how to play quarterback.

Obviously, my signing was much better by now since I'd had some practice with it, but I still found myself using a few phrases a lot more often than others, such phrases as "Thank you" and "Nice to meet you." And that stood to reason. Well, "Do you understand me?" was another. In fact, in retrospect, I probably used "Do you understand me?" an inordinate amount of time. Maybe that was because I had an inferiority complex about my signing skills. I always feared I was signing something other than what I intended and not knowing the difference, I worried I'd make a big mistake and offend someone.

As a coach, I always wanted to ensure that my players understood any technique or concept that I was teaching them before moving on to the next. So I'd simply ask them, "Do you understand?" I had to sign it with my hands. As a new signer, I'd developed the habit of speaking while I signed. I guess this helped me keep track of what I was trying to say while actually signing. But the odd thing about when I signed the words "Do you understand?" was that when I whispered to myself while signing it, I'd actually say the word, "Comprende?" I don't know why. "Comprende?" means "Do you understand?" in Spanish and I couldn't help but wonder if my brain was subliminally blending languages? ASL is just that, another language. Why else would I speak Spanish while signing in English? This made me wonder, do Hispanic people sign differently than non-Hispanic people or is signing universal? Was ASL limited to just the U.S.? In either case, did anyone of any origin understand my signing? Comprende?

Near the conclusion of our final footwork drill, I heard a commotion at the far end of the field. I looked up and saw players dashing toward to the goal post in the opposite end zone. They came from all directions and in small packs. My quarterbacks saw this and immediately followed suit. Ed had signaled an end to the morning practice and wanted the team to huddle around him. Finally, there was a little "hooting and hollering." I should better describe their celebrating as screeching, grunting, and howling. They didn't know the difference, they were just happy that their first practice was over. I jogged down to the end zone and joined them.

Ed signed to the team for several minutes. I had very little idea what he was saying since Ed signed faster than I could interpret. Although the players would often tell me that Ed wasn't a good signer, he was obviously good enough to get his point across to them. But, just as I had the tendency to repeatedly use the phrase, "Do you understand?" Ed seemed to have a personal affection for several words and phrases, too. One of those words was the adverb "really".

"I *really* want you to understand how important it is to be at practice on time," he told them, "and I want you to *really* focus in the classroom."

The sign for the adverb "really" was simple. You just cross your fingers as if crossing them for good luck, and then extend them away from your body. It was easy to interpret too, because after JC explained it to me I was easily able to see just how much Ed used the word. In fact, what I found out was that he often signed, "Really, really".

When Ed was finished with what I assumed had been a standard pep talk, the team broke their huddle and scurried off to the field house. I returned to the far end of the field to gather my equipment. But when I got there, I found a short, Hispanic fellow already packing the training gear into my green, military duffle bag. His name was Allen Carrasco and, like Damian, he was another student-manager working for Kris Gould. He was a very friendly young fellow, too, always smiling and always very eager to help me with my stuff. Allen showed me where he'd be storing the duffel bag under the stadium and told me that he would retrieve it for me before each practice. I thanked him as he carried the four-foot high bag to the Gator and drove off smiling.

The rest of the coaches were already on their way to the field house or chatting among one another somewhere on the field. On my way into the field house, myself, I passed within a few feet of the team's athletic trainers who were working near the watering station. Practice was over, but there were still a few players needing the attention of a trainer. I stopped and introduced myself as a new assistant coach. There were three of them.

Jon Vaughn was the Head Athletic Trainer. He was a young guy, maybe twenty-five or twenty-six years old, and in just his second year as Head Trainer. Originally from Virginia, Jon had graduated several years earlier from James Madison University. He was maybe five-foot ten inches tall with a slender build. Although his short, brown hair often appeared to me to not be groomed, it might have been the style then. And like Ryan, Jon usually had a few days growth of facial hair along his jaw line. We got along well, though, and often talked to one another on the long bus rides to and from away games. He wasn't deaf either, which as you might imagine, originally created some difficulty for him. As he put it, he was constantly learning how to improve his signing skills.

Allison Lindsay was in her first year as an assistant trainer. She wasn't deaf either, and her signing wasn't quite as far along as mine. In fact, I actually had to translate for her a few times early on. Imagine that. Allison was tall and thin and had straight, reddish-blond hair about shoulder length long. Usually, she kept her hair in a pony-tail. She was young as well, maybe in her mid-twenties. Originally from New Jersey, she'd graduated from Delaware University in 2003 and then earned her Master's Degree at George Washington University in Washington, D.C. At Delaware, she'd studied and worked as an athletic trainer with the football team, and enjoyed it. Unfortunately for Allison, George Washington University didn't have a football team.

And then there was Kayly, an undergraduate, student-trainer at Gallaudet. She was younger than Jon and Allison, maybe twenty years old. Kayly spent most of her time in the training room helping them. She was hard of hearing, so while we mostly signed to one another, there were also times when we spoke. Once summer practices concluded, though, and school resumed, we didn't see much of Kayly for the remainder of the fall.

Jon, being the only male on the staff, usually travelled with the team for road games while Allison remained behind at Gallaudet to work with the soccer and volleyball teams. Once or twice, Allison accompanied us for an away game, as did Kayly, but not regularly like Jon. They were a small staff, but very efficient, and I thought they did a very nice job with our players, who kept their training room pretty busy.

With the morning practice over and a few hours before our afternoon practice, I went to the locker room to freshen up a little bit. The weather was great and I'd hardly broken a sweat, so there was little need to change clothes like I usually did between two-a-day August practices. I met up with several of the other coaches near the coaches' office. Most of the coaches were preparing to head over to the dining hall for lunch, where Ed had arranged for the coaches to have dining privileges there during the summer practices. And so I joined them. I would not only eat lunch at the dining hall, but also breakfasts, and some dinners. This was definitely a big departure from coaching high school ball. Instead of rushing down the street to a local sandwich shop or fast food joint, we actually had a sit down, all-you-can-eat lunch. And it was great food, too. I remember my first lunch very well: baked ziti, Italian bread, Caesar salad, and about five glasses of sweetened iced tea.

Ed and Ryan remained behind at the field house to work on the afternoon practice plan. They didn't arrive at the dining hall until about half an hour after us. But, by then I was already enjoying my meal with Brian, Kerry, and Chris Burke. The dining hall was crowded, but pretty quiet since all of the conversations around the room involved deaf students signing to one another. There was an occasional chuckle, or series of grunts, as one student would try to get the attention of another. Of course there was also the sound of clanking silverware, chairs sliding across the tiled floor, and food trays being returned to the dishwashing area.

The dining hall was easy to navigate, but as I surveyed the various food serving stations, I began to worry a little about placing my order. I'd no idea how to sign for the words chicken, salad, pasta, or basically any food group. But, alas, cafeteria style dining at a deaf dining hall turned out to be pretty simple. You grabbed a tray, pointed out to the server the food that you wanted to eat, and voila, it was on a plate and handed directly to you. The servers, many of whom were Hispanic, appeared to struggle with speaking English, but seemed to understand basic signing. And that was okay with me, because not only did I speak Spanish, I also had very basic sign language skills.

While we ate our lunch, we talked about how practice had gone and how some of the players were doing with their drills and such. I was continuously distracted, though, by the shrill voice of a woman somewhere across the room. She was moaning off and on, loudly, and in such a way that it sounded as if she was having an orgasm. Kerry and I seemed to be the only ones who noticed it, though. However, Brian must have heard her too, because he would occasionally look up from his plate and glance quickly about the room, nervously. I doubt that she was aware she sounded like that. Most of the deaf people that I came to know made some form of guttural sound as they signed. Some laughed, some grunted, some squeaked, and I guess some sounded like they were having an orgasm.

Chris couldn't hear her, of course, but he was very intrigued when Kerry and I used a few select, but universal, language arts skills to describe what she sounded like. I mean, how else were we going to sign that?

The afternoon practice was again mostly conditioning and drill based, with a little seven-on-seven just to pique the interest of the players. The quarterbacks were a bit apprehensive, except for JC. Otherwise, they were excited for an opportunity to demonstrate their passing skills, as limited as the opportunity was. After the practice, we had a brief coaches meeting before departing the field house at 5:45 p.m.

Some of the other coaches were staying on campus for dinner and some for the night. Not me, I went home, cut my lawn, had dinner with my family, and then watched my eleven-year old son, Mark, play a scrimmage football game under the lights later that evening. This was just his second year of playing youth league football and he was pretty excited for me to see him play. After the game, we talked about how well he'd played and how proud I was of him. It wasn't long after we returned home that I went to bed. It had been a long day and I was exhausted. I was so tired that I woke up in the same position in which I'd fallen asleep, not moving at all during the night.

Sunday morning football practice was a new experience for me. In high school, we weren't allowed to practice on Sundays. Most coaches probably wouldn't practice on Sundays even it was allowed. Sunday is church day. Sunday is a family day. Sunday is a day of rest. At least that's how I think most of us felt, anyway. At 7:45 a.m. on Sunday morning I'd normally be resting, as in still in bed asleep.

Instead, I was at the field house on the campus of Gallaudet University getting ready for our third football practice. Following a brief, thirty-minute coaches meeting, most of the coaching staff left the building and headed to the dining hall for breakfast. It was a short, five minute walk from the field house, past the stadium, to the dining hall. The cashier checked our names off on a list and requested that we sign for our meals in lieu of a cash payment or the presentation of a meal card. The breakfast food smelled terrific and it wasn't very crowded inside. Other than our football players, maybe there were two or three other people in the whole place.

As Brian, Kerry, and I ate, Harold walked into the dining room. While waiting to sign in, he looked over toward us.

"Harold, my man!" I signed and smiled.

Harold got a kick out me trying to sign that little phrase. He laughed. I'm not sure I ever did sign it correctly, or if there even was a correct way to sign, "Harold, my man." But it always seemed like Harold understood what I was signing. He smiled and pointed at me as he walked past the cashier's stand and toward the breakfast bar.

Suddenly, a very serious look came across Kerry's face.

"Is everything alright?" I said to him.

Kerry raised his clenched right hand to his lips and choked a little. He then began to beat upon his chest a few times, using his fist. Brian looked up at Kerry as well, briefly glanced across the table at me, and then back at Kerry.

"Kerry?" Brian looked nervous.

We watched Kerry for the next few moments as he began struggling to breathe. Something that he'd eaten was lodged in his throat and his face began to darken. My wife was a nurse and she had always told me that a person choking on food could probably still breathe if he was making a choking sound. She said that the time to take action is when they put their hands around their throat, because when they do that, you know for sure they are in trouble. And so I watched for Kerry's hands to go to his neck, which I was sure was about to be the case. I thought about the Heimlich maneuver, I thought about CPR, and then I thought about getting ready to call 911.

Kerry bent over sideways in his seat and gagged, dislodging whatever it was that was stuck in his throat. He swallowed, shook his head a few times and then caught his breath.

"Phew," he said.

He used his napkin to dab the moisture from his eyes and then began eating again as if nothing had just happened. Without a word, Brian and I just looked across the table at each other, relieved that Kerry was okay and that we hadn't been forced into some life-saving act.

The thought of dialing 911, though, prompted me to look around the dining hall for a telephone. That's when I first realized that there weren't any telephones in the facility. Since my cell phone was back in my locker at the field house, I began to wonder how I'd have called for emergency help. How did a deaf person call for emergency services? What if I'd had to do CPR on Kerry? As a pre-requisite for coaching high school football, I'd been trained to perform CPR. But the second step in that process, telling someone to call 911, would be a little difficult for me at Gallaudet. Who would hear me, someone in the kitchen? And so I wondered, how did deaf people call 911 in an emergency? I made sure that I had my cell phone with me at the dining hall from that point on.

Following breakfast we assembled in Room G 40 for a pre-practice meeting with the team. Ed addressed the players for about twenty minutes, lecturing them again on team policies, campus rules, and so on. I was able to follow along that morning, because most of the time, like me, Ed spoke as he signed. I watched him sign while listening to him talk so that I could begin to correlate what he was saying with the signs that he used. I also looked about the room occasionally at the reactions of the players, learning a little something about each one's character along the way. Just like any other football team, there were players who dozed off or doodled with pen and paper. And then there were players who were more focused and paid close attention to what was being discussed. And just like most other football teams, it usually showed which players were which when the team got out onto the practice field, which is where we were headed after the meeting.

Upon leaving the field house with Ed and Chris Burke, a young man rode his bicycle down the ramp and right past us as we walked toward the stadium. He was a little guy with bushy, blonde hair and eyeglasses. I didn't recognize him. Ed immediately turned and glared at him. At the bottom of the ramp, the kid got off his bike and dashed into the field house, his bicycle falling on its side upon the pavement. Once the kid was out of sight, Ed continued to walk toward the practice field. Chris and I followed.

"Who's that?" I signed to Chris after tapping him on his shoulder.

"That's Shawn Shannon," he said. "He's a wide receiver."

"Yeah, the little fucker was off-sides all the time last year," Ed said. "He lined up off-sides, said he couldn't see all that well. He's JC's favorite receiver though."

Shawn Shannon was five-foot seven inches in height and weighed only 150 pounds. He wore eyeglasses when he wasn't on the football field. He probably wore contact lenses when playing football, and when he didn't I guess he lined up off-side. He dressed like a surfer boy from California, although he and his twin brother, Robin, were actually from Honey Creek, Iowa. Robin was also on the football team, a defensive back, and about the same size as his Shawn. But unlike his brother, Robin kept his hair very short, didn't wear glasses, and was always very intense. Robin wore jersey number "3" and his brother, Shawn, wore number "4".

As we continued our walk to the practice field, I wondered why Shawn had been a wide receiver if he couldn't see very well. After all, if he couldn't see the line of scrimmage, how on earth could he see the ball in order to catch a pass from JC? Oh well, if Ed was ok with it then I guess I should be, too.

As I watched the players during Flex, I noticed Allen working over in the stadium. He was unloading my practice gear from the Gator. In the same part of the end zone where we'd worked on Saturday, he began setting up the agility ladder. I walked over to help him out, but by the time I got there, he'd already finished and was getting ready to move on to another assignment. I thanked him again for his help. He smiled. I told him that I had to make sure that we moved the ladder around each day so as not to destroy the grass beneath it. Allen indicated that he understood and from that day forward set my gear up a few yards away from where we'd worked the day before.

After Flex, Ed assembled his special teams unit to work on special teams plays. All of the other players, who didn't participate on the special teams unit, reported to their individual position coaches. The special teams unit on a football team is that group of players who are on the field whenever the ball is being kicked. They could be kicking the ball or receiving it from the opponent. And kicking the ball could mean that it was being punted, kicked from a tee, or from the hold of another player, such as on field goal attempts and extra points. Fletch was on the special teams unit, so he didn't get much time to do many of our quarterback warm-up drills. A.J. and Scroggins were on the special teams units as well. So, just JC and Jimmy were with me at the beginning of practice that day.

As I warmed up the quarterbacks, I heard Ed screaming from the middle of the stadium field. Something really had him fired up and it didn't take but a few seconds for me to find out what it was.

"Why are all of the fucking footballs over there with the quarterbacks?" he yelled with his hands raised high in the air above his head.

Although he wasn't yelling at me personally, or even in my direction for that matter, the inference was that I'd taken all of the footballs. Well, I just had the same four footballs that Kris had given me to use for practice on the day before. I didn't know where all of the other footballs were, though they were probably still inside the field house. Someone else should have been responsible for the footballs used by the special teams.

Jimmy had a good, strong arm, so I had him throw two of our footballs to Ed at midfield. I hated it when other coaches took our good throwing balls and used them for kicking. It ruined the footballs. I could use the same four footballs all year long for quarterback workouts and seven-on-seven drills and still manage to have them in great condition for the following season. Then I could send them to the special teams and get four new balls for the quarterbacks. That was good resource management.

"The same shit happens every year," I heard Ed say as he directed a couple of players to catch the balls thrown by Jimmy.

JC and Jimmy warmed their arms up by throwing to one another until Fletch joined us after working with the punt team.

We had a great practice and the guys really got into it. I was very pleased with their athleticism and attitudes. We worked specifically on their footwork for passing, both the three-step and the five-step drops. Three-step drops are used on shorter passing plays and require the quarterback to establish his passing platform, or stance, very quickly. Five step drops take a little bit more time to establish, but allow receivers to get much further down the field. Therefore, the quarterback has to throw the football much further. I was very excited by just how quickly they were able to pick up on the concept and rhythm of the short passing game. They also did very well with the five-step drop, although we only worked on it briefly.

Ryan had instructed the quarterbacks to use a hand signal to indicate to the center that they were ready for the ball. So I incorporated it into our drills since they needed for the hand signal to become second nature. Personally, though, I thought that it would be an easier signal for the center to see if the quarterback just lifted his foot up, even though for most teams that was the signal for a particular player to go into motion. We were not most teams, however, and our quarterbacks simply waved to a player that they wanted to send in motion. But Ryan was in charge and he insisted on the hand signal. And so they worked on doing just that before every practice snap, signaling with their hand to begin a drill.

I really enjoyed the transition from coaching the high school athlete to college athlete. It was always rewarding to see the dramatic development of the high school athlete. But watching the physically superior college athletes immediately implement and utilize the skills and techniques that you taught them was a blast.

JC and Fletch got most of the work in the first seven-on-seven drill with Ed and his defensive unit. That portion of practice was simply called "Skelly", which was short for "skeleton" since there wasn't a complete unit on either side of the ball, only the skilled position players. "Skelly" isolated the offensive backs and receivers against the defensive backs and linebackers and the offense only practiced its passing plays.

Each of the quarterbacks did pretty well, especially consid-ering their lack of familiarity with the new playbook. JC needed more reps reading the defenses, and Fletch needed a lot more help with his footwork and passing mechanics. Jimmy got in a few reps near the end of the period also. Ironically, of the three players, I actually thought that he looked to be the most comfortable in the position.

Near the end of practice and while the team was conditioning, I made my way around the field and retrieved the footballs that were used by the special teams unit. From that point on, I made sure that we used them only for passing.

Ed brought the team together at the conclusion of practice again and talked to them for just a few minutes before giving them the rest of the afternoon off. With the news that they were done for the day, the team was quite jubilant and enthusiastic as they headed back to the locker room. The coaching staff met briefly af-ter practice, and that's when Ed informed us that Daniel Dosema-gen, the big kid from Wisconsin, had already quit the team. His heart was just not into playing. Following our meeting, most of the coaches sauntered over to the dining hall for lunch before leaving the campus.

While at lunch, I took advantage of the opportunity to eat at a table with JC, Dima Rossoshansky, and Robin Shannon. Being around the players was about the best way for me to learn how to sign. And I enjoyed the time that I was able to spend with them. However, it took me a lot longer to eat when dining with players since I couldn't use my fork and sign at the same time. While I'd been taught as a child never to talk with food in my mouth, it was apparently okay to do if you were deaf since you didn't have to open your mouth. I couldn't do it, though. I still spoke while I signed, albeit under my breath, and not talking with food in my mouth was a manner that had been permanently engraved into my psyche.

6

Boys Will Be Boys

Some things in life are just a given, I guess. The sun will rise in the morning, it's always cooler in the shade, and boys will be boys. With just a week and a half to go before our first scrimmage game, our practices started become more intense, and so too, did the attitude of the players. Well, most of the players anyway.

In one of our offensive team meetings before practice, Ryan introduced several new plays that we'd be using during that practice. While he was diagramming the plays on the dry erase board at the head of the classroom, a commotion arose from the right side of the room. Several players began to shuffle their chairs away from the area while others got up and found seats on the opposite side of the room. They howled and grunted as they laughed and made fun of one another.

"What the hell is so funny?" asked Ryan as he snapped his head around, obviously annoyed by the disruption.

Adam Brimmer, a senior offensive lineman from Indianapolis, pinched his nose closed and made a farting sound with his lips, "Pthhh!" One of the other players had passed gas. I knew that sign. Several of the players just waved their hands in front of their faces and grimaced.

"Would you guys grow up?" Ryan scowled as he returned his focus to drawing plays on the board. He stopped and turned around after just a few seconds. "Jesus? Who did that?" The smell had made its way to the front of the room.

Ryan continued to diagram plays on the board, turning frequently to face the players as he did so that he could sign instructions to them. I wondered if skilled teachers of the deaf could sign with one hand and draw at the same time with the other. I knew that I couldn't and I didn't expect that Ryan could either. And he couldn't.

"Pthhh!" Adam Brimmer made the farting sound again.

Ryan went on drawing and paid no attention to Adam. I was seated on the far side of the room and glanced back and forth between both he and Ryan. I didn't know Adam very well yet, and wasn't sure if he was trying to get the best of Ryan, or just having fun with the guys.

"Pthhh!" There it was again.

Without moving my head at all, I shifted my eyes from Ryan to Adam to see if Adam was the one who'd made the sound again. Sure enough, he had, and this time he was smiling at his teammates after doing so. Ryan turned around briefly, but continued to ignore Adam. A few players chuckled. So they, too, must have heard the sound of Adam's lips.

"Pthhhhhhh!"

"That's enough, already," yelled Ryan.

He walked over to Adam with a look of disdain on his face, and said to him, "I can hear you. So stop it." The other players laughed aloud at Adam getting chastised. I thought the whole incident was a little funny, too. But then again, I wasn't the one trying to teach the offense how to execute new plays.

Beginning on Monday, the team's morning practices primarily consisted of conditioning drills and plyometric exercises. Ed didn't require the part-time coaches to be on the field in the mornings any longer. He understood that it was our full time jobs that put food on the table at home and not our part-time coaching salaries. And so he, Ryan, and Brian would conduct the morning practices for the next two weeks leading up to the commencement of the fall semester. I voluntarily went to a few of their early morning practices, but not many. Sometimes I couldn't make it because of work and sometimes I couldn't make it because I had to help my wife get our boys off to school. Whatever the reason, meeting one's personal responsibilities as a husband and a father should always take priority over those as a football coach, within reason, of course. Because if things at home were not in order, how on earth could I focus on being a good football coach on the field?

And so beginning on Monday I'd usually plan to arrive on campus around 2:45 p.m. Our team meetings in room G40 would begin between 3:30 and 3:45 p.m. The hour or so beforehand allowed me time to change clothes in the locker room, maybe grab a snack across the street, and review the daily practice plan that Ryan had prepared for us. Following our team meetings, the players had about fifteen minutes to suit up and get out onto the practice field by 4:30 p.m.

On that Monday afternoon following our first weekend of practice, the team lined up for Flex in both helmets and shoulder pads for the first time. Ryan got his opportunity to beat on the drum and he did so without injury to either himself or anyone else. Holding it with both hands, he pounded the mallet into the side of the drum with all of his might, as if trying to bust a hole in the drum skin. He clenched his jaws tightly each time that he pounded on the drum, and looked up afterward, smiling ear to ear, like a little kid. He enjoyed it. When the players finished their stretches and lined up for the agility portion of Flex, Ed walked over to Ryan and handed him a clipboard.

"You need to get attendance before they start hitting today," he told Ryan.

"Ok," Ryan said.

He set the mallet down on the side of the drum cart and took the clipboard from Ed's hand. He glanced down at the attendance sheet, lifted the paper up, and then looked back at Ed.

"Where's the pencil?"

"Don't have one," Ed replied.

"Why not?" asked Ryan.

"I don't need one. You do."

"What the hell?" Ryan chuckled, thinking that Ed was kidding. "You don't have a pencil?" he asked Ed again.

"No," said Ed, "I don't. If I were you, I'd go ask Jim if he has a pencil. He's probably prepared. I'll bet he has one in his fanny pack."

I was about ten feet away. I heard the entire conversation and Ed knew it. He was pretty wily, and generally knew at all times what was going on around him. He grinned devilishly as Ryan lowered the clipboard to his thigh and looked at me.

"You got a pencil," Ryan said to me, "in your fanny pack?"

"I don't carry a pencil in my fanny pack, Ryan. Sorry," I said. "I have a pen, though. Would you like to use that?"

Ed threw his head back and chuckled out loud as he walked away toward the trainer's tables near the sideline of the practice field. I took a pen out of my fanny pack and held it out. He grabbed it and went on about the business of taking attendance.

After Flex, the team broke into small groups for the Indy segment of practice. The quarterbacks and I made our way over to the end zone in the stadium where we usually worked on our drills. Kerry, meanwhile, was with his offensive linemen on the practice field near the baseball diamond, and Ed was just beyond them, working with his defensive players.

A few minutes into the practice segment, I heard Ed calling out to Kerry. But Kerry couldn't hear Ed because he was busy bellowing out commands to the linemen, even though his players could not hear them. He was very busy demonstrating to his players a particular stance and step drill. It's a very common, but effective, drill that's used at every level of football from the youth leagues to the pros. The primary objective of the drill is to get the linemen to use their hands and feet when pass blocking. It's important to teach them how to get their hands out in of front of them with their thumbs together and their elbows slightly bent. The players then need to learn to move their feet in order to maintain a position in front of an opposing defensive lineman. While doing so, they should be "punching" their palms up and into the chest of the defensive player. Well, apparently, it was Kerry's method of teaching the linemen how to do this that had caught Ed's eye. One of the linemen was having difficulty keeping his hands together and inside the framework of his chest. And so Kerry, using his ingenuity, had secured the player's hands together using plastic zip ties, the kind that electricians use to secure multiple wires together.

Unable to get his attention by calling out to him, Ed eventually left his group of defensive players and trotted over to where Kerry and his offensive linemen were working.

"Hey, coach?" Ed said. "What are you doing?"

"What do you mean?" Kerry said as he finally looked back at Ed.

"You can't handcuff a deaf person!" Ed said loudly.

Kerry's turned beet red and the expression on his face reminded me of Curly from the Three Stooges. I was waiting for Kerry to start finger-slapping his own face.

"Oh, yeah, I guess you're right," he said. "He needs his hands for more than blocking, doesn't he?" At first Kerry seemed pretty embarrassed, but he quickly shook it off and went right back to work.

Each practice presented me with another opportunity to improve my signing skills and I got a little better at it every day. Still, the key to my learning sign language was the patience of the players. When I signed to them, they could have anticipated what I was trying to say and interrupted me, but they didn't. If I had to, they'd let me spell out entire words one letter at a time. But what required the most patience on their part was when they signed to me. Being very fluent in ASL, they signed very rapidly, no matter how simple the message. Following along and understanding what they were telling me was extremely hard for me. I had to interrupt them constantly to ask them to slow down, repeat, and even spell out many words and phrases. And yet they never seemed to mind. Chris Burke explained to me that, being deaf, they had learned to be patient.

For me, learning to sign was much the same as learning to speak Spanish. I learned to say basic phrases in Spanish relatively quickly. But learning to interpret those same words was much more difficult for me, especially if spoken fluently. To make things a bit harder, I spoke Spanish well enough that the listener would often assume that I was more fluent than I actually was. And their response was usually so rapid that I couldn't understand them. Signing was pretty much the same. I'd become pretty good at signing a few basic things, enough so that someone might think that I could carry on a normal dialogue. But I couldn't.

As simple as they were, my conversations with the players began to open doors for me, doors that would allow me access to the deaf community. I began to understand the players much better, and where it was that they were coming from emotionally, which is very important for a coach if he wants to communicate effectively with his players, regardless of the communication process. I learned, too, some things about other coaches that helped me to better understand them as well. For example, I discovered that "Harold, my man!" was a personal trainer, working out of Northern Virginia, which explained how he was able to keep himself in such great shape.

I also learned that JC was engaged to be married and that his fiancé had been Gallaudet's Female Athlete of the Year in 2006. She had since graduated and the couple was awaiting his own graduation in January before proceeding with the ceremonies. Phil Endicott, the offensive lineman that I met in the eatery earlier that summer, was engaged to be married, as well. And so by knowing a lot of the things that I was learning, I wasn't only able to understand their motives for playing football, and better coach them as players, but also better able to mentor them as young men.

Practice went smoothly for the remainder of the afternoon and without incident. Ed did pick up the pace and intensity as the evening drew near, and that actually seemed to motivate the players, and in turn generate excitement among the team.

At the end of practice I ran across the field to where I saw that Ryan and Kerry were talking as they headed for the field house.

"Coach," I said to Ryan.

"What's up?" he replied.

"You got my pen?"

"Yep," he said, and pulled the pen out of his pocket to hand it to me. "Thanks."

"No problem," I said as I took the pen and placed it back into my fanny pack. Kerry smiled at me and shook his head as we all three walked back to the field house together.

*

The following day was August 14, my birthday, and it has always coincided with the beginning of the football season. When I was a player, I had to practice football on my birthday. As a coach, I had to practice football on my birthday. And this year was no different. But it didn't bother me. I had grown accustomed to celebrating my birthday on the football field a long time ago.

A funny story, though, from a few years back. On registration day for football at Severna Park High School, a freshman approached me just before leaving the gymnasium where the registration process was taking place.

"Excuse me, Coach," he said confidently.

"Yes, what is it, son?" I answered.

"I'll be missing the first day of practice," he said. "I just wanted to make sure that someone knows that I won't be able to be there. Is that okay?"

"Well, the first day of practice is pretty important, you know? It's never good to miss it if you don't have to," I said. "What's going on?"

"Well, it's my birthday."

I smiled at the thought of his innocence.

"Well, that's kind of bad luck, son," I shook my head. "You see, it's my birthday, too!"

He had a blank expression on his face.

"But, how about we have a cupcake together after practice, okay?" I said somewhat sarcastically. "I'll see you on Saturday."

He didn't seem too excited about my response. Maybe he didn't like cupcakes.

Occasionally, the team would sing to me, or a coach would acknowledge my birthday at the end of practice when addressing the team. But usually, it was just another day of practice for me and I didn't make a big deal of it. I certainly didn't expect that the Gallaudet players would sing to me, and they didn't, of course. I didn't even expect that any of them would know that it was my birthday, but they did. To my surprise, about a dozen or so players wished me "Happy Birthday" as I walked into the field house on Tuesday. And when I passed by the equipment room on my way to the locker room, Kris Gould poked his head out and said, "Happy birthday, Coach!" I was indeed pleasantly surprised that he knew as well, and I stopped to thank him.

"How did you know that it was my birthday, Kris?" I asked him.

"A few of the players told me," he smiled.

It turns out that the players discovered it was my birthday while surfing the internet in search of information about me as one of their new coaches. I'm told that most deaf kids are very skilled at finding information on the Internet and that they cruise it with zeal. It's a much more integral part of their daily routine than it is for many of us. When I mentioned to Ed that some of the guys had found out that it was my birthday, he told me that if there was something about me on the Internet, the whole team would know about it before long. Well, I didn't have a page on MySpace and Facebook didn't exist yet, so information on me had to be some-what limited.

Sitting on the bench in front of my locker before practice that day, I began to think about how quickly I was approaching the age of fifty. I remembered playing little league football as a kid and lying on the ground during warm-ups, the smell of fresh cut grass wafting across my facemask. Looking up out of my helmet, all I could see was blue sky. I remembered that so well. I also remembered being able to play football all day on a vacant lot a few blocks away from our house, and then again on the little league field at night. We'd get up again the next morning and be right back at it without so much as a single ache or pain. Those were the days, I thought.

As a coach, I guess I was in pretty good shape compared to most men my age. But that didn't mean that my legs didn't ache after practice, or that my lower back didn't hurt after standing on the field for several hours. In fact, they did, and I went through ibuprofen like they were Tic Tacs. Perhaps all of those years of playing football were beginning to catch up to me now. Regardless, because of the aches and pains, I'd begun to think about just how much longer I wanted to coach. And as I got older, the sun seemed to zap me of my energy much quicker than in years past, no matter how much sunscreen I wore, or how wide the brim of my hat. By the end of the day, I was ready for a good night's rest and falling asleep was seldom a problem. But, getting out of bed the next morning was a different story.

As I thought about my physical ailments and discomforts, an old man walked into the locker room carrying a small, white plastic bag in his left hand. He was in his late sixties, maybe even in his seventies, had short, white hair, and walked with what I thought was a cane in his right hand. But I realized very quickly that the cane was actually a walking stick and that the old man was blind. He used the stick with his right hand to feel his way to the end of the same bench that I was sitting on. He sat down upon the bench and placed the white, plastic bag on the floor in front of him. Without a word, he paused for just a moment before kicking off his shoes and feeling in front of him for a locker. As he did, the little white, plastic bag fell over near his feet and a canister of underarm deodorant rolled out of the bag and across the floor behind him.

"Let me help you with that," I said to him as I got up and reached for the deodorant. I picked it up and placed it on the bench beside him. "There you go."

There was no response from the man as he continued to undress and change from his trousers into a pair of gym shorts. I watched him stand up to pull his shorts on and when he sat back down to put on his sneakers, his hand knocked the deodorant onto the floor again. And again, I picked it up and placed it next to him on the bench.

"Might need that today," I said. "It's getting a little hot and muggy out there." Again, there was no response from the man. "Actually starting to feel like August," I added as I tied my turf shoes and began applying sunscreen to my face and neck.

But the old man still didn't say a word. I was closing the lock on my locker when I saw another man walk into the locker room, dressed neatly in a sport coat and slacks. At his side, he carried a gym bag out of which protruded the handle of a racquet ball racquet. He appeared to recognize the old man and approached him. Setting his gym bag on the floor beside the old man, he reached out with both of his hands, and then placed his right hand into the clasped palms of the old man. He was signing to him and the old man was using his hands to "feel" what the other man was signing. The old fellow smiled, patted the back of the other man's hand with his own, and then stood up as his friend walked away.

Not only was the old man blind, but he was also deaf!

Suddenly, I felt guilty. My aches and pains were nothing compared to the physical impairments that he had to overcome. I wanted to pat him on the back of his shoulder as I left the locker room, but didn't. I somehow felt that since he didn't know me that it might be considered intrusive to do so. I also didn't want to startle him, although somehow I had the feeling that he didn't startle easily anymore. And so I walked out of the locker room through the restroom area toward the exit. When I got to the door leading out of the locker room, I held it open for a moment and looked back at him. He wasn't too far behind.

A couple of interesting things happened out on the practice field that day. During Flex, I noticed that a new player had joined us on the field, jersey number "93", a big guy. But, much to my chagrin, the jersey he was wearing was navy blue. Our offensive line was undersized and this kid looked to go maybe 300 pounds, at least. We sure could have used a little more beef up front. My assumption was that Ed must have liked the boy's size as well, and as head coach decreed that a new defensive lineman had arrived.

"Hey, Coach?" I called out to Ed, who was standing behind the formation with his arms crossed, watching the team stretch. "Who's the new kid?"

"What new kid?" he responded without so much as even a glance toward me.

"Over there, in the back," I pointed "number 93."

"He's not new," Ed said, looking up from under the brim of his white visor, "that's Dosemagen."

"Dosemagen?"

"His daddy refused to pay for his airfare home, so he has to stay here," Ed explained. "And since he can't afford his room and board otherwise, he has to be on the football team, or pay up."

Dosemagen actually did fairly well with the conditioning drills and seemed to be ready to play football again. The coaches each made an effort to encourage him whenever the opportunity presented itself, and I was no different. I'd learned how to sign, "Nice job, looking good!"

When the team went to "Skelly", I got the opportunity to call plays for the offense. Ryan had been drawn away to help Damian, who was having a problem with a video camera. We filmed every practice. The practice segment went very well, and I felt pretty comfortable using the simple signs that Ryan had created for each of the plays. I also was doing okay communicating with the quarterbacks, who were executing the plays much better than I'd expected. They had a lot of questions about the routes that the receivers were running and which one they should throw to. Apparently, they didn't have too much experience recognizing or understanding defensive formations and coverage responsibilities. Ironically, as I worked with them on reading defenses, the biggest problem they had to overcome was their lack of patience on the field, something that I would have thought would have been one of their greatest assets.

Walking to the sidelines during a break in practice, I looked toward the end zone at the far end of the stadium. There I saw a player wearing a blue jersey emerge from behind some bushes along the outfield fence of the baseball field. He was very short, the shortest kid on the field in fact, which made it very easy to identify him. And I realized that I'd seen him over there several times during the course of the practice. The kid unfortunately had a medical condition that required frequent urination and, well, those short little legs hustled back and forth to the bushes the entire season.

When practice concluded, and I began to leave for the field house, I once again saw Allen packing up my gear on the part of the field where I'd worked with the quarterbacks. I still felt kind of guilty about not doing it myself, but was getting used to the luxury pretty quickly. I thanked Allen for his help every opportunity that I got. Before crossing the running track, though, as I made my way out of the stadium, I stopped to wait for several joggers to pass by. First, there were two middle-aged women walking together on the inside lanes of the track. Then a man and a woman running side by side went by me at a pretty good clip. And then, finally, there was a much older man jogging slowly along in the far outside lane. After he passed by me, I crossed the track. After doing so, I turned around to take another look at the older guy jogging in the outside lane, because he looked familiar to me. He was the same old man from the locker room who was blind and deaf.

I stood for about ten minutes and watched him run around the track in the outside lane. His stride was smooth, though short and deliberate, and he pumped his fists downward as he ran. I was amazed that he didn't veer or stray outside of his lane. And he didn't use his walking stick. Two times he went around the track as I watched, and not once did he appear to cross the line or stumble off of the track. The other runners seemed unfazed by his presence, too, but very conscious of his whereabouts. They didn't run in his lane, nor run alongside of him, and they made sure not to cross in front of him as they left the track. The thought went through my head that he should probably be heading back in soon, since daylight was beginning to diminish in the later hours of the evening and there were no lights around the track. But then I realized that that wouldn't matter to him. He was blind.

While leaving the parking lot after our post-practice coaches meeting, a brand new Honda Accord zipped past me en route to the main gate. As it darted across the front end of my car, and through the beams of my headlights, I recognized the driver. It was JC.

Like many of the players, JC lived off campus, though not in the dangerous neighborhood across the street from the school. It was my understanding that he lived with his fiancé and that they had a pretty nice place somewhere north of the city. That didn't surprise me, though, since JC was a lot older than most of the players and had his act together. Although he was a very athletic individual, he was equally as smart, and that's pretty much what made him the best all-around player on the team. But it wasn't his smarts and athleticism that made him the team's undisputed leader, but rather his unselfish character. JC always seemed concerned about the welfare of his friends and teammates. He never seemed to bask in the glory of success, either real or perceived, and he genuinely wanted his own success on the field to translate into success for the team. In fact, when I mentioned one time after a game that he had played well, he smiled for a second, but then shrugged it off, almost embarrassed to accept credit for his performance.

Alright, so JC was a good guy. How was that good guy able to afford a new Honda? When I was in college the only guys driving new cars around were those guys whose parents had big bucks. From what I knew about JC, his background wasn't one of wealth, but very middle class. So how was he able to afford that new car and an off campus apartment? Well, as a Gallaudet student, JC had the advantage of two great benefits that most college students don't enjoy.

The first benefit of being a student enrolled at Gallaudet was the incredibly low cost of the education there. Tuition, room, and board, was less than $12,000 per year as of 2007, including health insurance. That's because Gallaudet was a federally chartered institution, created by Congress, and serving governmental objectives. As such, the university received the bulk of its income in the form of an annual appropriation from Congress, which is overseen by the U.S. Department of Education. And so the university doesn't have to rely so heavily upon tuition-based income in order to survive.

Secondly, in addition to the grants, loans, scholarships, and other financial aid programs available to almost every college student, Gallaudet students had the unique opportunity to participate in Vocational Rehabilitation Programs. These programs were designed to help students obtain a college degree and achieve their career objectives. By enrolling in the program, a student would receive what was called Vocational Rehabilitation Money, or as our players called it, "VRM". I still don't know exactly how the actual program worked, but by the way that some of the players described it to me, it sounded like a student could "borrow" money against any future income that would exceed $30,000 per year. While in enrolled at the university, a student could receive as much as $1,000 per month. That should more than pay for a new Honda Accord.

The following day, near the end of practice, the team got its first taste of live contact. Ed allowed the offense to scrimmage the defense in goal line situations for about fifteen minutes. The play-ers were excited to finally hit one another and the coaches were eager to see their units in action. It was a very lively, but limited, practice segment. On offense, we primarily utilized our two her-alded freshmen running backs, Scott Lehman and Pierre Price, to run the ball. And they did very well, scoring a few touchdowns. But JC did not throw any passes, nor did he run the ball himself. And just like I'd seen at the high school level on the first day of full contact, some of the guys that I didn't expect to be hard hitters were. And some of the guys that I thought would be bone crushers were not. Fortunately, everyone walked off the field in good shape.

As we progressed through the week, the weather warmed up and became very hot and humid, which required more frequent water breaks for the players during practice. And with the team engaged in full contact drills, it didn't take long before ice bags be-gan to appear on the scene. Jon and his training staff started getting pretty busy after each practice. I would stop along my way back into the field house to watch them treat the players. One of their more common procedures was using large rolls of plastic wrap to secure bags of ice to injured shoulders, arms, and necks. The clear, plastic wrap was similar to the kind you might stretch across an open container of food, only a lot thicker. I thought using the wrap to secure ice bags against an injury was a great idea, and I was surprised that I had not seen the technique used before. I asked Jon if the plastic wrap in my kitchen drawer would suffice should one of my boys suffer an injury at football practice. He didn't think so, believing that it probably wouldn't be thick enough. And so he gave me a half-used roll of the wrap to take home. I've used it a few times, but fortunately not too much.

After a particularly long practice on Thursday, I had to do double-time it to pick Mark up from his own football practice. I got there about ten minutes before their practice was over. Most of the parents from his team knew by then that I was coaching football at Gallaudet and would frequently ask about it. One of the fathers told me that there was a player on the ten-year olds' team who was deaf. He didn't know which player, but pointed out where his team was practicing on the other side of the practice field. And so I thought that I might visit the boy before he left the field and say hello to him. I waited for my son to join me.

Mark and I walked over to where the coach of the ten year olds' team was speaking to his team after practice. When he finished talking to his players and released them for the night, I introduced myself, telling him that I'd hoped to speak with the deaf player. He quickly introduced me to the boy's father, who in turn introduced me to his son. It turned out that, although the boy was deaf, he wore a special hearing aid, which rendered him hard-of-hearing. He didn't practice, or play games, while wearing the hearing aid, though. And so on the field of play he was deaf. The kid had a great attitude, though, and spoke very well. I think that he'd become pretty skilled at reading lips, too. To my surprise, he didn't know ASL. The hearing aid and lip reading sufficed for the young boy. The family's plan was to have a cochlear implant inserted when he was older.

I told them of an athlete at Severna Park High School who was also deaf and had a cochlear implant. He was one of three boys in his family, each of whom was a tremendous athlete, although he was the only one of the three who had been born deaf. Unfortunately for our football team, his family was afraid that playing football might cause problems for him and the implant, and so he didn't play football once he got to high school. He did play basketball and lacrosse, though, and like his brothers, played lacrosse at the University of North Carolina in Chapel Hill. The ten year old was very inspired by the story, as was his dad.

Back at Gallaudet, the end of our first full week of practice was upon us, and so too, was a senior writer from ESPN the Magazine, accompanied by a local freelance photographer. They were on campus because ESPN the magazine wanted to feature a story about how the team was preparing for its inaugural NCAA season.

Several newspapers and magazines had published articles and stories about Gallaudet football in the recent past and I'd already read several of them, myself. And, of course, I'd seen the documentary that ESPN had produced a few years back about Gallaudet football.

I was somewhat familiar with the press from coaching high school football, but this was different. As a high school coach, you might talk occasionally with a reporter or two from the local newspapers, usually beat writers. But you seldom spoke with such an accomplished sports writer; someone whose work had garnered national attention. And that made me a little apprehensive about speaking with this guy. You see, I had a weakness in my game at that point, signing, and I really didn't want it to be broadcast to the world that a coach with a deaf football team wasn't very good at signing. So, for one of the few times in my life, I managed to keep a pretty low profile while they were on campus. I did speak with the writer briefly, though, as he walked along side of me between practices on Friday. It was mostly small talk, but I did find one of his questions to be pretty interesting.

"So, what do you think of Coach Hottle?" he asked me.

Well, there's a loaded question, I thought. Was my response going to show up in the article and if so, what would Ed think? And as an assistant coach, how was my opinion of Ed of any relative importance to the feature? Wasn't the story about the team? I paused before telling him what I thought.

"Ed's a good football coach," I replied, lifting my eyes up from the ground before me and over toward him. "He knows the game and manages the team very well."

"That's why he's the head coach," he said. He looked at me with a blank look upon his face as if he expected more of an answer. "He seems a little intense."

"And he can be a little intense," I added.

"A little?" said the writer with a wry smile upon his face.

"Okay, he can be very intense," I said. "But he's otherwise a very good head coach."

"Don't let him fool you with the loud bark," said the writer. "It's just a facade."

The writer presented his opinion of Ed as if it were a matter of fact. But, I didn't know Ed well enough yet to know what he was like away from the game. I suspected that he was quite a bit different when around his family and friends, though. The writer probably already knew that, having witnessed firsthand Ed's personality both on the field and off while interviewing him. Again he smiled wryly as he opened the door to the field house for me.

We walked into the field house and down the hall toward Room G 40. As we passed by the training room I looked in and saw three players in the same one-man whirlpool tub. Two of them were immersed up their necks and the third to his waist. At first I thought it odd to have three guys in the same tub, but it was the only tub that Jon had and I guess that he was making the most of it. Swirling in the water between the players was a yellow, rubber ducky. I shook my head and smiled, wondering whether or not the writer had witnessed the same sight. And if he did, and decided to incorporate it into his story, would he write about how our trainers treated multiple players, or would he write about the rubber ducky?

7

Let's Get Ready to Rumble

Saturday morning's weather was like no other August morning I can ever recall in the region. Temperatures were in the low 70's, humidity was nearly non-existent, and the skies were crystal clear. It was weather that made you feel good about being outdoors and it seemed to energize my aging legs. So many times in the past I remembered my legs just aching as I stood on the football field, socks wet with dew, and the urge to continually swipe what felt like a steamy sweat from behind my knees. When I felt like that, I often wanted to squat down to stretch out my thighs and relieve some of the stress from my calves. But whenever I squatted down, I could feel the dew that had popped up from the soles of my shoes as I walked, squish between the skin of my calves and the backs of my thighs, and it made me even more uncomfortable. Not today, though, not today.

The team had less than a week to go to before its first scrimmage game on Friday night against Shenandoah University. But our weekend practice had more or less taken on the feel of getting our house in order, rather than that of continuing to build it. It felt as if we were taking a step back to assess what we had at that point, and making adjustments. Ryan was visibly upset on the field about the offensive unit's lack of timing and execution, although I thought that it was to be expected at this stage of installing a new offense. Initially, I tried to support and encourage Ryan, even though his lack of patience was beginning to irritate me. I thought that he expected too much from the players, too quickly, and that he needed to respect the learning process. The new offense was a big adjustment for them, both physically and mentally. And whenever I tried to reassure him that he was doing a good job and that things would eventually come together, he would have none of it.

"Coach, this isn't high school football, this is college football," he'd say in a very condescending voice. "You need to understand that. These guys should be executing these plays by now."

I was relieved, sarcastically, of course. For a few days there, I'd been wrestling with what I thought was the early onset of dementia. Where was I? What was I doing all day in this strange place? Thankfully, Ryan had eased my worries by reminding me that I was actually coaching "college football." And I smiled to think that it was just one year ago that Ryan was on the field coaching about two dozen high school players on a small team back in Ohio. Meanwhile, at the same time I was several hundred miles away coaching about a hundred fifty. Now, he had twice as many players on the field with him. Maybe that was causing him to stress him out?

Things weren't going as well with the installation of the offense as Ryan had planned, and that was definitely frustrating him. And I don't think he could come to grip with the idea that it might not entirely be the fault of the players. Most of our starting players were veterans and, though still in transition, they seemed to have a very good sense of what Ryan was asking them to accomplish as an offensive unit. I thought there was a considerable amount of trepidation in the play of several key players, mostly backs and receivers, related to their individual roles within the offense.

I got the sense that they were confused. After all, I was somewhat confused by our offense, myself. When a player is confused, he's going to slow down, make mistakes, and eventually lose confidence in himself. And that's what I saw our guys doing, slowing down, and worrying about whether or not they were doing the right thing, and if they should even be on the field. They weren't playing like the confident athletes that they were, which was crazy to me since I'd come to admire the self-confidence that all of these guys exuded.

Long ago, our old football coach at Annapolis High School use to say, "Keep it simple, stupid." More simply put, Coach Larimore called it the KISS Principle and over the years he had tons of success coaching both football and basketball by just sticking to that principle. I told Ryan that I felt we needed to embrace that same principle, at least initially, whether that meant that I was thinking like a high school coach or not. Didn't Vince Lombardi coach the Green Bay Packers? Of course he did. And I've often read that Coach Lombardi liked to keep things really simple and that his World Champion Packer offense basically ran just three or four plays. But they ran them well. So was that coaching with a high school mentality? If it was, well, then the National Football League's Super Bowl trophy is named after a man who coached with the mentality of a high school football coach! And I think that's pretty darn impressive.

Perhaps it was my insistence that some of our offensive formations were too confusing, or maybe he felt Ed breathing down his neck, but Ryan announced that he was going to make some adjustments to the offense. In our morning meeting, he abolished the use of color coded personnel packages. In other words, up until this point, the color red might have indicated that he wanted two wide receivers, two tight ends, and a running back out on the field to run a particular play, or series of plays. The color blue maybe meant that he wanted two wide receivers, one tight end, and two running backs. I don't remember what they all were, but we used several more colors. There were several players, like Fletch, who played multiple positions. Those guys, in particular, were having a really tough time trying to remember which of the colored packages they were supposed to be in on, and at what position? For example, he could be the running back when the red group of players was on the field, but a slot receiver in the yellow group. And maybe he wasn't on the field when the orange group was called upon. Forget learning the plays, or just how to execute them, they weren't even sure if they were supposed to be on the field! It was a mess, and I was glad that Ryan decided to go back to basic formations with an assigned position for each player.

Ryan started using signals to essentially change a formation. It was much simpler than constantly changing colors, player packages, and identifying the direction of a play. Now, we could just signal a formation, a motion, and the name of a play. It was far easier for the players on the field and I welcomed the change, regardless of why he made the changes. Plus, it meant that I no longer had to try to remember ASL signs for all of the colors. Other than for our colored personnel packages, I really didn't have a need to know the signs for colors. Think about it, how often do you actually need to say the name of a color in your daily dialogue?

Well, the players responded well to the changes and our offense began to operate much more efficiently that afternoon. And of course, once JC was on board with the changes, the rest of the team fell right in line. He was as close to a player-coach as I think a college team could have. JC directed player movement on the field, encouraged his teammates to play with confidence, and settled them down whenever frustration affected a player's performance. We also pared our quarterback stable down to three: JC, Fletch, and Jimmy Gardner. At Ed's direction, I explained to A.J. Williams and Joe Scroggins that they would see little, if any, playing time at the quarterback position. And so I sent them to work with different position coaches. They were disappointed, but understood. A.J. went to work with the wide receivers and Joe exchanged his yellow jersey for a navy blue one. That would give me more time to work with our primary quarterbacks, but at the same time I'd also lost the two players who could hear me and help translate to the other three.

During the afternoon practice on Saturday, Ed was visited by a woman and her family on the sidelines. They stayed for the entire practice, too. While she mostly looked after her boys, the husband seemed to be interested in practice. She and her family were my first glimpse into the personal side of Coach Ed Hottle. The woman was his sister. She and her family were in town for the weekend and stopped by to visit him. When he introduced me to her, I found her to be warm, friendly, and soft spoken, not at all like the person that her brother projected himself to be. Had I peeked behind the façade that the sports writer spoke of?

The temperature outside began to rise dramatically on Sunday morning and it suddenly felt like typically hot, August weather again. But the stifling humidity didn't seem to bog the offense down at all, and it continued to show signs of steady improvement. JC appeared to be more comfortable with our offensive objectives. And Fletch, although working primarily as a slot receiver, was also showing signs of improvement as the team's back-up quarterback. At that point, Jimmy was spending most of the practice as an observer, watching JC and Fletch. But he wasn't just watching. Instead, he would stand near to me and ask questions about strategy and play-calling. Jimmy was learning, preparing for his chance to play, whenever that might be.

The weather wasn't the only thing heating up at Gallaudet that weekend. The level of intensity among the players on the field began to escalate as well, especially during the team segment of practice that morning. Not to be outdone by Ryan and his offensive unit, Ed tried to motivate his defense to improve as well. He did so by challenging them to match the intensity of the offensive unit, both physically and emotionally. Of course, this wasn't accomplished by simple words of praise, but rather with vein popping, fist pumping, and dirt kicking fervor. That was Ed's way and it worked. The defense began to redirect every stride forward made by the offense. They won some battles and they lost some, but all in all, the field of play was evening out. Some refer to that as the offense catching up to the defense. But, whatever you wanted to call it, the two units had begun to strengthen one other as a result. Although neither the offense nor the defense emerged as the dominate unit that morning, it was perhaps a good thing, because after lunch it was time for team photographs. It's always better when you're one big, happy family on picture day.

*

There were some city blocks along my drive to the campus where I felt that my personal security might be at risk on any particular day. But the first time that I actually came face to face with the real possibility of physical injury occurred on the practice field that Monday afternoon. It happened about half way through the practice, with the two units scrimmaging live against one another. The offense was working on its passing game and the defense, of course, was trying to defend against the pass. Now when one unit is doing really well during a football scrimmage, it usually means that the other unit probably is not, and that was the case for our team that day. And when you're having a bad day in a physical game like football, it's pretty easy to get frustrated and lose one's cool. Sometimes, a little extracurricular activity occurs when a player tries to vent some of that frustration, like a little push here or an extra shove there. Well, the offense was doing pretty well and the defense was not, especially one linebacker in particular.

Ricky Bailey, who wore the number 40 on his blue jersey, was a freshman linebacker from Willingboro, New Jersey, just north of Philadelphia. Ricky was a black kid listed in the program as 6'1" and 240 pounds. Like many athletes, his lower body was very muscular and well developed. The kid was thick, as we like to say in football, meaning that his body had a solid base, including strong legs and usually a larger than average posterior. Ricky's posterior was bigger than most. In fact, I'm surprised that Kris Gould found pants to fit him. Nonetheless, he had a body made for contact sports.

During the team segment of practice, Ricky just wasn't getting the job done as a defender in pass coverage. JC was able to complete passes to just about any receiver operating in Ricky's area of responsibility, which didn't sit well with Ed. And at one point, he approached Ricky with some very colorful dialogue to let Ricky know that he wasn't impressed with the linebacker's performance. And, of course, Ricky didn't appreciate his coach jumping into his facemask to scream at him after what seemed like every other play.

Things began to get a little dicey on the very next play.

Cole Johnson and Shawn Shannon were running shallow crossing routes, Cole from the right side of the offensive formation, and Shawn from the left. That means that each player was running laterally across the field, about ten yards deep, but toward each other from opposite sides of the field. The play called for them to pass within a yard or so of one another, making it difficult for defensive players to cover both receivers. Usually, one of the defensive players will get "picked off" by one of the receivers at the point where they pass by one another. As a result, one of the two receivers will usually be 'open' to receive a pass from the quarterback.

On the play, Ricky was responsible for covering Shawn in man-to-man coverage. Shawn made his cut right in front of Ricky, and then began running full speed across the field toward Cole. Ricky, running full speed himself, was behind Shawn, trying to keep up with the speedy receiver. As the players neared one another in the center of the field, Shawn angled slightly to his right to avoid running into Cole, who was not looking forward, but rather at the quarterback. Well, Ricky didn't take that slight angle to his right, as Shawn had done ahead of him, and as a result collided head on with the 170 pound sophomore from Edina, Minnesota. The impact of the two colliding was so vicious that it could be heard by everyone on the field that could hear, including those who were hard of hearing. It wasn't a good moment to be Cole Johnson.

I'm pretty sure that Ricky saw the play unfolding in front of him and could have avoided the hit, at least the way that it unfolded. But like I said, he was in a sour mood by that point, and knowing that he was the much larger body of mass, he probably decided to just let it happen. The hit, though, was not a problem. You see, Ricky had a really great smile, and that smile was normally accompanied by a sharp giggle. I don't know why, it just was, always. And I don't really think that Ricky knew he giggled when he smiled. I think it was just part of the deal. Well, after the hit, Ricky stood up, Cole still on the ground below him, and for whatever reason, looked down at Cole and smiled. Of course, when he did, he giggled.

Adam Brimmer saw Ricky standing over of Cole and didn't like what he'd seen happen to his receiver. And so the big offensive lineman charged Ricky, hitting him chest high and taking him to the ground. Ricky hadn't seen Adam coming, either, and landed flat on his back with Adam on top of him. They landed with an enormous thud. They began fighting and the two of them went at it with an unbridled fury. At first, it was just Ricky and Adam, but as several of the other players tried to break the two apart, they themselves got hit and consequently joined in the fracas as well. Soon, there was an all-out brawl that most of us coaches thought would be short-lived, including me. It's not uncommon for a fight to break out at some point during a hot, summer football practice; it's the nature of the beast. Things weren't any different at Gallaudet. But when players began to join in from every corner of the field, things got quickly out of hand.

"Coaches, get in there and break it up!" yelled Ed after he realized that that this was no ordinary fight.

Ryan and I had been standing behind the offensive unit during the play and were just a few yards from the initial fight. At Ed's command, Ryan rushed into the fray without hesitation, the good soldier that he was. I was right beside him for a moment, until I came to my senses.

Like they might say in the military, that's a bad order, I thought to myself. These guys were big and strong, throwing wild punches, and wearing equipment. And what was I going to do, run in screaming, "Break it up! Break it up!" to a bunch of deaf guys? It wasn't like they'd hear me and come to their senses. I thought for sure that they'd feel me wedging my way in and assume I was just another player and then slug me once or twice. No way was I going into that mess. I looked at Ed, who was standing and watching from about 30 yards away. He was angry as hell, I could tell. But he was smart enough to stay out of the mess himself and, doggone it, so was I.

Ryan, though, had leapt right in, God bless him, and was being pushed around pretty good amid the pile of humanity. I'd see him surface for a brief moment and then back under he would go. Brian and Harold were able to pull a few players away from the perimeter of the fight and seemed to be holding their own. Kerry charged in after Ryan, but was thrown to the ground himself. He quickly realized the error of his ways and worked himself back out to the edge of the brawl, near where I stood. As Brian and Harold, and I guess, Ryan separated the players from one another, the rest of us coaches kept them from joining back in. Although no physical match for Ricky, Cole was still a pretty strong athlete, and by the time that the fight had settled down, he'd gotten back to his feet. Fortunately, he suffered no serious injuries as a result of the play.

It took about ten minutes for any semblance of order to emerge and as it did, a light rain began to fall. Ed got the attention of the team and commanded them to assemble in the end zone, except for Ricky Bailey; he dismissed him to the locker room. I wasn't sure at that point whether Ed was dismissing him from the team or not, though it appeared so. Later, he and Ed would have a one-on-one discussion and Ricky ended up staying with the team.

Ed directed each coach to establish a position at points up and down the field no less than twenty yards apart from one another. The lines on the field were fading as the grass grew longer, and so he was using us as field markers. He signed to the players for a few short minutes and then threw his arms down to his sides. And with that the running began. I stood at the forty yard line nearest the end zone from where the players began running. Brian was twenty yards in front of me and Ryan was twenty yards behind me. Ron and Kerry were at the far end of the field.

Every time the players ran twenty yards to where a coach stood, they'd touch the ground, return to the end zone, turn around and run to the spot where the next coach stood. Again I had very little idea what Ed had actually signed to them since in his anger he'd signed it so quickly. But it wasn't hard to figure out. Call them gassers, ladders, or suicides, whatever you want to call them. Ed was doling out his form of discipline for the team's fighting. Quite simply, it was called running.

As the clouds darkened, the rain began to fall harder and harder. Eventually, I had to pull down on the bill of my hat to keep the rain from hitting it and running across the underside of the brim and onto my face. My shirt was soaked with rain, as were my shoes, and I was glad that I'd purchased the extra set sitting in my locker. I watched the players run by me, and each of their faces was without expression. They knew that what had happened was unacceptable, that there was a price to be paid, and they were paying it. I heard a grunt here and there, but nothing more as they began to slip and slide in the muddy turf of the stadium field. I could also hear the wet plodding sound of each player's cleats as he ran.

Occasionally, I'd acknowledge a player with a slight nod of my head, but otherwise, I just stood in place like the rest of the coaching staff, and observed. I'd been there before, both as a player and as a coach, and knew the drill. Ed stood motionless at midfield just behind me and to my right, his arms crossed over his chest. He stared out from under his baseball cap toward the end zone, his eyeglasses fogging up. The longer they ran, the harder it rained. After about thirty minutes had passed, Ed dismissed the team for the night.

In the locker room afterward, Harold and I discussed what had happened. As we changed into dry clothes, Ricky Bailey entered the showers. Sometimes players showered in our locker room if their own was too foul, or congested. I waved to get Ricky's attention and he walked over. Slowly, but as best as I was able, I tried to explain to Ricky via signing that what had happened was wrong, and that he could have avoided the big hit on his teammate, Cole. I also acknowledged that he had the potential to be a tremendous athlete, and that I hoped he'd make good use of the physical abilities that God had blessed him with.

Ricky didn't smile this time, he just listened respectfully to what I had to say. Regardless, he acknowledged that he understood what I'd told him and then headed off to the showers. As we walked toward the locker room exit, I glanced over at Harold and asked him if my signing to Ricky had been understandable. He gave me the thumbs up and a facial expression indicating his approval of my message to Ricky. I felt good about that.

Whether we realize it or not, God uses us all to do His work on a regular basis. We just don't always know it at the time. We're sometimes well down the path of life before we see the light and come to understand a particular role that we've played in someone else's life. And when that happens, I think that God's revealing His work in and through you, which itself is a blessing. And that's the way I feel about much of my experience coaching the boys at Gallaudet, including Ricky.

*

On Tuesday, I noticed a man standing on our sidelines observing practice. He was a tall, broad shouldered man, casually dressed, and wearing a baseball cap and sunglasses. The man nodded to me on a few occasions as we either moved from one spot on the field to another, or he moved about and happened to cross my path. And when we broke into our Indy period, and the quarterbacks and I began to warm up, the man slowly made his way to a position behind us, just a few yards away. It didn't bother me so much that he was there, but I was a little self-conscious about my signing and what he might think of my instruction since I still presented it in such remedial terms. I acknowledged him and signed "hello," but he didn't return my sign, simply offering a small wave instead.

"Did you play football?" I signed to him.

He dropped his arms with his hands out toward me, palms down, and shrugged his shoulders slightly. I immediately knew that he wasn't deaf.

"You can hear me?" I asked, pointing to my ear.

"Yes, I can hear you, Coach," he said. "I'm sorry. I don't mean to disturb you. I was just interested in the drills that you were doing with your quarterbacks."

"No problem," I smiled. "Watch all you want. If you have any questions just ask."

"I will. Thanks, a lot."

His deep, confident tone of voice carried well, even in the hot, dense summer air. Oddly enough, I had the feeling that I knew this man, his voice, and his friendly smile. I couldn't place him at first, but he looked very familiar. He seemed to be having the same idea about me.

"Do you live around here?" I asked the man as I looked back at JC and Jimmy warming one another up. Fletch was still with the punt team and would join us in a bit.

"No," the man said. "I'm from Ohio. I'm just visiting for a few days."

"Okay, because you seem pretty familiar to me for some reason." I smiled.

The man shook his head. "In fact, this is only the second time that I've ever been in the area. The first time was this past spring when I visited the Naval Academy with a group of co-workers from back home."

I immediately knew why he seemed so familiar. He recognized me, too, and smiled.

"Cliff Hite," he said, offering his hand.

"Jim Overmier," I replied, shaking his hand.

"You were the guy that gave us the tour of Annapolis this spring," he said.

"That was me!"

Several months earlier, one of my Coach & Courier drivers was late picking up his passengers at BWI Airport near Baltimore. And so I hopped into one of our full-sized vans and headed off to the airport so to pick them up myself. There were about eight or nine of them, all educators from the same school district in Ohio. They had been invited by the Naval Academy to visit the Annapolis campus to become more familiar with the educational experience the Naval Academy offers its students.

Well, this fellow sat in the front bench seat of the van, right behind me. And being the friendly sort of guys that we each were, we'd struck up a pretty good conversation about the area and the Academy. I offered them the scenic approach to the Naval Academy, including a brief tour of historic downtown Annapolis. And being first-time visitors, they gladly accepted.

As I drove them across the Severn River and toward Annapolis, I mentioned to the man that I coached a local high school football team, and that several of my former players were now playing at the Naval Academy. He told me that he, too, had been a high school football coach, in addition to being a teacher and state legislator. The man went on to tell me of how he wouldn't be remembered for winning championships, though, but rather for playing his own son at quarterback instead of a kid that turned out to be better at the position. He didn't mind that he'd become sort of a local enigma as a result, but actually enjoyed the role instead. You see, the other kid went on to win two Super Bowl rings as an NFL quarterback. The other kid was Ben Roethlisberger, and the man was Cliff Hite, the father of Ryan Hite, our offensive coordinator.

Cliff was a good guy, very jovial and friendly; quite the opposite of Ryan. We spoke several times during his brief stay to visit his son, and about a variety of things including Ryan, politics, and of course, football. His wife had accompanied him on the trip, but hadn't come to the school, and I never got a chance meet her. He appreciated some of my suggestions on where they could get a good meal or two in Annapolis, and some local points of interest that I thought they might enjoy visiting. He came to watch several practices and during those visits, I would watch as he and Ryan walked about the field. Cliff was obviously very proud of his son. But after watching the chemistry between them, I had the feeling that there might be a little distance between the two of them, maybe a little tension, or some disagreement. As a father myself, I had a feeling that Cliff was in town to make sure that his son was doing okay.

Until then, all I really knew about Ryan was of his playing days at Dennison University and his short coaching stint at North Baltimore High School back in Ohio. Well, before the end of the day, I had a little better idea about what had actually brought him to Gallaudet. I'm sure that Ryan believed he was taking advantage of an opportunity to break into coaching college football. But, if you asked me, it seemed more likely that he was a young man running away from some difficulties back home.

For starters, his short marriage was already on-the-rocks. And although Ryan would offer that there might be a shot at reconciliation, he never really sounded as if he wanted that to happen. With him in Washington and her in Ohio, the other coaches and I never thought that that had much of a chance anyway. And as the Youth Pastor of his church back home, Ryan had had a falling out with the congregation, or the church administration, or both, and he'd been asked to step down from the position. Ryan probably harbored a lot of resentment about that situation, which would help to explain why he might be struggling with his own faith. I began to see Ryan in a different light and regarded him as less of an adversary and more as a man that God wanted back in His fold. Did I have a role in facilitating that? I wondered.

Back on the practice field, the team was substantially smaller as a group for a few days. The freshmen were not allowed to practice from Wednesday until Friday. They were required by the university to attend new student orientation classes. From the practice field, we would see several of them walking across the campus from time to time. Occasionally, one or two of the freshman players waved to us from the street outside the stadium. We weren't sure if they'd be able to participate in that Friday night's scrimmage game against Shenandoah or not, which made game planning a bit more difficult.

With fewer numbers on the practice field, the veterans saw increased repetitions in drills, and much more frequent contact during team segments. While working on the inside run, several players went down with injuries. It was obvious that the adrenaline that had carried them through their first week and a half of practice was dissipating. They were getting tired. Ed sensed this and cut practice short, sending them back to their dorms.

For the first time, I saw the boys as not quite the group of athletes I thought college athletes should be. They were worn out a bit, perhaps due to a lack of pre-season conditioning, perhaps because they simply weren't that athletic. Many of them looked as if they hadn't been in the weight room for some time, if at all. While some were overweight, others might have been just too downright small to play college football. Either way, I began to wonder just how well we would do on Friday night.

Ed kept Thursday afternoon's practice very light. We began the practice by working on the kicking game: punt, punt return, point-after-touchdown, and kick-offs. Ryan ran the offense up and down the field a few times, calling plays from the sideline while the team worked without a huddle. We ran the plays "on-air," or without any defensive players on the field. After each play, I'd take the football from the ball carrier and place it five or ten yards further down the field, until the offense reached the end zone. I'd alternate where I placed the football. Depending on the conclusion of the play, I'd place it on either the left hash mark or the right; sometimes between the two. That way, Ryan could practice of calling plays according to where the ball was on the field. During the drill, if there was a problem with how the quarterback executed the play, I'd try to talk him through it, though Ryan had little patience for that.

"C'mon Coach! Let's go!" Ryan screamed as I answered a question from JC regarding his footwork on a play-action pass. JC frowned as I quickly jogged away to place the ball on the ground for the next play.

While the offense was going through its pre-game practice, Ed was in the end zone working with two of the student managers, Damian and a kid named Dustin Cutrer. Dustin seemed to be easily frustrated and didn't cope with anxiety particularly well. But he was out there in the pending darkness giving it the old college try. They were attempting to assemble new end zone camera equipment that Ed had managed to procure the funds for.

The new equipment included a telescoping unit upon which a video camera was affixed. The idea was to erect the telescoping unit behind the goal post and film from there, well above the action on the field. Combined with the camera from the sideline, this would provide us with the valuable coaching tool of multiple angle game film. It looked like they were having a time of it down in the end zone, though. When we wrapped things up on the stadium field, Ed briefly joined us at midfield to give the team some instructions for the following day. He then dismissed us from practice and returned to the end zone to oversee the ongoing project there. After changing clothes I walked out to my car, which was parked behind the field house. As I drove off, I saw Ed and the managers still trying to figure out how the telescoping pod worked. Ed didn't look happy.

8

Under the Lights vs Shenandoah University: Our First Test

Playing football on Friday night was nothing new to me since most of our high school football games were played on Friday night. What was new to me, though, was the sight of the two air-conditioned, charter buses parked out in front of the field house when I arrived on campus. The weather that afternoon was hot and humid, and the sight of those two buses was a welcome one. No more cramped and smelly, yellow school buses like the ones we used to haul our high school players around in. The trip to Winchester, Virginia to play Shenandoah University would be done in style. It was just another facet of coaching college ball that I was beginning to enjoy. The only drawback was there wouldn't be any more 20 minute road trips like in high school; they'd be more like eight or nine hours. The road trip to Shenandoah University was only two and a half hours, the shortest bus ride we'd have all year.

When I approached the front of the field house after parking my car, I saw the team managers already loading the buses with gear and equipment, including the big, bass drum, of course. At the same time, Jon and his staff were checking their medical kits and making sure their duffels were loaded on board as well. Kris Gould appeared to be overseeing both ends of the operation. I checked in with Ed, who was pacing about on the concrete sidewalk between the buses and the field house, and then proceeded to the equipment room to bag a few new game balls. Before each game, home or away, I'd pack up a few practice balls and several new game balls. I also brought a scrubbing brush and scrubbed the new balls to remove the sheen from the surface of the new leather. Otherwise, they could be somewhat slippery and difficult to handle.

Offensive players boarded the first bus and defensive players the second as we departed Gallaudet at 2:00 p.m. to begin our journey through D.C. traffic en route to Virginia. The freshmen had joined us as well after completing their orientation. Neither Ed nor Ryan felt that the buses were in very good condition, but I thought they were pretty comfortable. Once I got settled into my second row seat, though, I began to look around inside the bus and I could see what they meant. The windshield was cracked, several of the arm rests were broken off, and a few of the small, overhead televisions were inoperable. Initially, there was a strong smell of urinal deodorant that wafted throughout the passenger compartment. It either went away or we quickly got used to it, though, because after a very short time I didn't smell it anymore.

Regardless, travelling to a game in a charter bus was a new experience for me. And, like I said, it was a whole lot more comfortable than the traditional, yellow school bus with six players more than there were seats on the bus. I reclined in my seat, reviewed the play calling sheet that Ryan had prepared for the offensive coaches, and then watched a movie with the rest of the team.

I don't remember which movie we watched on the way to Virginia or on the way home for that matter. What I do remember was wondering how difficult it must be for the players to follow along with the movie. It was a little naïve of me, I guess, but I didn't figure that having the volume up as loud as they did would make it any easier on a deaf person. It might help those who were hard of hearing. So, when Brian popped up out of his seat to adjust the

DVD player, I realized for the first time that DVD's are also closed captioned. All you have to do is activate the option through the DVD menu and voila, the words begin to appear at the bottom of the screen. I never knew that. But then again, I never needed to. At first, I found myself reading the words and missing out on some of the movie action above them. The stupid thing was that I didn't need to look at the words because the volume was so high, too high really, but I did anyway. About fifteen minutes into the movie, though, I was reading the closed captions and following the action at the same time, as if I'd done it all of my life. In fact, at times, I thought that I might be reading the words and ignoring the voices of the actors and actresses. That was a little puzzling. But I couldn't ignore the sound though; the volume was just too loud. I thought it to be peculiar that I was on a bus with about thirty deaf football players and yet the loudness of the movie was deafening to me. Ryan seemed unfazed by the loudness and gazed intently at the show. I thought to myself that he was a young guy and was probably used to loud music and movies.

The football stadium at Shenandoah University sits on a parcel of land adjacent to Interstate 81 North just outside of Winchester, Virginia. For those of you unfamiliar with the area, Winchester is in the northernmost portion of Virginia, just below where the small arm of West Virginia juts into the state of Maryland. Interstate 81 actually separates the stadium from the main campus of the school. The stadium sat on the east side of the highway. Motorists travelling from the north had a clear look into the stadium. In fact, I'd passed the stadium on dozens of occasions in the past and must confess that although I'd taken notice of it, I'd never really given much thought to what team played there or to what school it belonged. It was a very nice, but small stadium, and had a seating capacity of about three thousand, the bulk of which sat on the home team side in the main structure. On the visitors' side were a few sections of stadium like bleachers that faced to the south. My guess is that they probably held a few hundred people at the most.

Our buses drove onto the Shenandoah University campus at about 4:30 p.m. and we were escorted to Shentel Stadium. There, we were directed to a small, white building that sat behind the goal posts at the east end of the field. The one-level, cinder block building housed dressing rooms and showers for both teams, each with their own entrance. It sat in such close proximity to the field that there was a large net that hung above it to catch footballs kicked through the uprights from the playing surface. Without the netting, the footballs would likely have landed on the roof of the building, or in the parking lot on the other side.

When the doors of the bus opened we were rudely reminded by the extreme humidity that it was still late summer. And it was hot. There were towering cumulonimbus clouds approaching from the south, almost as if funneled through the valley toward Winchester. And although the hot sun shone brightly upon us at the time, the smell of rain was in the air. I used to think that my mother was crazy when she said she could smell rain. But over the years I guess that I'd inherited her keen sense of smell because it definitely smelled like rain. The players grabbed their gear bags and headed inside to our locker room. I grabbed my bag of footballs and muddled my way in among the herd. While they stored their gear, I walked on through the building, out the exit on the opposite side, and onto the turf field of the stadium outside. Ed had preceded me and I stood next to him as I looked out across the stadium.

Immediately to my left, and a good bit higher than the crossbar of the goal post, was the scoreboard. I had to look through the netting and up at the score board from where I first stood outside. The grass playing surface was immaculate and the field had been freshly painted; the white lines were sharp and bold. A small crowd had already assembled and the smell of food cooking on the grill led me to believe that there was either some tailgating going on nearby or the concession stands had begun preparing for the game. What a great environment to play a football game, I thought to myself.

The locker rooms were not air-conditioned and so a few of our players began to come outside for some fresh air. There was a nice little breeze picking up ahead of the thunderstorms. At the same time, several of the Shenandoah players emerged from their locker room as well, dressed in their white game pants, cleats, and t-shirts. Our guys had yet to begin dressing, but Ed was in no hurry to have them suit up as it appeared that a delay was imminent, at least until the thunderstorms had cleared the area. He did, though, take them back inside for a little pre-game instruction and review of the game plan, commonly known as a "chalk talk."

"Jimmy?" Ed said to me as he strolled back toward the entrance to our locker room, "The quarterbacks will get taped up first. When they're ready and we get the okay to take the field, go ahead and take them out to warm up."

"Okay," I said.

"When you're done, bring them back in to suit up and we'll send out the specialties."

"Fifteen minutes?" I said.

"That's fine. Whatever you need," he said, looking at me over the tops of his sunglasses.

Sure enough, there was a delay for thunderstorms in the area, but it didn't last long. The storms passed by within thirty minutes and with little more than a brief shower and a few gusts of wind. The humidity was still significant, but not nearly as thick as before the storms. The temperature though, had dropped quite a bit, perhaps by ten degrees or more. His pre-game talk with the team wrapped up and Ed emerged from the locker room to join me outside of the entrance to the locker room. As we waited out the rain delay, we watched the sun reappear from across the valley. And as it did, so, too, did the players from the locker room, visibly antsy and ready to go. JC was the first, followed by Fletch. They were dressed in their white game pants and white game jerseys without shoulder pads.

"Ready?" JC signed to Ed.

"Waiting for the okay to take the field," Ed signed back.

"Where's Jimmy?" I asked JC.

"He's getting the footballs," JC signed back.

A field maintenance worker stood a few feet away from us and watched as we signed to one another. It was the first time that I actually felt like part of "the team," probably because I understood what JC was signing and realized that I was one of but a few people nearby who did, except for our players and coaches. Just as Jimmy appeared in the doorway carrying the mesh bag of footballs, several Shenandoah players bolted from their own locker room and headed out onto the stadium field. They had received word that the coast was clear.

"Let's go," Ed said aloud and signed simultaneously. And with that, I took to the game field with our quarterbacks for the first time.

Standing on the twenty yard line at the far side of the field, and near our own sideline, I watched as the three quarterbacks kneeled about ten yards apart from one another to begin their warm-up routine. As they began to pass the ball between them I was impressed with their apparent composure and focus. None of the three seemed jittery or nervous, and I wondered to myself if being deaf actually helped them contain their emotions. I was excited to get the game underway and the stadium music, along with the other team ranting and raving on their side of the field, only added to my enthusiasm.

Like most athletes, music and shouting before a contest had always worked to get my adrenaline going as a player. As a coach, though, I'd become much more reserved. Deaf players, though, have to rely on whatever stimuli works for them if they need additional motivation or inspiration. And since that can mean something completely different for every kid on the team, the Gallaudet players didn't give the appearance of being a high energy unit.

We spent about fifteen minutes going through our standard warm-up drills, and when JC felt that he was ready we headed back to the locker room. Along our way, we jogged past several Gallaudet fans making their way to the bleachers behind our bench. They signed words of encouragement to the boys. Others pumped their fist as if to say, "Go get 'em!" JC, Fletch, and Jimmy each signed back to them, but I just smiled and waved, wondering if any of them realized that I'd no idea what it was they were signing to us. And then there was the Shenandoah trainer and his assistant standing at the entrance to the building who nodded to us as we passed by.

"Hmmm, pretty good size," he mumbled to the young man next to him.

"Yeah," the younger man said, "but let's see if they can play ball."

While the people who were signing to us may have thought that I was deaf, I quickly realized that these two guys didn't know that I wasn't. And I was a little conflicted because I didn't necessarily feel compelled to tell them, though that may have been the polite thing to do. Instead, I began to think of ways that this could work to my advantage, and the team's. It was sort of like being able to read people's minds, I guess. Maybe it was more like being the proverbial fly on the wall.

Inside our locker room, the three quarterbacks worked their way to their lockers, donned their shoulder pads, and readied their gear as Ed began to address to the team one last time before sending them out onto the field. He delivered the standard motivational speech that most coaches traditionally give their team before a game, just without verbalizing it. The players responded by pounding on one another's shoulder pads with their fists, butting helmets, and grunting loudly as they prepared to take the field together. At Ed's direction they left the locker room and headed out onto the field where they assembled en masse in the far end zone.

It doesn't really matter what sport you play, your opponent's fans are always eager to see what kind of "game" you have. Oddly, they'll pay a lot more attention to you and your team during pregame drills than they will during the game itself. Once the game

starts they tend to be more focused on their own team's performance, especially that of their favorite player, unless of course you
should have some impact upon that performance. During pre-
game, the fans of the other team like to watch you warm up, both
individually and collectively, and they assess the size of your squad,
how organized your team is, and who your star players might be.

The hometown team hadn't yet returned to the stadium from
their locker room when we took the field for pre-game stretch and
agilities. And when we did, I immediately noticed a much more
curious nature about the fans than I might have otherwise expected, and really, it was quite understandable. I mean, after all there
was a big bass drum right there in the middle of the field.

With the boys gathered in a large huddle under the goal post,
five or six of the players broke away from the group and ran to
the forty-five yard line. They lined up across the field shoulder to
shoulder, about five yards apart, and turned to face their teammates who were still huddled together under the goal post. Fletch
was one of those five or six players. With a stern look, he raised his
hands above his head, crossed his forearms and looked toward the
end zone at the rest of the team. The stadium went silent. A moment later I saw Fletch smile through his facemask. Suddenly, he
pulled his arms away from one another and down to his sides. And
with that, the silence was broken.

The team huddle broke apart as the players ran from underneath the goal post in as many directions as there were players. As
they did, Damian beat wildly on the bass drum at midfield behind
Fletch. The players sprinted out onto the turf toward their five or
six teammates, making whatever noises their vocal chords could
produce and as loudly as they could. The team's choreographed
conquest of the field was Ed's version of "The Herd," a similar performance used by the Thundering Herd from Marshall University
whenever their team took to the field. And within about ten seconds, each player had a found his pre-determined spot on the field.
That spot would line the boys up directly in front of, or behind, one

another, five yards apart, and in a straight line looking forward at one of the five players standing at the forty-five yard line. They'd assumed their Flex positions and once each player was in place, the screaming and the banging of the drum stopped, just as suddenly as it had started. It was pretty cool. The people watching from their seats inside the stadium just stood and stared.

A few moments later, as our boys progressed through their routine stretching exercises, the Shenandoah team raced out onto the field and the music blared once again. If it hadn't been for the cheering of the crowd, rather than standing and simply watching as they had when our team had taken the field, it would've almost seemed anticlimactic. The home team's arrival into the stadium is supposed to steal the show. The players in red and blue swarmed the field, much to the delight of their home town fans. I say "swarmed the field" because Shenandoah's mascot was a hornet. With the exception of an occasional glance here and there by a few players, our guys seemed pretty much unaffected by the hooting and hollering of the Shenandoah players and their kin folk. I loved all the noise and the commotion. It just made me want to suit up and get out onto the field myself. I felt a little badly that our guys couldn't experience the same sense of excitement. What I didn't realize was that, in their own way, they could.

After both teams had completed their warm-ups and the team's respective captains met at mid-field for the coin toss, the announcer asked everyone to rise for the playing of the national anthem. The Shenandoah players assembled along their sideline, removed their helmets, and turned in unison to face the flag. Our players, though, were still milling about our bench area, drinking from water bottles, and making last minute adjustments to their equipment. They could not hear the public address announcement. A few of them seemed to be aware of what was happening, but not many.

"Hey? Get their helmets off and get them up here. Let's go," Ed yelled out for any of us coaches who could hear.

I removed my cap and began to do as I'd always done on the sidelines before a game, call out to the players to get their helmets off and face the flag. But that wasn't going to work since they couldn't hear me. So, along with a few of the other coaches, I hurriedly darted about the crowded sideline getting the attention of every player and team personnel that I could get in front of. I motioned to each of them to remove their head gear and face the flag. As they did, they'd try to get the attention of players around them to have them do the same. Somewhere between "the twilight's last gleaming" and "the perilous fight," we finally got our act together. I made a mental note to next time get a head start when preparing the team for the playing of "The Star Spangled Banner."

And then it was game time. I stood on the sideline next to Chris Burke and awaited the opening kick-off. Chris was probably more fired up about the game than most of the players. We watched as our kick-off team took the field. Their white jerseys, trimmed in navy blue and gold, stood out in stark contrast against the surrounding array of colors throughout the stadium and the darkening skies beyond. One of the changes in NCAA football that year required that teams kick-off from the thirty yard line, instead of the forty. And so a kicker would need a little more leg than in years past if he wanted to help his team establish decent field position.

Our kicker was a defensive back from Carmichael, California named Justin Wilson. One of but a handful of black kids on the squad, Justin was a very good athlete, but a little slight of build at 5'9" and 175 pounds. He could kick the football well, though, was pretty fast, and could tackle. So, it was a big plus for the kick off team to have an extra defensive player on the field instead of a kicker whose specialty was something other than tackling. The referee blew his whistle and motioned to Justin with his arm to begin play. Justin approached the football ball and kicked it straight down the field, high into the night, while his teammates pursued it. The trajectory of the ball carried it through several shades of evening sky until it descended into the hands of the Shenandoah player at about the ten yard line. The players in white collided with the players in red and blue, and the sounds and voices from among the wreckage on the field were loud, violent, and unmistakably football. At that point, I realized that speed and impact were not the only differences between the college and the high school football, but so too was the volume. For the Gallaudet players, though, there was no difference between the sound of college football and high school football, even Pee Wee football for that matter. To them, it was always silent, and always had been.

While the defense was on the field I made sure that JC was warmed up and ready to go. He was a veteran and he knew the routine, patting his hand on the shoulder pads of the offensive linemen and fist bumping his receivers and running backs. Standing next to me on the sideline, JC shifted his weight back and forth from his right foot to his left; he was ready to play. Using his index finger, he tapped me on the chest and pointed across the field to the Shenandoah team, moving his finger from left to right showing me how many more players they had on their sideline compared to ours. They stretched from one twenty-five yard line to the other, two and three players deep. They must have had over a hundred players dressed that night, maybe more. I counted at least four sets of matching numbers on players' jerseys. I shook my head and puckered my lips, indicating that I was impressed by the number of players on their team. JC just smiled.

Once our offense got the opportunity to take the field, I redirected my focus toward facilitating successful transitions both on and off of the field for our offensive players. With Ryan calling plays from the coaches box up in the stadium and Brian signaling them to the team on the field, I primarily watched the play of our quarterbacks when we had the ball. When they came off of the field, we discussed a variety of things from how they felt physically to how the defense was responding to various formations. We reviewed the types of pass coverage that the defense was employing in certain passing situations, as well as the benefits of making a pre-snap read. And we identified certain techniques that they needed to work on in order to improve their efficiency. Most importantly, we discussed what they'd learned about executing the offense.

JC played the first quarter and Fletch played the second and third. Jimmy got a few reps in the final quarter. JC played well, as expected. Despite working in a new offense, I thought he maintained his composure and focused on playing within the framework of the system. It would have been understandable had he prematurely improvised a few times, whenever he perceived that a play was going awry, and tried to make things happen on his own, but he didn't. JC was a team player and kept his expectations and approach to the scrimmage in proper perspective. He seemed to understand that the game was a learning situation and, while he and the offense did enjoy some success on the field, he wasn't frustrated by some of their mistakes.

Fletch had an interesting first few plays once he got into the game. He took the reins at quarterback after our defense had intercepted a pass and returned the ball all the way down to the Shenandoah one yard line. On his first play from under center, Fletch turned and handed the ball to Dima, who scored a touchdown on an inside run. On Shenandoah's following possession, our defense continued its stellar play and forced Shenandoah to punt the football. Our punt returner ran the ball back across midfield and into Shenandoah territory, giving our offense great field position.

On the very next play, just Fletch's second play of the game, he received the shotgun snap and looked down the left hash marks at receiver, Cole Johnson. Cole was running a deep slant toward the middle of the field on a play that we called "Irish," and he'd cut in front of the defensive back guarding him, about nine yards downfield. Fletch threw a laser of a pass to Cole, who caught the ball in stride, ran away from the cornerback, and past the safety for forty yards and a touchdown. On his first two plays as a quarterback,

Fletch and the offense had scored two touchdowns! And he was just as giddy as he could be when he ran off the field, giggling loudly as he hugged me on the sideline. Although we wouldn't score again that night, Fletch continued to play very well and we were both very pleased with his performance.

At the beginning of the fourth quarter, Jimmy got his chance to play. Throughout the first three quarters of the game, Jimmy stood by my side and we discussed what was going on out on the field. Jimmy was a smart kid, like JC, and had an insatiable eagerness to learn. I don't know whether it was at Ed's direction or not, but Ryan did not call many passing plays with Jimmy in the game, even though we trailed on the scoreboard. But when he did, Jimmy threw the ball with accuracy and good velocity. Unfortunately, the receivers that accompanied Jimmy onto the field weren't quite as ready to succeed; they dropped several passes and ran poor routes.

Overall, I thought it was a pretty successful night for all three quarterbacks. I felt good about their performances, and they did as well. All three had gained some confidence while out on the field, which is such a huge step in the maturation process for a new quarterback like Fletch or Jimmy. For JC and his years of playing club ball, it was more of a confirmation that he could indeed play inter-collegiate football.

At the conclusion of the contest, the teams lined up for the traditional hand shaking ceremony at the fifty yard line. Shenandoah sure had a lot of football players. I've never shaken that many hands in that short a period of time before, and haven't since. After the handshaking was done, we headed back to our locker room. A lot of the Shenandoah players, though, remained on the field to meet with their friends and families.

Inside, Ed spoke briefly to the team and encouraged them. He told them that he thought that they'd played very well and the fact that we came up a bit short on the scoreboard wasn't significant. What was important was that the team had garnered some valuable experience and was in the process of developing a solid foundation on which to build.

The players showered, changed into their street clothes, and met us at the buses outside. Kris and his staff were there in the parking lot to assist them with their gear. Ryan had arranged for a local Subway Restaurant to deliver sandwiches, chips, and soft drinks for each of the players and the food awaited them at their designated bus. Once we knew that each of the players had received a meal and was on a bus, the coaches picked from what food remained and hopped on board as well. By 10:00 p.m. we were on our way back to Gallaudet.

For whatever reason, the video system on the bus wasn't working when we pulled away from Shenandoah University. Without the loudness of the movie, the bus ride was a lot more peaceful than the ride earlier that afternoon. That and the players probably fell asleep after a tough game and some fast food. They probably didn't mind that there was no movie. Brian was seated across the aisle from me, and we spoke about the game and what we needed to do to prepare for the season opener next week.

I tried to sign to Brian as I spoke with him, because I was comfortable practicing with him. Like most of the players, he was very patient with me. Even so, when he told me to turn on the overhead light so that he could see what I was signing, I felt a little bit stupid. Out of curiosity, I turned and looked over the headrest of my seat toward the rear of bus. Sure enough, there was row after row of overhead reading lamps shining from above each set of seats. I guess the fellows weren't so tired after all. Either that or they had quite a few war stories to tell each other about.

We arrived back at Gallaudet just before midnight and after helping to unload the bus, I left campus about forty-five minutes later. By the time that I rolled into my driveway it was nearly 1:15 a.m. As I walked toward the front door, I could see by the light in our bedroom window that a lamp was still on inside. I walked quietly down the hallway toward the master bedroom and gently pushed open the door so as not to startle my wife, Mary-Ellen.

She'd dozed off in the bed while watching television and lay sleeping. The boys were in the room next door, asleep themselves, nestled into their bunk beds. While checking on them, I pulled the sheet up under their chins, adjusted their pillows, and as I had the habit of doing, said a short prayer over each of them.

After cleaning up and changing into a tee-shirt and gym shorts, I turned off the lamp and tried to slide into bed without waking my wife.

"Hey," she said softly, "how'd it go?"

"Pretty well," I said. "I was trying not to wake you, sorry."

"It's okay. I'm glad you're home safely," she said. "Are you going to take Mark to his football scrimmage in the morning?"

"What time?"

"He has to be at Cardinal Field by ten o'clock," she said, her eyes still closed.

"Hmm," I moaned, "I have to be on campus for a ten o'clock team meeting."

"That's alright," she sighed, "I'll get him there." She momentarily lifted herself up and kissed me on the forehead. "I'll see you in the morning."

"Okay," I mumbled, knowing that it wouldn't be the last time that she'd have to get him to his game on her own. I regretted not being able to take him myself because I knew that he looked forward to me being at his games, and I enjoyed being there to watch him. Exhausted, I fell asleep wondering if I had made the right decision in coaching collegiate football.

9

Getting Ready
for the Big Day

Saturday, September 1, 2007 had been circled on Ed's calendar for God knows how long, maybe a year or more. It marked the day of his first official game as the head coach of a NCAA football team. It was Gallaudet's first game as a NCAA Division III program and it was also our season opener on the road in Latrobe, PA against St. Vincent College. St. Vincent College was a school that hadn't fielded a college football team in forty-five years. So, it was a big day for them as well. It was also just a week away. Everyone had a lot of work to do.

I arrived at the field house on Saturday morning just before 10:00 a.m. and wondered how many of the boys were in the training room with Jon following the Shenandoah scrimmage. To my surprise, when I walked by the training room and peeked inside I didn't see a single football player. There was a soccer player and two young women from the volleyball team, but no football players. I waved to Jon.

"No football players?" I asked.

"Haven't seen a one," he said, shaking his head.

"Wow, that's pretty good, eh?"

"Not really," he said as he looked up from taping the ankle of one of the volleyball players. "They'll just all come in at the same time after breakfast."

"Oh," I tapped my fingers on the door frame and nodded to Jon. "See you later."

"So long," he said.

The weekend practices were surprisingly relaxed. In our team meeting on Saturday morning, we watched the game film of our scrimmage game against Shenandoah. During the film review, Ed decided that he wanted the quarterbacks to stop using their hands to signal for the snap of the ball. Instead, he wanted them to simply lift their foot off of the ground. When he said that, I noticed Brian look up at Ryan, who was seated just in front of him. He then glanced over at me with a smile. Brian remembered that earlier in the summer I'd suggested to Ryan that the quarterbacks use a foot signal and Ryan had dismissed the idea, referring to me as a clinician.

After the meeting, we ran the boys through a few light conditioning drills on the stadium track to work out any kinks from the night before. They were released after lunch to enjoy some personal time that afternoon and evening.

Sunday was much the same. So relaxed was it that when I arrived at the field house at 8:00 a.m. I found no one around but Kris. We shared a few words about the big game ahead and parted ways when, eventually, the rest of the coaching staff began to arrive, about twenty minutes later.

Brian had worked for several days with new computer equipment Ed had purchased for breaking down game film. That morning we used the new set up to watch film of St. Vincent playing a scrimmage game against a team from Marietta, Ohio the week before. With the new film breakdown capabilities, the defensive unit was able to watch only those plays involving the St. Vincent offense. Meanwhile, in another room, we were able to watch film of their defensive unit. This made for a much quicker and more efficient film study of our opponent's game tendencies.

After the film sessions, and before breaking for an early lunch, Ed brought the two units together for a short meeting. Among other things, he told the team that after the St. Vincent game they'd be off on Mondays for the remainder of the season. Of course that announcement was met with a great deal of enthusiasm and celebration by the players.

The team lifted weights that afternoon and afterward Ed addressed the group one more time before releasing them. Since classes were scheduled to commence the next morning, Ed repeated what expectations he had of them as student-athletes. The start of school meant a lot of things to a lot of guys. But to Daniel Dosemagen, the big kid from Wisconsin, it meant that he no longer had to remain on the football team in order to pay for his room and board. And so, for the second time in as many weeks, he quit the team.

With the eased workload over the weekend, the players all seemed pretty well refreshed and their spirits clearly lifted. They appeared ready to take on the task of preparing for the team's season-opener against St. Vincent that following weekend. Fletch was beginning to communicate with me more often, and about personal issues as well as football, such things as his faith, friends, and family. I interpreted this as a sign that he was becoming more comfortable with me, not only as his position coach, but as someone he felt he could trust. Meanwhile, when Jimmy walked into the field house on Monday afternoon, I pretended not to recognize him. You see, occasionally, I would tease him about his unruly, or seemingly unkempt, hair. Well, when he walked in the door that day, he had a fresh haircut, a clean shaven face and neck, and a smile that extended from ear to ear. He looked great. And although I'd been generally just teasing him about needing to get a haircut, it was pretty rewarding to think that I might have had a hand in bringing about such a change. Jimmy's self-esteem was improving daily.

Monday afternoon's practice began with an offensive staff meeting. Ryan had prepared a game plan for the game against St.

Vincent and his practice plan reflected the new offensive strategies he hoped to employ. For starters, we were going to use a hurry-up, no huddle offensive approach, and I complimented Ryan on the idea. At the same time, he wanted to utilize the short passing game and a zone blocking scheme to run off tackle. Basically, he was going to continue to simplify our offensive plays. And since the plan was to use a rapid tempo on offense that weekend, practice during the week had to be executed in the same manner.

Out on the field, during stretch and agilities, I noticed a new jersey in the Flex formation, number 29 in white. He was a dark-skinned, black kid who, although not very big, appeared to be very athletic. Although I was happy to see another athlete in an offensive colored jersey, I couldn't help but wonder why Ed hadn't given him a navy blue jersey. The boys whom I spoke with referred to the player simply as "Q". Apparently, he'd been on the team the year before, but left the university suddenly. I walked over to where Ed was observing the team stretch.

"Number 29 looks like he might be a player," I said. "Where'd he come from?"

"Oh, Q's a player, all right," Ed said, but without changing either his stance, expression, or the direction of his stare. "He just doesn't play with a full deck. The boy saw monsters in his dorm room last year. He saw monsters in the bathroom and in the hallways. They had to ship him out of here."

"That's a shame," I said, "because he looks like a good athlete."

"He is," Ed sighed. "He just doesn't want to be at the school. His old man makes him come here. He's quitting on Friday."

"What do you mean he's quitting on Friday?"

"He already told me that he's quitting on Friday."

"Why is he bothering to practice then?"

Ed, his arms folded across his chest, used his left hand to slide his sunglasses down the bridge of his nose a bit, and then turned to look up at me.

"The boy sees monsters in his dorm room, Jim. I don't know

why the hell he's out here. I don't know how the hell he got back into school to begin with."

I nodded. He had a good point.

"Coach?" Ryan called out to Ed as he made his way toward us. There was a little extra pep in Ryan's step, and for a change a smile had replaced his frown. "Who's the kid wearing number 29?"

Ed, expressionless, looked at Ryan and then back at me. Without saying a word, I turned and began walking toward the area where the quarterbacks were already warming up.

The individual skills portion of practice went well, as usual, and the boys moved quickly into their warm-up drills after the team broke following Flex. I introduced a weighted football into a few of our quarterback drills. It's a two pound, rubber football that obviously slows the quarterback's delivery down quite a bit. But it requires the player to be much more deliberate with his delivery and passing techniques, while at the same time helping to strengthen the muscles in and around the shoulder. Obviously, after throwing the weighted ball for a few drills, when the boys returned to using a regular football, it seemed to zip right out of their hands at warp speed. This they found to be quite funny, especially Fletch and Jimmy. JC just smiled at the playful attitude of his two teammates.

Practice went fairly well as we installed the new plays that Ryan had introduced during the offensive pre-practice meeting. Most of our seven on seven segment of practice was on air instead of "Skelly." This enabled the backs and receivers to focus their attention on running their routes properly without worrying about getting hit by a defensive player. Once Ryan was satisfied that the unit had grasped the concepts of the new plays, we finished the segment against the defensive unit.

Throughout the afternoon, we emphasized the importance of practicing with a higher level of intensity and focus. We also ratcheted up the tempo of the practice as well. The team bought into the concept and challenged one another to "expand the envelope," if you will.

JC's stature as the team's leader was becoming more and more evident as the team followed his example without hesitation. If JC picked up the pace, so, too, did the team. If JC became frustrated, so, too, did the team. Thus, it was becoming more and more important for me to ensure that JC understood the objective of the plays and the pace at which we wanted to execute them.

Practice was supposed to conclude at 7:00 p.m. following a short conditioning period, but during that time I asked Ed if I could leave early. I needed to get to the practice fields back in Crofton by 8:00 p.m. to pick up Mark.

"See you tomorrow, Jimmy," Ed nodded.

"Thanks, Ed," I said as I began to jog off the field. "See you tomorrow."

The ride home was a little quicker than usual, or so it seemed. Sometimes, when you've got something on your mind, or if you're listening to a good radio talk show, time can seem to pass more quickly. That night, it was a little of both, I guess. The topic of discussion on the local ESPN sports radio affiliate was the transition experience of college football players to the professional level. I began to think about where I was headed, the little league practice field. The players on that field, including my son, would be wearing youth-sized jerseys, tiny little cleats, and helmets with little mouthpieces dangling from their masks. The older kids on that field would soon make the transition to high school football. And beyond that, some might advance to the collegiate level.

And how quickly that time would fly by, I thought. For me, it seemed to have come and gone overnight. I was happy to be coaching the college players, but I began to wonder if maybe I should've been out there coaching my own young sons. A little guilt was beginning to set in.

At practice the next day, I began to work with the wide receivers and defensive backs, as well as the quarterbacks. During the inside run segment of practice, where the offensive unit practiced their inside running plays against the front seven defensive players, I moved off to the side of the field with the backs and receivers. For twenty or thirty minutes, the defensive backs worked on their set-ups and pass coverage skills. At the same time, the offensive receivers practiced running their routes and catching passes from a quarterback. And that quarterback was usually Jimmy Gardner, since Fletch and JC were over with the unit practicing the inside run. It gave me a lot of extra time to work with Jimmy.

It also allowed me to get to know several of the players among those backs and receivers. One such player, a particularly athletic kid, was Kevin Alley. Kevin wore jersey number 18 and was deceptively quick with great hands. Besides football, he also played baseball for the school. I immediately liked Kevin. He was a clean cut, polite, and hardworking young man and, like the others, very patient with me and my signing skills, or lack thereof. Kevin was a junior from Lebanon, Oregon, stood about six feet tall, and weighed about 185 pounds. He'd become the team's most reliable receiver and JC looked his way often. He conveyed to me that his goal was to become a Physical Education teacher and one day, a coach himself. When I found out that he was engaged to be married, I was a little surprised.

"How old are you?" I signed, pretending to stroke a long beard from my chin.

"Twenty-one," he signed, "soon to be twenty-two."

Still a little young to be getting married these days, I thought, but at the same time a little old to still be a junior in college. As it turns out, many of the guys were even older than Kevin. I guess deafness had presented a significant obstacle to learning during their primary education and, as a result, had left them a few years behind other children who could hear. Perhaps that is why so many of the players at Gallaudet were much older than I'd have expected. Most of the varsity high school players who I'd coached were just sixteen or seventeen years old. Most of the freshmen players at Gallaudet seemed to be at least nineteen.

Unfortunately, things were not going so well across the field. I could hear Ryan yelling while smacking his hands together and signing extra passionately. Apparently, the players on the offensive unit were not setting up quickly enough for him and he was getting very impatient. At the conclusion of a play, Ryan expected the linemen to hurry back to the line of scrimmage to get set up, and then look immediately at him on the sideline for the next play.

"Set up! Set up!" he hollered and signed.

I guessed that the sign for "set up" was to form a 'thumbs up' with one hand, place it at rest in the palm of the other, and then raise both together, because that's what Ryan was doing. He was clenching his teeth, though, as he did, and raising his hands forcefully. The hurry-up, no-huddle offense was a new concept to them, though, and from what I could see the linemen were getting back to the line of scrimmage pretty quickly, but waiting for the backs to get into position before looking over to Ryan for the next play call. They'd just figured out that Ryan wouldn't call the play until everyone was set, that's all.

In terms of linemen, well that corps was getting a little thin. Eric Jindra, a 280 pound tackle from San Mateo, California, had hurt his shoulder and was walking off the field with the trainer at his side. And it looked like our center, Justin Lathus, might soon join them as he was having trouble with his bad hip and not moving particularly well. He'd always had problems with the hip, but maybe the physical demands of the game and the size of the defensive linemen were beginning to take their toll. At just 215 pounds, he was pretty small for a college football lineman, even in Division III. But JC had confidence in him and as long as he knew that, Justin was going to give it all he had.

Meanwhile, after practice, Ed was a bit riled up that our game uniforms had not yet arrived from the distributor, and we were just a few days away from their debut. And to annoy him just a little more, the players began to complain that their travel gear from our team sponsor, New Balance, ran small in size and didn't fit so

well. Agitated by it all, Ed instructed the players to begin switch-
ing out the navy blue warm-ups with one another, trying to get as
many guys as possible into gear that actually fit. But after all of the
swapping was over, only a few players were happy with the results.
Ed was in his office and on the phone with the sales representative
from New Balance as I left the building. I could hear the conversation from the stairwell.

When I arrived for Thursday's practice, the first thing I noticed
was a bunch of the players walking around in new warm-up suits.
And they all seemed to fit just fine. New Balance had replaced all of
the warm-up suits. That's impressive, I thought. Ed definitely had a
way of making things happen, which didn't surprise me. After all,
in just a few short days, Gallaudet University was going to play a
NCAA Division III football game with a team of deaf football players who just one year ago were basically playing sandlot football at
the club level. Ed had made that happen as well.

The practice was light, but spirited, and we focused mainly
on special teams throughout. Fletch sat out a good portion of the
practice, nursing a strained calf, but he was playfully attentive on
the sidelines. Kevin Alley was punting and Justin Wilson worked
on his field goal kicking. I hadn't anticipated that he would be the
kicker type, but Ed was comfortable with Justin and that was good
enough for me. What I didn't know was that Ed had very little
expectation that he'd be asking much more of his placekicker than
an extra point here and there. I was more accustomed to having an
experienced kicker who I could utilize as an offensive weapon to
score points.

When Ed pulled the team together after practice, he lectured
them for a short while on his rules of traveling to and from away
games. In other words, he reviewed the team's code of conduct
when on the road. The returning players were loose and ready to
go. The freshmen were eager to go as well, but appeared a bit nervous, as one might expect. They paid keen attention to Ed as he
signed to them. Of the fifty-five players making the trip, sixteen

were freshmen and it would be their first collegiate game. Well, actually, it would be the first collegiate game for all fifty-five of them.

Ed assigned me the responsibility of ensuring that we traveled with at least six new game balls, and instructed me to see Kris about making sure that the balls were on the bus in the morning. I didn't want to take any chances so I went to Kris directly after practice and asked for the new footballs. He gathered them for me from within his equipment room and placed them into a mesh bag, squeezing each one a few times to make sure that they'd been properly inflated. He then held the bag out for me to take.

"Oh," he said, "take this as well, Jim." He handed me the worn down, wooden scrub brush. I threw the brush into the mesh bag with the footballs.

"Thanks, Kris."

"Would you mind doing something for me?" he asked.

"What do you need?"

"On your way home, will you be going by a store that sells large, plastic trash cans?" he asked.

"Yes," I said, "Kmart. Why?"

"I want to try something," Kris grinned devilishly. "I thought I'd fill the trash cans with water and detergent, and then after the game put all of the dirty uniforms in them before we loaded them onto the bus. They could soak all the way home and it would make them easier to get clean the next day."

"You mean put them on the bus, full of water?"

"I'll need cans with lids, eh?" Kris said.

"I would think," I nodded.

"Can you look in Kmart on your way home? I'm staying on campus tonight or I'd get them myself," he said.

"No problem, Kris. I'll get them for you."

"Don't worry, I'll reimburse you," he said.

"Okay."

"Thanks, Jim. You're the man." He smiled as he turned and walked back into his equipment room.

A few miles from home that night, I stopped at Kmart and purchased three 32 gallon, plastic trash cans, with lids. I left them in the back of my mini-van, so that I wouldn't forget them when I returned to Gallaudet the next morning. Driving home from the store, I could hear the cans vibrating on the hard, plastic floor strips in the rear of the van. I thought to myself, this just might work. The vibrating cans might do more than let the uniforms soak, they might actually wash them.

I arrived at my home a little after 8:30 p.m. and there was chaos in the halls of my castle. Our ten-year-old, Mark, had just returned home from football practice and was running back and forth between the laundry room and the bathroom, half naked. My wife had asked him to undress in the laundry room and then proceed directly to the bathroom to shower. And so he took off part of his uniform and ran from the laundry room, through the kitchen, across the foyer, and down the hallway to the bathroom. Each time that he reached the bathroom, he realized he was still wearing a part of his uniform. And so he'd run the gauntlet all over again until he was completely naked and back toward the bathroom. From the kitchen where she was trying to put together a family dinner, she was yelling at him for running in the house. Our seven-year-old son, Tyler, was glued to the television set in his bedroom, which, judging by my wife's ire, he shouldn't have been. Her greeting was anything but heart-warming.

"This is what you leave me with?" she yelled at me from where she stood at the kitchen sink as I entered the house. "And I'm supposed to handle this all by myself?"

A better man would have walked over to her, put his arms around his wife, and told her that he appreciated her holding the fort down while he was gone. At least that's what my wife tells me that a better man, another man, would do. But there was something about an angry, Italian woman with a paring knife clenched tightly in her hand that made me think otherwise. Instead, I mumbled a few words under my breath and decided to come to her rescue by getting Tyler to the dinner table, and Mark into the shower. Just don't say anything and let the storm blow over, I thought to myself. When Mark and I joined Tyler at the dinner table, I poured them each a glass of milk and opened a can of soda for myself. As I did, Mary-Ellen approached the table with plates of food.

"What would you like to drink?" I asked her.

"I don't need anything," she said, angrily. "You think you can just waltz in, sit yourself down, and expect dinner to be served?"

Uh, oh, I thought, the storm had not blown over as planned. I could tell by the looks on my boys' faces that they were having a similar thought.

"Why don't you try helping out around here sometime instead of being Mr. Big Shot on the football field?" she said. She put the plates on the table in front of us and left the room.

"Aren't you eating with us?" I asked.

"I need some down time," she said and retreated to our bedroom at the end of the hall.

I sighed. Mark sighed. Tyler sighed. Then we ate our dinner. My wife comes from a family of four girls. She knew almost nothing about sports, dirty uniforms, and three word, male communication habits. But now, it was becoming a lifestyle that she really wanted no part of, but was stuck with at this point in her life. And she wasn't handling it well. How in the world was she going to deal with things when Tyler began to play? That just might push her over the edge, I thought. And maybe it wasn't a good time for me to be going away with the football team for two days. Then again, maybe it was!

The weather on Friday morning was sunny and pleasant. And I was glad for that because the rush hour trip into Washington was not. When I arrived on campus I noticed the two large charter buses parked out front of the field house again. There was a flurry of activity all around them as the players stowed their bags and equipment in the cargo areas below and their pillows and snacks inside the bus. The trainers were loading their medical kits, water coolers, and field tables while the managers carried out their video equipment, tool kits, and of course, the large bass drum. They'd have to leave room for the three trash cans, too. But there was plenty of room as Kris had already made provisions for them under the bus that he was traveling in.

Ryan stood beside the first bus directing pedestrian traffic. He didn't seem too happy, perhaps because he was nervous about how smoothly our departure would go. Ryan was in charge of planning the itinerary and being accountable to Ed had to be tough for him.

"Good morning," I said.

"Morning," Ryan said without as much as a tiny smile. "This bus is the offense's bus," he said, pointing to the bus behind him.

"Okay. Thanks," I said and boarded the bus with my one personal bag and a cooler of food. "Anything you need me to do?"

"No. Just make sure that we have the footballs."

"I'm all over it!"

I put my bag in the overhead compartment above the second row of seats to the left side of the aisle and sat my cooler on the floor in front of the seat next to mine. While the players generally occupied but one seat, the coaches had two, which gave us a little more room to spread out. I then hopped off the bus and jogged down to the equipment room to grab the bag of new footballs that Kris had gathered for me the night before.

When Kris and I returned to the staging area outside of the buses, Ed and Ryan were standing and talking next to the second bus, the defense's bus, Ed's bus.

"Morning, Jimmy," Ed gave me the good, old Boy Scout salute.

"Good morning, Coach," I nodded as I boarded the first bus.

With the exception of Kris, Ryan, and a few disheveled players, most of the team was already on board and dressed in their New Balance travel suits. Some were eager and excited about the trip and others were already asleep in their seats. Brian was fumbling about inside the overhead compartment above the first set of seats, directly behind the driver. He was trying to figure out how to get the on-board DVD player working.

"I've got some movies for the trip," he said, smiling at me as I sat in my seat.

"All right, let's get going," Ryan said as he boarded the bus.

He stood at the front of the bus and gazed toward the players in the back, his jaw jutting forward. Judging by the rapid cross movement of his eyes, it looked like he was getting a final head count.

"Yep, we're ready," he said.

And with that, the two chartered buses rolled off campus and onto Florida Avenue. Once we cleared the brutal rush hour traffic of Washington, the trip along Interstate 270 North was a smooth ride all the way through Western Maryland. Brian wasn't able to get the DVD player working so we couldn't watch any of the movies that he'd brought along. But that just gave me plenty of time to practice my sign language with some of the players. For instance, I was able to communicate fairly well with JC, who was very excited to point out the house in which he'd lived growing up. The house was in the rural town of Middletown, Maryland and not far from his high school, The Maryland School for the Deaf, which was in Frederick, Maryland. Actually, we had maybe a half-dozen players, or more, who'd attended the same school, including the twins, Robin and Shawn Shannon, two of JC's best friends.

We drove past the city of Frederick and then west, through the small town of Boonsboro, Maryland. Yes, that would be Boonsboro as in the early American pioneer, Daniel Boone. The town, though named after him, was actually founded by two of his cousins. From Boonsboro, we crossed the Potomac River into Shepherdstown, West Virginia. Shepherdstown is a very quaint little village nestled in the lower Shenandoah Valley. It's a pretty popular weekend getaway for folks from Washington, D.C. and Baltimore. Shepherdstown is actually the oldest town in the state of West Virginia. It's also the home of Shepherd University where the Shepherd Rams play NCAA Division II football. Ed knew the football coach there and had arranged for us to conduct a short practice at their practice facilities. The stop provided a nice opportunity for the players to work off a little nervous energy.

Wearing shorts, game jerseys, and helmets only, the team went through their stretch and agility routine and then proceeded through a standard pre-game walk-through. Each of the units reviewed their plays, responsibilities, and assignments under the watchful eye of their head coach. Afterward, we gathered outside of the buses for a lunch that Ryan had ordered from, again, the local Subway. Unfortunately for Ryan, this particular Subway wasn't quite as prepared as the one in Winchester, Virginia the week before. They were late delivering the sandwiches, chips, and soft drinks and that, of course, angered Ed, who blamed it on Ryan. Ryan called and spoke with the delivery driver via his cell phone, and guided him to the practice field at Shepherd University. Once the food finally arrived, Ryan could stop sweating, although not entirely until he was back on the offensive bus and away from Ed. We each grabbed our food, boarded our respective buses, and off we went, eating our lunch along the way.

For the next several hours I mostly just sat and watched the scenery go by. Occasionally, though, I read the daily newspaper or reviewed Ryan's offensive game plan. I also used my cell phone to call my office at Coach & Courier a few times to see how things there were going back home. Most of the time things were going pretty smoothly at the office, although occasionally they would need my direction. I had responsible folks handling the day-to-day business activity, but it gave me piece of mind knowing that there weren't any emerging crises in the works. And if there were, at least I wouldn't be surprised by them upon my return.

Just a short distance outside of Shepherdstown, the defensive bus began to experience some sort of maintenance issue and, as a result, was unable to keep up with our bus through the mountains and hills of Southern Pennsylvania. So we slowed down to allow them to catch up on several occasions. Ed called Ryan several times via cell phone about the situation and apparently their bus also had a problem with its air-conditioning unit as well. Ed wanted to change buses with the offensive unit, but for practical purposes that never happened, thank goodness. Because of the reduced speed of travel, we didn't arrive at the Sheraton Four Points Hotel in Greensburg, Pennsylvania until 5:00 p.m., much later than Ed had planned. The hotel was only about 15 minutes from the town of Latrobe and the campus of St. Vincent College.

Ryan departed our bus and accompanied Ed to the hotel's front desk where they received and organized room keys for each player and coach on the team. While they were doing that, the rest of the team rode in the two buses to the parking lot at the rear entrance of the hotel. As we were unloading our personal gear from the bus, Ed and Ryan emerged from within the building to join us and distribute the room keys. We stayed two to a room in double occupancy quarters, except for Ed; he stayed in a private suite. My roommate was defensive backs coach, Ron Cheek. Still outside the buses, and before sending us off to our rooms to freshen up for dinner, Ed told the entire team that dinner would be served in the Keystone Room at 6:30 p.m., followed by a short team meeting, and then a few hours of personal time. Lights were to be out at 10:00 p.m.

The hotel's main dining room was reserved just for us, and I sat at a table near the entrance to the room along with Ed, Ryan, and Chris. We watched as the servers attempted to engage the players in small talk while offering them beverages. When the players obviously didn't respond in kind, the serving staff appeared a little perplexed, maybe even taken back a bit. It didn't take too long, though, before they realized that most of the boys were deaf and couldn't hear them, much less carry on a normal conversation with them. You would have thought that the hotel management would have told them that we were a team of deaf football players, wouldn't you? And so when our server arrived at our table to offer us drinks, she didn't say a word, but simply looked around the table at us and offered up a pitcher of iced tea in one hand and another of soda in her other hand.

"Iced tea, please," I said.

"Oh?" She was a bit startled. "Ok. I'm sorry. I, uh…"

"It's okay," Ed said, "some of us can hear just fine. I'll have iced tea also, thank you."

"Absolutely," her voice wavered with relief. "And what would you like to drink, sir?" she asked Chris Burke, who was watching a table of players across the room.

"Not him, though," said Ryan, "he's deaf."

Ryan snapped his fingers in front of Chris's face to get his attention.

"What do you want to drink?" Ryan asked Chris.

Now the poor woman was really confused. Why, if Chris was deaf and couldn't hear her, would he be able to hear Ryan? Chris looked briefly at Ryan and then smiled at the server.

"Iced tea, please," Chris said in his raspy voice.

"All right, then," she said with a whimsical smile. She poured iced tea into Chris's glass and added, "Why don't I just leave this pitcher here for you all, okay?"

"That would be great, ma'am," said Ed, "thank you."

A few minutes later, at the buffet table, I explained to the poor woman that Chris could read lips and that's how he understood what Ryan was saying to him. I was tempted to tell the woman that it was the decibel level at which she spoke that prevented Chris from hearing her and that it was a certain talent that Ryan, and we coaches, had developed that enabled us to communicate with the deaf. Although I didn't have the heart to actually tell her that, I suddenly realized that many other such amusing opportunities might lie before me. And indeed there would be.

While we ate our dinner, Ed explained that he wanted me, Harold, Chris, and Brian to monitor the halls and enforce the ten o'clock curfew. Both he and Ryan would assume the duties of issuing the players their eight o'clock wake up calls in the morning.

Breakfast was to be served at 8:30 a.m. in the same dining room as dinner, and the buses would depart for St. Vincent College at ten o'clock.

I was curious as to how they would give our deaf football players a wake-up call. Until then I had never really had the need to consider the matter. Obviously, having the front desk ring the telephone in the players' rooms would be futile. Knocking on their doors wouldn't work either. Would they use a second room key to go in and awaken each player? No, the keys weren't numbered; plus, what a logistical nightmare that would have been. And, of course, the hotel wouldn't allow us to use a master key.

What Ed planned on doing was having each of the players leave the door to their room ajar, propped open by the small, swinging device on the door frame. Ed and Ryan would have to go to each room and physically wake each player with a tap on the foot, a nudging of their shoulder, or, if necessary, a couple of slaps to the face if the player was an extra heavy sleeper.

I learned that deaf people have many different means of waking themselves in the morning. Some have timers on their lights, some have vibrating devices, and others have alarm clocks with bright, flashing lights. Deaf college students try to avoid early morning classes.

Following dinner, the players retreated to their rooms to watch television, horse around a little here and there, or in some cases just read and relax. Me, I broke out my laptop, got online through the hotel's Internet service, and called in to my fantasy football draft. I was a veteran fantasy football guy, having played since 1986, when the player drafts were conducted using a "draft preference card" delivered by mail. Now, with computers and cell phones, we held what were called "live drafts." I couldn't let a little thing like being in a Greensburg, Pennsylvania hotel with a deaf football team ruin my successful fantasy football draft history of 21 years.

The halls were pleasantly quiet at ten o'clock and it appeared that the boys had obeyed Ed's curfew. And then Ron and I heard room service knocking on the door across the hall around 10:15 p.m. Ron looked out and saw a young man knocking on the door of the Shannon brothers' room. Obviously, there was no answer. I stepped across the hall and opened the door to their room to find them watching television. The server stepped in behind me and asked them if they'd ordered room service. They didn't answer him, but they did jump up out of bed to take the trays of food from his cart. I explained that the boys were deaf and that they hadn't been able to hear him knocking. He brushed off the inconvenience, placed the last tray of food on the desk, and departed.

"What's this?" I signed to the players.

Robin, dressed only in a pair of gym shorts, walked over to the desk, removed the tin cover from the plate, and looked up at me. It was a plate of potato skins, that's what it was.

"You have a 'lights out' at ten o'clock, you know that?" I signed.

"We know," Shannon signed just before turning off the lights.

"Okay," I signed by the hallway light. "See you in the morning."

Ron and I returned to our room where I sat at the foot of my bed across from the television. We'd been watching ESPN Sports Center before the room service waiter arrived. Ron crawled back onto his bed and propped a couple of pillows under his head. Of course, we were watching College Football Game Day.

"Jim?" Ron asked without removing his gaze from the television screen.

"Yes, Ron?" I said, turning in his direction.

"How did those guys order room service?"

I thought about it for a moment, but had no answer for him. I could only shake my head and shrug my shoulders.

A few minutes later there was another knocking, this time upon our door. I stood and opened it to find Brian standing in the doorway, both hands deep into the pockets of his jeans. He grinned as he walked by me and sat in a wing backed chair.

"You guys want to split a pizza?" he asked, grinning.

"Nah, I'm good," said Ron, "but I could go for a beer."

"Hey," I said, "there's an idea."

"Call room service," Ron said as he sat up.

We called room service, but at that hour the kitchen was only offering food service. The man on the phone told us that we could still purchase alcoholic beverages, but we'd have to go down to the lounge and get them from the bartender ourselves. And so I volunteered to go to the lounge and get us a six pack of beer. Still dressed in my khaki pants and a sports shirt, I slid into my sneakers and headed off to the lounge.

The main entrance to the lounge was located in the hotel's lobby and directly across from the front desk. It sounded pretty loud as I approached from the elevators down the hall, and the folks going in and out on that busy Friday night seemed to be mostly middle-aged and dressed in casual attire. As I walked across the lobby I saw Ryan at the front desk speaking with the night clerk. Near the revolving door entrance of the hotel was a small, open room for business clients with a desk, a few chairs, a computer, and some other light office equipment. Inside the room, I could see Chris Burke and Harold Catron, sitting in front of the computer searching the Internet. Harold saw me and waved as I headed across the lobby to see what Ryan was up to.

"Is everything all right, Ryan?" I asked as I neared the front desk.

"Yeah, fine," he said with a slight grimace. I knew he'd been in Ed's room reviewing the team's departure plans for the morning. "I'm just making sure they have breakfast set up for us in the morning. We won't have much time."

"Eight-thirty, right?" I asked.

"Yes, eight-thirty."

Ryan and Ed requested that breakfast already be in place, with food served on individual plates and waiting at the tables when the players arrived. Standard fare was expected: scrambled eggs, hash brown potatoes, sausage, and a piece of fruit. Drinks could be served by wait staff. A buffet line would take too long with fifty-five guys. This way ensured that most of the players would finish eating around the same time and then exit the dining room together.

"See you then," I said as I turned and walked toward the lounge.

"What are you doing?" Ryan asked me, "Where are you going?"

"I'm getting a few beers for me, Brian, and Ron. Would you like one?"

"No," he shook his head, "and you can't go in there."

"I have to," I shrugged. "Room service for alcohol ended at 11:00 pm. They said to get drinks from the bartender in the lounge."

"Ed doesn't want anyone in the bar. We have a game in the morning, Coach."

I stopped and looked back over my shoulder at Ryan. The young woman behind the registration desk looked at me and rolled her eyes, which I thought was pretty funny.

"Ed doesn't want any of us hanging out in the bar, getting plastered, and making a fool out of himself, or the football team," I said calmly. "That's probably what Ed doesn't want." Besides, I thought to myself, I'm 47 years old, away from my family, and only making about forty-five dollars a day. If I want a beer, I'm having a beer. Plus, it wasn't like I was actually playing in the game the next day.

"Whatever," he said, probably resigning himself to the fact that he wasn't going to convince me not to go into the bar. If invoking Ed's command wasn't stopping me, what else could he have said that might?

"Suit yourself."

"I'll see you in the morning," I smiled.

The bar was pretty much at capacity and the disc jockey's large speakers pounded the room with the sounds of good time oldies from the 1960's and 70's. That was my kind of music, but it was a bit too loud. My folks had always told me that playing my music so loudly would eventually cause me to go deaf. Imagine that. Cigarette smoke wafted through the air along with all kinds of perfumes and colognes. Like any other middle-aged bar on a Friday night, Rodney Dangerfield and Bob Uecker look-a-likes cajoled, strutted, and glided around the room trying to impress women who fancied themselves as a contemporary Suzanne Sommers or Angie Dickinson. A few more years and I'd fit right in, I thought. Shuffling through the crowd, I made my way across the room until I reached the bar. I remembered the routine from days long gone by, and with my size had little problem getting to the oasis.

"I'd like a six-pack of Miller Lite," I told the bartender. He cupped his ear, motioning for me to repeat my request. "I'd like a six-pack of Miller Lite to go," I raised my voice.

"I don't have six packs, but I can give you plastic cups," he yelled back.

That might be a little tough getting six cups of beer back to my room, I thought, especially through that crowd. He saw me trying to visualize doing so and must have seen the response before.

"I can give you lids and a tray. Will that work?" he said.

"That'll work."

While I was waiting for the bartender to pour the beers, I looked about the room. I felt a tap on my shoulder and turned to find Chris and Harold smiling at me. I must have become a bad influence, because now they, too, were in the bar in violation of Ed's directive. I signed to them that I was getting beer for Ron, Brian, and myself, but struggled to do so. Again, I usually spoke aloud to myself while I signed and the loudness of the music was distracting my thought process. All the while, both Chris and Harold watched patiently as I tried to sign. Chris was also reading my lips and trying to enunciate what it was that I was attempting to sign. They weren't distracted at all. In fact, it was in situations like this, I remember thinking, that deaf folks held an advantage in communicating amid all the noise.

One, they could communicate across the room with relative ease, as long as they had good vision and a decent line of sight, I guess. And the accuracy of their communication wouldn't be so adversely affected by the loud music. Deaf guys also wouldn't have to repeat themselves so often or scream into one another's ear. And they probably wouldn't get Michelob Light beer instead of Miller Lite.

"Here you go," called out the bartender, "six Mick Lights."

"Michelob Light?" I asked. He cupped his ear again after setting the tray of beers on top of the bar in front of me. I didn't bother to complain, I just settled for the six beverages already on the tray.

"That comes to fifteen dollars," he said.

I reached out to hand him a twenty dollar bill and as I did, I glanced over and saw Chris and Harold a few feet away. They were rocking back and forth to the loud beat of the music's drums and bass guitar, and watching the folks out on the dance floor. They really were in their own little world. I nodded toward Chris and Harold as the bartender took the bill from my hand.

"Give them each a beer as well, will you?" I said as I forked over another ten dollar bill. "And keep the change."

"Thank you," said the bartender.

While he twisted off the top of a couple beers for Harold and Chris, I signed to them that I'd bought them each a drink. Chris smiled and patted me on my shoulder.

"Thanks, buddy!" he mouthed out loud.

I gave him the thumbs up, took the tray of beer from the bar top, and began to walk away. As I did, the bartender reached across the bar, holding two bottles of beer for Chris and Harold.

"Here you go guys, two Miller Lites," he said.

What? I did a double take back at the bartender and frowned as I saw him hand each of them a bottle of Miller Lite. Harold and Chris smiled broadly and raised their beers in my direction as I walked out of the lounge.

10

Game Day: St. Vincent College Hosts Gallaudet

The big day had arrived. Saturday, September 1, 2007 began with a beautiful, sunny morning in Latrobe, Pennsylvania. Our departure from the hotel went smoothly, for the most part. The only glitch was in the dining room where, instead of individual meals in place at the tables as Ed had requested, the kitchen staff had set up a buffet. Ed was a little perturbed at first, but calmed down quite a bit when he figured that we would still be on schedule. Regardless, I kept my distance a few feet behind him at the front of the buffet line. The players queued up along the wall and waited patiently for their opportunity to fill their plates.

While eating my scrambled eggs and sausage, I noticed a middle-aged woman standing beside one of the player's tables and talking to the boys as if she knew them. She had a continuous smile and signed with ease. Later, she made her way to our table and wished us luck. She was the mother of Chester Kuschmider, a junior wide receiver from Olathe, Kansas. She'd come to support her son on behalf of both herself and his father, who had died three years earlier in a bus accident following one of Chester's high school games. Chester's dad had also played football for Gallaudet, back in the late 1970's. I wondered if I'd played against him when I played quarterback at Anne Arundel Community College. Whether he had or hadn't seemed insignificant, although if he had, it was interesting to consider that our paths had crossed once again, thirty years later.

The team bus departed the hotel at ten o'clock, right on time, and it was a very short ride to the school, maybe fifteen minutes or so. St. Vincent College is a small, Catholic school of about 1800 students. The 200 acre campus is nestled among the scenic, rolling hills of southwestern Pennsylvania. Upon our arrival, we immediately saw the football stadium out of the windows on the left side of the bus. The main playing surface lay between two unmistakable, yellow goal posts with stadium seating on just one side of the playing field, directly behind the home team's bench area and sidelines. The facility was pretty much brand new and on that particular day it was being dedicated to Chuck Knoll, the former coach of the NFL's Pittsburgh Steelers. The stadium, and the two lined practice fields between it and where our buses eventually parked, was the home of the Steelers summer training camp.

We were escorted to the visiting team locker room in the basement of a building a few hundred yards away from the stadium itself. The building was old and space was limited, but the facilities were sufficient. There were showers and lockers, but not enough room in the locker room for Jon and his training staff to work on the players. So they set up their training tables in the hallway downstairs and began taping players. Outside the entrance to the building, Ed met with us coaches one final time to discuss strategy and procedures. Shortly thereafter, he signaled for me to take the quarterbacks down to the stadium for pre-game warm-ups ahead of the team's arrival.

I went into the locker room to find JC, Fletch, and Jimmy. They had been taped first and were ready to go. So I flipped a new football to each of them and told them that it was time to head out. They emerged from the locker room wearing their game pants and jerseys. The white pants were dressed with navy blue and mustard stripes along the sides. And the white jerseys were emblazoned with large, navy blue numbers outlined in the same mustard gold as the pants. They left behind their shoulder pads and helmets, knowing that they would return after warming up. We made our way across the two practice fields and onto the grass playing surface of the new stadium.

I set us up for our pre-game drills near the St. Vincent sideline, between the twenty yard line and the goal line. On away games, I generally preferred to have the quarterbacks warm up in the shadows of the opponent's sideline to give them a feel for what could be a potentially hostile environment. Sometimes we heard a few boos and at other times a little heckling, but usually nothing that was too irritating. Trash talk from players on the opposing team, though, could get under your skin a little, if you let it, or heard it. Of course, my guys were deaf and couldn't hear any of that, but they could sense it for sure. Although being deaf diminished some of the benefit of warming up in a semi-hostile section of the field, just sensing the tension helped escalate their competitive psyche.

Another thing that was easy to sense, for both the players and I, was the curiosity of the St. Vincent fans throughout the stadium as they watched the boys warm up. They were eager to see what they might consider to be the spectacle of a deaf football team. And while the boys had no idea what was being said around us, I certainly did, even though I pretended not to. I have to admit, it was very amusing for me to hear people make remarks like "How wonderful is it that these boys are "trying" to play college football?" and "How do they know when the play is over?" They weren't being mean, mind you, they just didn't know. But they would soon find out.

The St. Vincent team had not yet arrived on the field, not even their special team's units. So there were no players anywhere near us or the St. Vincent bench for that matter. There was, however, a small group of female cheerleaders about ten yards or so from where we were warming up, maybe eight to ten of them. The young women were stowing their gear along the base of a concrete wall just below the first rows of seating; things like megaphones, pom-poms, duffel bags, and the sort. They were dressed in green and gold, traditional cheerleading skirts and tops, with a smattering of glitter across their youthful faces. And, of course, they were quite spirited, exhibiting what, to me, was an annoying effervescence. That annoyance was yet another indication that I'd become a middle-aged man.

When I was thirty-four years old, I played basketball in a men's league at a local gym in Bowie, Maryland. That was when I first tasted the bitter reality of becoming an aging male. While I'd always been a very good athlete, most of the guys in that league were a dozen or more years younger than me, and they could jump through the roof. But at the age of thirty-four, I could no longer play the game anywhere near the rim, much less up in the rafters. I couldn't beat them down the floor, either.

When I was forty-years of age, I injured my shoulder while bench pressing three hundred fifteen pounds. I probably shouldn't have been working with that much weight, but I had something to prove to myself: that I could still put up three plates and, more importantly, still hang with the some of the stud muffins in the gym. I managed to prove that I could still put up three plates, all right. But I also proved that my body wasn't willing to keep up with my mind. And my mind was obviously was in denial about aging.

On the stadium turf of Chuck Knoll Stadium, I'd find myself at odds with reality again, at the age of forty-seven.

"Oh my God," blurted out one of the cheerleaders. "He's gorgeous."

For a sheer, fleeting nanosecond, I had this wildly insane idea that she was speaking of me. And during that incredibly brief passage of time, I was transported back nearly three decades to when I was a college football player and maybe worthy of such admiration. As exciting as that felt, I didn't flinch, but rather pretended not to hear anything being said just a few, short yards away. I continued to sign instructions to the guys.

"Number five or number two?" asked another young woman's voice.

It was over. It was fastest nanosecond of my life, and it was gone. They were speaking of JC and Fletch, respectively, of course, and I suddenly felt stupid. I mean, really stupid. After all, what was I thinking? I was forty seven years old and my college days of wooing coeds had long since passed, decades ago!

"Either one, my God," the first voice said.

"Hey?" asked another cheerleader. "What if they can hear us?"

"They're deaf. They can't hear us," said another.

"They'd have looked our way by now if they could hear us."

Just then, JC glanced in the direction of the cheerleaders and from among them came a collective gasp. He then took a few steps toward them and not a single girl dared to move. A football had fallen to the ground and bounced to within a few feet of the girls. He picked up the football, smiled at them, and then resumed warming up with Fletch and Jimmy.

"I'll take number five," one cheerleader said.

"In your dreams, girl," a sarcastic voice chimed in, "in your dreams."

"You guys can fight over him while I ride off with number two," giggled another.

And so it went, on and on, or so it seemed. But the guys paid it no mind at all, not that I could tell, anyway. Instead, they appeared to be focused on the task at hand instead, winning a football game. They may not have heard them, but the boys knew that the cheerleaders were nearby, especially Jimmy. Occasionally, he would glance over at them and then smile back at me. Poor Jimmy, I thought to myself, he had no idea that number nine wasn't even in the conversation, and I wasn't about to tell him.

After about fifteen minutes, we wrapped things up and I signed to the guys that it was time to head back into the locker room. They each smiled and nodded that they were ready to roll and began to saunter off the field. As they did, I heard the girls once more.

"Oh! Goodbye, gorgeous," one of the cheerleaders called out softly toward us.

I couldn't help myself. I just had to do it, just had to. And so before I began to jog off with the three quarterbacks, I turned and looked in the direction of the cheerleaders.

"You wouldn't be talking to me by any chance, would you?" I asked the group.

The ebullient spirit of the entire cheerleading squad suddenly turned to horrified, panic-stricken fear as they jockeyed about to try and cower behind one another. And their previously effervescent, young faces turned ashen the instant I spoke. You would have thought that Saint Vincent himself had just appeared before them.

"I didn't think so," I smiled, "but that's all right. Good luck, today."

And with that, we left the stadium and jogged back to join our team.

*

Two by two, the players quietly left the locker room following Ed's final words of encouragement. They walked across the street and down a short flight of concrete steps. From the base of those stairs an asphalt pathway lead us to the stadium a few hundred yards away. As we walked by the two lined fields that the Pittsburgh Steelers practiced on just a few weeks earlier, the glare of the sun reflected brightly off of our players' gold helmets. The glare acted like a beacon, signaling to those in the stadium that our arrival was imminent.

I don't know if the guys were just focused or nervous, maybe a little of both, but over the last fifty yards or so, before we walked onto the stadium grass, they were unusually quiet. There were no high pitched screeches, no grunts, or off key laughter. In fact there was very little sound at all other than the sound of their cleats grinding into the walkway below their feet. At that moment in time, if not for the sound of those cleats, I'd have been almost completely in sync with them and their deafness.

That moment in time would pass quickly, though, as we approached the stadium sidelines and took the field to warm up. The stadium had come to life since the quarterbacks and I had left the field about twenty minutes earlier. The sights and sounds of game day had taken over the placid, rural morning and St. Vincent fans, eagerly anticipating the school's first football game in forty-five years, filled the stands from top to bottom. There were folks lined up along the walkways that led up to the stadium from the east and in the direction of the dormitories to the west. People sat in lawn chairs and on blankets atop the crest of a large, tree lined hill that surrounded the west end zone to our right. And not lost in it all was a small section of bleachers, just behind our bench, off a bit toward the open side of the stadium. In it were about two hundred Gallaudet football fans cheering for us as the players began to assemble in the end zone. They weren't a bit shy, either, demonstrating a fervent support for their boys. And I could hear all of it.

Although the players couldn't hear their families and friends cheering for them, but they knew that they were there, they could see them. After gathering in a large huddle under the east goal post, the players started jumping up and down as they suddenly became explosively enthusiastic. Finally, they appeared to be a team that was excited to play a football game. That excitement seemed to work its way up and throughout the stadium, too, as the curious St. Vincent fans rose their feet. The home team had returned to their locker room after their pre-game warm up and was not yet back on the field, so our boys were the only act in town. The fans all watched as the famous Gallaudet bass drum was carted onto the field. Undoubtedly, they had all heard about Gallaudet's big, bass drum and were excited to see and hear it for themselves.

BOOM! BOOM! BOOM! The sound of the bass drum echoed throughout the stadium as the players scattered from under the goal post and charged onto the field toward their pre-determined positions for Flex formation. Ed's routine was pretty cool, even though it was just orchestrated chaos.

BOOM! The players simultaneously began their first stretch.

BOOM! Ten seconds later they relaxed in unison.

BOOM! The next stretch began. That was the routine and so it went.

The fans were busy pointing toward the big drum at midfield, smiling and gesturing with amusement at the unusual sight of how a deaf football team prepared for a game. They seemed, for a time, captivated simply by how we warmed up. It wasn't until the Bearcats of St. Vincent College finally took to the field themselves that the fans turned their attention away from us and toward the opposite end of the field. They began to cheer wildly for the arrival of their home team and as they did, the stadium grew much louder.

The St. Vincent players, wearing green and gold uniforms, jumped up and down themselves as they entered the stadium. As they did, a lot of their players waved their arms high above their heads, extolling their fans to cheer louder. I gazed across the stadium at the celebratory atmosphere, taking in the sights and sounds of college football. The noise of the crowd and the rhythmic beat of the music blaring from the stadium loud speakers had me pumped up and ready to get the game underway. But when I looked at our players going through their warm-ups, I realized that those same sounds had very little effect upon them. Music didn't help them to get pumped up for a game. They had to rely a little more heavily upon on the same source of motivation that all athletes relied upon, that ravenous desire to compete. The boys from Gallaudet were no less competitive than the players on any other team that I'd coached. Still, I couldn't help but think that hearing the music gave the St. Vincent players that little extra motivational edge.

I don't know if it was arranged by Gallaudet University, or simply the hospitality of St. Vincent College, but while the national anthem was being sung, a woman stood in the end zone nearest us and passionately signed the words of "The Star Spangled Banner." The manner in which she presented the anthem was very engaging and inspirational. I could see many of the people across the field from us, hands across their chests, watching her as well. For many of them, I thought, it might be the first time that they'd seen sign language in action. It was the first time for me that I'd seen a song sung by a person who was deaf.

Once we received the opening kickoff from St. Vincent, though, the focus of everyone at the game shifted away from our team's deafness to the game itself. And it was surprisingly good football, too, considering the two teams were new NCAA programs playing their first games. It didn't take but a play or two before the referees began to seek out coaches on our sideline who could hear. They wanted to know who, besides the head coach, they could communicate with if Ed was not nearby. Rapid and effective communication during the course of a football game wasn't limited to just players and coaches, but rather busy officials and coaches as well. And although I'm sure the referees knew beforehand that Gallaudet was a deaf football team, I doubted that any of them had polished up on their American Sign Language just to referee the game.

"Where's the big drum?" asked the side judge as he approached the sideline, put his whistle back into his mouth, and turned around to face the field.

"We don't use it during games anymore," I said as he held his right hand up to signal to the referee on the opposite side of the field that he was ready for the next play. "We only use it for timing the cadence of our stretch period now."

"Yeah, I see. You guys are using a silent count," he said with his teeth clenched upon his whistle. "That's great."

"Kind of makes sense, doesn't it?" I said.

"Yep, I it sure does."

Things were a little chaotic on our sideline at first. What, with Ed being so calm and everything. Of course I'm kidding. But, then again, every sideline during a football game is nothing less than designed madness at best, and at every level of the game. It wouldn't be very long before we had things under control, though, meaning having the right players in the right place at the right time and so on. Then it just became a matter of getting JC calmed down, both on the bench and the field. JC had played four years of college level club football, and with a great deal of personal success. But this was real college football, in a real stadium, against a real defense. He felt the difference.

JC seemed shaky and nervous for the first quarter and a half. He wasn't comfortable in the pocket, he was hurrying his throws, and his footwork was just awful. In fact, most of the passing plays that Ryan called became running plays when JC pulled the ball down and instinctively tried to run instead. And that wasn't working too well against the well-disciplined St. Vincent defensive players, and a college caliber defense. It may have served him well in the past against club teams, but it wasn't a good tactic now and he was growing visibly flustered. And when he did pass the football, he was often throwing off his back foot instead of stepping into the throw.

On the sideline between offensive series, I tried to get JC to calm down. I told him that he needed to trust that his linemen will protect him and that he needed to step up into the pocket to throw the ball. He also needed to regain his focus and composure, normally his strengths. I explained to him that when a quarterback loses his composure, one of the first things that he abandons are his pre-snap reads. In other words, he'll stop taking the time to assess the defensive coverage before calling for the snap and beginning the play. Before beginning each passing play, a successful quarterback will attempt to determine which of his receivers will have the best chance of defeating the defense, which is basically what football coaches refer to as "reading a defense." Well, JC was not doing that, and the speed of the game at this level was not allowing him to make decisions at whatever pace he'd grown accustomed to before.

My inability to sign proficiently was definitely an obstacle for us, especially with the pressure of trying to communicate within the definitive time constraints of a football game. But JC was a very intelligent guy and he understood what I was trying to convey to him: calm down, look across the line of scrimmage before each play, and try to determine what coverage scheme the defensive unit is trying to employ. Doing so would help him identify, before the play even began, the receivers that will be best positioned to defeat the defensive coverage. Once he receives the ball from the center, he should look to those receivers first. He needed to play to his primary strength: intellect.

Well, I must have been somewhat effective at communicating this to him because JC settled down just fine midway through the second quarter. The offensive line did a nice job of protecting him from the St. Vincent pass rush and as a result, his confidence began to flourish. A few minutes later, he threw a beautiful touchdown pass to Kevin Alley. And we'd score a few more times, too, including another touchdown pass late in the second quarter to take a 19-0 lead into the locker room at halftime. And Ed's defense was playing superbly. Robin Shannon had a pair of sacks and safety Rantz Teeters successfully defended several Bearcat pass attempts. At the same time, the St. Vincent offense appeared to have no answer for our Alaskan Pride Fighter, defensive end Josh Ofiu.

Josh was a raw athlete at 6'2" and 235 pounds, who ate ten pounds of King Salmon every day, and had a motor that just wouldn't quit. I called him our Alaskan Pride Fighter because Josh wasn't only from the Great State of Alaska and of Eskimo descent, but also an aspiring mixed martial arts fighter. He'd had two wins under his belt before giving it up to play football at Gallaudet. And he was fighting like hell out there on the football field. Quick and brutally strong, Josh just couldn't be contained. In the first half, St. Vincent's offense had tried everything from screen passes to counter plays to neutralize him, all to no avail.

At halftime, we left our sideline and headed back toward the locker rooms, passing right by our fans in the bleachers behind us. Wearing school colors and waving Gallaudet Bison banners, those that had made the trip were getting their money's worth and enthusiastically showed their support for our team. Seeing all of them made me feel good myself, so I knew that the boys had to feel good about themselves, too. Inside the locker room during half-time, there was joy and glee among the players, unlike the anxiety before the game. Ryan and I stood in the hallway and discussed what second half adjustments might be made by the St. Vincent defense and how we might counter those changes.

"Do you know how lucky you are?" he asked me.

"What do you mean?" I asked.

"JC is the smartest quarterback in college football," Ryan said. He reached into his mouth with the thumb and index finger of his right hand and adjusted a wad of chew that rested inside his cheek. "He hardly needs a quarterback coach."

I wasn't quite sure what his point was, or why he was even compelled to say such a thing, so I didn't answer, or acknowledge the comment. I just grabbed a cup of Gatorade and ventured back inside to talk with our brilliant quarterback. Cary, meanwhile, was fired up by how well the offensive line had played and was chest bumping each of his linemen. And Brian was smiling ear to ear at the prospect of potentially winning our first college football game. He was very loyal to the team and took pride in how they played the game. I got the feeling that both Brian and Harold wished they were still playing, not unlike us over the hill guys. Ed was a little fired up as well, but still went about his business, checking in on those players who were a bit dinged up. Jon was taking care of those players in his makeshift training room. Thankfully, there were no serious injuries since we had very little depth at most positions.

By now the locker room was full of hooting, laughing, and the playful "yips" and "yaps" from some of the players. One of those voices was Josh's and I immediately recognized it. Now, while I wouldn't mess with Josh, I did find it amusing that this brute of a guy had such a squeaky, little voice. And on occasion, I'd test the waters to see just how much teasing he could take about it. He was remarkably good natured, though his young life had been one tough road.

Josh's parents died tragically when he was just three years old, so he was raised by his older brothers and sisters. Those older brothers and sisters, all of whom could speak, probably hadn't known much sign language at that point, nor did they have the patience to learn it for that matter. So Josh had to learn to read lips. He also taught himself to mimic the lips of his brothers and sisters when they spoke certain words, words that he recognized the meaning of. And so by learning to produce such a variety of discernible words with his mouth, Josh was able to communicate with his siblings much more quickly, if for no other reason than to let someone know his basic needs. Thus, he'd developed an ability to speak and I could have a somewhat normal conversation with him, even though one could tell by his manner of speech that Josh was unmistakably hearing impaired.

Ed walked in and grabbed the team's attention by raising his hands above his head and speaking loudly so that the players who were hard of hearing took notice. With those players focused on their head coach the others quickly settled down and watched Ed as well. Like most good coaches at halftime, he signed to them words of encouragement and motivation. He reminded them that while they'd played a very good first half, there was still another half of a game to play and that St. Vincent wasn't likely to just give up. A seasoned coach with a passion for the game, Ed spoke loudly and signed firmly. His jaw protruded outward as he stared intently at his players; he tried to do what all coaches seek to do at half-time, re-energize his team. As coaches, we all knew that we'd have to survive at least one second half surge by the Bearcats.

The route from the locker room to the stadium was the same as before the game, but this time the boys were far from solemn. With the coaching staff preceding them, they gathered themselves well behind us at the foot of the concrete steps, waiting for all of their teammates to join them from the street above. We were a good fifty yards ahead of them when the last players stepped down onto the walkway. At that point, the herd of players broke away en masse. Hearing the team's thunderous approach, we hopped off the walkway and began to jog along the grassy practice field, attempting to get out of their path to the stadium. But it was too late and they were upon us in no time flat. They were like warriors charging into battle. They were like teenage girls chasing The Beatles. They were like a stampeding herd of Bison. And we were right there in the middle of the herd, surrounded on all sides.

My jog had become a light, gliding run when I looked to my right at Ed, who was just about ten feet away. Being a much shorter man than I, Ed was almost in a full sprint. He looked over in my direction, noticed me glancing at him, and smiled. We were both surrounded by players in white uniforms making a dash for the stadium, some passing us on to either side and others passing between us. Ed seemed very pleased at that moment, very proud of how he had been able to get the team to that point, and rightfully so. For me, it was more surreal, a moment in time that seemed to last far longer than it actually did. And to this day I can remember exactly how I felt at that moment. I was part of the herd, and it felt good.

The St. Vincent offense did indeed get its act together in the second half, and on their first drive of the third quarter they marched the ball right down the field for a quick touchdown. Apparently, their head coach had succeeded in re-energizing his team as well. The crowd began to sense that all wasn't lost and that their Bearcats were on the prowl. We were unable to move the ball on our first series of the second half, but a great punt by Kevin Alley pinned St. Vincent deep in their own territory. Looking out onto the field from the sideline, JC stood next to me toweling off his shaven head and taking sips from a water bottle. It had become a very warm September afternoon, but JC showed no signs of losing his cool, even after the Bearcat offense took another swipe at us.

On the first play of their next drive, the St. Vincent quarterback took a quick, three-step drop and fired the ball out to his wide receiver, not far from where we were standing. The pass was a quick hitch and the ball was delivered low, down around the feet of the receiver. The receiver dropped to one knee to make the catch, but quickly rose and began to run down the field with the football. In college and high school football, when a ball carrier's knee contacts the ground, the play is over and the referee blows his whistle to indicate such. And so believing the receiver to have been down as a result of his knee touching the ground, the Gallaudet defenders ceased to give chase. It didn't matter that our players couldn't hear the referees whistle, because there was no referee's whistle to be heard. The referees had missed the call, and the kid ran the ball eighty-six yards down the field and into the end zone for a long, St. Vincent touchdown. Ed was furious and complained to the officials, but to no avail. After a failed extra point conversion by St. Vincent, our lead was just 19-13 at the end of the third quarter.

Suddenly, the temperature on the field was much hotter, and the stadium crowd had become fully engaged and very loud. I sensed that the game might be slipping away from us and that our guys might become overwhelmed by the crowd noise as momentum had clearly swung St. Vincent's way.

The roar of a partisan crowd is definitely a home team advantage. It can have a chilling, negative effect on the morale and confidence of an opposing team, and thus play an integral part in the eventual outcome of a game, unless you were playing against Gallaudet. Then, no matter what the decibel level of the crowd noise was, it didn't have any effect on our players. And so without the distraction of the cheering St. Vincent faithful, our offense was able to go right back onto the field and recapture its confidence with a few modest gains and a couple of first downs.

In fact, just a few plays later, JC scrambled out of the pocket to his right to avoid a blitz by the defense and connected with Kevin Alley, who outraced a Bearcat defender to the end zone for another touchdown. Alley had a great game and would finish the day with eight receptions. JC ended up having a great game, too, completing 20 of his 33 pass attempts for 227 yards and three touchdowns. And Ed's defense was just as dogged as the offense. Josh and his cohorts along the defensive line continued to harass the Bearcat quarterbacks throughout the second half, and 5'9" defensive back Robin Shannon tallied three sacks and five tackles for a loss. In the face of such pressure from our defense, the St. Vincent offense failed to mount any further scoring threats. And so we had survived the St. Vincent surge that we anticipated. When it was all said and done, it was an opening day victory for the Bison.

GALLAUDET 32 ST.VINCENT 13

Like the cheerleaders during pre-game warm-ups, the St. Vincent players didn't know that I could hear. During the customary, post-game handshake at mid-field, I listened as the players filed past one another.

"Good game," said most of the St. Vincent players to each of our guys. "Good game, good game, good game …" came the obligatory greetings.

But a few dozen of their players actually signed, "Hello! Good game," as they passed along side of our team. I thought that was impressive as they must have planned on doing so well before game day. That was great sportsmanship and several of our guys were very impressed by the thoughtfulness of those players' gestures. Our boys mostly nodded toward the St. Vincent players as they shook their hands, although many attempted to mouth the words, "Good game."

At game time, I'd have estimated that Chuck Noll stadium was filled with two or three thousand people with several hundred more watching from outside the stadium complex. Maybe a few had departed by the time we finished with the handshaking, but for the most part the crowd had remained. Most of them likely wanted to greet their sons or friends as they either left the field or emerged from their locker room. Others, though, were still very curious about the Gallaudet football team, and watched intently as our players were joined on the field by their own friends and families. The scene appeared to be one of celebration, but was so quiet that someone who didn't know any better might have thought that they were watching it on television with the sound turned off.

The President of Gallaudet University, Dr. Robert Davila, had made the trip to watch the game, too, and addressed the team and their families afterward. There were several former Gallaudet players on hand as well. And just like all of those folks over in the stadium, I was just a spectator as well since Mr. Davila and all of those other folks just signed too darn fast for me. So I stood off to the side of the Gallaudet crowd, accepted a few congratulations here and there, and watched the happy faces of our players and their families.

While the team showered and prepared for the four hour bus ride back to Washington, I called home to see how my eleven-year-old son had done in his own game that afternoon. My wife told me that his team had lost their season opener to a perennial powerhouse, and that his team was very disappointed. When he got on the phone himself, he went on to tell me that he'd played a pretty good game and made a bunch of tackles. He also reminded me that it was the first time that I'd missed one of his football games. That kind of stuck in my craw a bit, as you might imagine. But, I guess I'd known that that was coming sooner or later.

When my wife got back on the phone, she told me how proud I'd have been to hear the announcer saying, "Mark Overmier on the tackle, Mark Overmier on the tackle."

Yes, I was very excited to be on the college football field with the Gallaudet players. And yes, I resented the fact that I wasn't on the field with my own son, especially since it was me who encouraged him to play the game of football. I was definitely conflicted, and I thought about it for a good while on the journey home. Why was I coaching college football again? Was it because I loved coaching the game of football and wanted to experience it at another level? Was it the esteem? Was it the excitement? Was it worth the sacrifice?

And, yes, I was very proud of him.

11

Injuries and Illness: Playing Walter Reed Hospital

I f you don't love the game of football, and I mean really love the game, then coaching college football isn't something you should aspire to do. It's a seven day a week job for the most part, even at the Division III level, and the days can be excessively long. If Ed had had things his way, we'd all be on campus sixteen hours a day with a cot in the locker room for napping the other eight. But considering that most of us were part-time coaches earning a fraction of what a full-time coach would earn, Ed was somewhat relaxed with our schedules at times. I also believe he was afraid that some of us might quit if our schedule became too burdensome on our families or full-time occupations. Perhaps that had been his experience with prior assistant coaches. Ryan and Brian were the exception. Ryan was a full-time, paid coach and Brian was receiving tuition assistance as a Graduate Assistant. Ed pretty much expected those two to be at the field house from sun up to well past sundown and at times midnight, for that matter.

On Sunday morning, Ed cut everyone some slack though, even Ryan and Brian. Our bus had gotten back a little after midnight the night before, and most of us hadn't headed home until about an hour after that. So Ed scheduled our coaches' meeting for two o'clock in the afternoon and directed the players to arrive at four. It would be an easy day for them with a review of the St. Vincent game film, a little conditioning, and some light lifting in the weight room. Of course, the players were very appreciative of the opportunity to sleep in. And I was appreciative of the opportunity to go to church with my family once again. After attending the eleven o'clock worship services at our church in Crofton, my family and I went back to the house where my wife prepared lunch for me and the boys. I left for Gallaudet shortly thereafter.

Usually, on Sunday afternoons in the fall, I could be found on my couch watching the Baltimore Ravens play football on television, or in my seats at the stadium in downtown Baltimore, but not now. Instead, I watched the tape of Gallaudet playing football against St. Vincent. Brian had spent much of the night preparing the game film for Ed and Ryan to review with us. That was the job of a GA, according to Ed, and he expected Brian to put in some ungodly weird hours doing so. There were times when he wanted the game film to be ready for him by six o'clock the next morning. That's why Brian remained in the field house well after we'd all departed.

As a result, while most of us watched the film, commented on what we saw, and made notes to discuss later, Brian nodded off in the corner of the cool, darkened classroom. Harold and Ron Cheek weren't at the meeting, and I didn't know where they were, though Ed did not seem to mind too much. So with Brian asleep there were essentially just five coaches watching the film. That made it very difficult for me to inconspicuously turn on my cell phone and check the live game scores on NFL.com. You see, I was heavily into fantasy football and needed to know which professional players had scored and what their game statistics were. I managed it each Sunday, but I'm pretty sure I wasn't always inconspicuous. While turning the sound off on the phone was a given, the little screen on my phone sure emitted an awful lot of light.

About ten minutes into the offensive film review, Ryan pointed out that the wide receivers were not very effective with their downfield blocking. Ed grimaced a bit and then looked over his left shoulder at Ryan.

"What the fuck is their problem, Hite?" he asked.

"It looks to me like they're turning their asses so they can get between the ball carrier and the defensive backs," Ryan said. "What the hell? They should be cutting their man!"

Now Ryan knew all too well what the wide receivers were attempting to do even before he'd pointed out their inadequacies. Just a few days earlier he'd caught a glimpse of me working with them on their stalk blocking. He'd asked me why I was teaching them to turn their hips in response to pressure from the defender. He didn't like my rationale and scolded me for coaching high school blocking techniques to college athletes, though he offered no alternative or preferred method.

"Did they get that shit from you?" Ryan looked past Ed at me.

"I explained to you a few days ago what we were doing, Ryan, after you guys finished with your inside run," I responded calmly.

"I mean, that's bullshit," he said.

"Yeah, they were a little tentative, being it was their first game and such, but they'll improve," I assured him. "I mean, you're the receivers coach aren't you? Just give me a few drills that you prefer and we'll work on getting them more proficient." If Ryan was trying to discredit my coaching acumen, it hadn't worked.

Ed sat, with his arms folded across his chest, staring at the game film on the wall. He calmly turned his head toward Ryan.

"Fix it, Hite," he said in his stern, commanding voice. If Ryan was trying to deflect responsibility, well, that didn't work either.

Ryan's jaw dropped a bit in frustration as he returned his focus to the game film. The rest of the hour was pretty civil with very little contention, especially since the quarterback play was pretty impressive. What could there have been to complain about? And, after all, we'd just won our first game, hadn't we?

Once the boys arrived we broke off into offensive and defensive groups and watched the game film with our players. Afterward, we took them to the stadium track for a short period of stretching and light conditioning. About thirty minutes later we led them through an abbreviated lifting session in the weight room before releasing them for the day. While working with the quarterbacks in the weight room, Fletch asked me whether or not I'd gone to church with my family that morning. I told him that I had and that it was nice to have done so. He smiled and confided in me that he, too, was of the Christian faith. And then, out of nowhere, he said that he thought the team should have a team bible study. That was the moment that I first realized that there were some signs of faith there at Gallaudet.

Monday was Labor Day and with Walter Reed on the schedule the following Saturday, there was very little concern from Ed regarding our opponent. They were a team comprised of military personnel assigned to Walter Reed Hospital, a military medical center near Washington. They had some size, a little speed, and some pretty good former high school athletes. But with player coaches and very little time for organized practices, they'd be no match for Ed's well-oiled Gallaudet machine. So Ed gave us the day off. For the coaching staff, it would be our first day off in the past twenty-four, which made the holiday a little extra special for a change. In high school football, we weren't allowed to practice on Sundays, so practicing on Labor Day was essential to preparing one's team for its season-opening, Friday night game. But this year I'd spend the bulk of the day at the Crofton Country Club pool with my family. And it was a welcome break.

*

Tuesday's practice was a harbinger of things to come for the rest of the week. JC had apparently injured his thumb during the game on Saturday and was unable to practice for most of the week. Jimmy was struggling mightily with seasonal allergies and pretty much practiced at half speed. Fletch wore down pretty quickly picking up the slack for the two of them, both emotionally as well as physically. Not only did he work with the special teams to begin practice, he would then drive the sled with the line, and then almost immediately hop under center to take reps with the first unit offense since JC was out. So, predictably, Fletch had a few days of just awful practice at quarterback, especially during the team's "Skelly" segments.

Now when a team's quarterback is in a funk, you can almost take it to the bank that the rest of the team won't be far behind. And that was especially true for the Gallaudet football team that week. With their emotional leader, JC, sidelined and Fletch being off-kilter, the team's approach to practice was both lackadaisical and unenthusiastic. The practice tempo was way off from the prior week. Maybe the two days off had been too much time away for the boys. Maybe there was an anticlimactic atmosphere following the build up for the inaugural game against St. Vincent. Whatever it was, Ed and Ryan were beside themselves with frustration about the team's lack of intensity on the practice field. Several key players on both sides of the ball were unable to practice at 100% due to nagging injuries from the game. And the number of sidelined players seemed to grow by the day, the hour even, until it almost appeared that there were more players who were unable to practice than those who could. Not good. College football was a very physical game, maybe more so than many of the boys had expected.

On Thursday afternoon, I decided to grab a soft drink before leaving my office at Coach & Courier in Crofton and heading downtown to practice. And so I walked across the parking lot in front of my office to a nearby convenience store. There was a big commotion on the roadway in front of the store. I saw a couple of police cars with their emergency lights ablaze, and two pretty banged up passenger sedans. One sedan had crashed into the other as the driver was attempting to pull out of the store parking lot and onto the street. A county policeman was re-directing traffic and another, one of our local town officers, was checking on the drivers. Our local officer appeared to be a bit perplexed as he spoke with the driver of the sedan that had been struck broadside. The other driver, a young woman in her early twenties, sat on the curb crying. I knew the local policeman pretty well, and being the busy-body that I am, I was all too willing to render assistance.

"Is everybody all right, Dave?" I asked him. I didn't know if one had been called, but an ambulance had yet to arrive upon the scene.

"Yeah, Jim," he said as he walked back toward his cruiser. "She's a little messed up, though," he said as he pointed toward the girl sitting on the curb. "I can't get a word out of her, she's so nervous."

When I looked over at the young lady, I could see what Dave meant. The girl was in tears and fumbling with her cell phone. Apparently, the phone had either been damaged in the accident, or the battery had died, because she just couldn't get it to work. I walked over to her and asked if she was okay.

"Are you okay?" I asked her. She didn't answer, but continued to look down at her phone. It looked to me like she was trying to text someone. "Do you need me to contact anyone for you?" I asked. "You can use my phone if you'd like," I said, holding my cell phone out to her. She looked up at me and, like Dave had said, was nervous and trembling. Otherwise, she appeared to be okay.

"Are you okay?" I asked her again.

This time, though, she set the phone down in the grass behind her and tried to speak to me, and at the same time gestured franti-cally with her hands.

"Dave?" I called over to the policeman, but maintained eye contact with her.

"Yeah, what's up, Jim?" He came over, stood by my side, and looked down at the girl sitting on the curb in front of me.

"She's deaf," I said.

"Great," he sighed, "how the hell are we going to find out if she is okay? Let me get a pad of paper."

While he fumbled in the pocket of his shirt for a pen and a small note pad, I tried signing to her and asked her if she was okay.

She said that she was.

"She's fine," I told Dave. I continued to sign to her, but apologized for not being better at doing so. She didn't care how poorly I signed, though, she was just happy that I could. Dave watched as she and I continued signing to one another.

"She says that it happened so fast that she couldn't stop," I said as Dave just stood and stared at me. "Her name is Amanda and her license is still in the car."

"When exactly did you learn sign language?" Dave asked me.

"Uh," I paused, "a few weeks ago."

Dave chuckled as he walked over to the girl's damaged car and retrieved her license from the console inside. I continued to interpret as best I could, which was more than good enough for all involved. Eventually, the girl was able to give me her mother's telephone number and most of the other information that the officers requested. Dave called her mom, who wasn't deaf, and she arrived on the scene a short time later. She expressed to me her gratitude for intervening on her daughter's behalf. Thankfully, her daughter and the other driver were both okay, although their cars were not and had to be towed from the scene. On my way to practice, I was very pleased by the thought that God may have prepared me for His service in helping out that day. And I was very eager to tell my story to the team, and did so throughout the practice that day. Most of the boys thought my story to be very cool, smiled, and patted me on the back of my shoulder as they did.

When Friday's practice rolled around and we went through our pre-game walk-through, I felt a sense of déjà-vu. To me, it seemed like the team had pretty much just finished a weeklong walk-through, considering how poorly they'd practiced. And with so many guys among the walking wounded, I thought to myself it was a good thing we were playing a team from Walter Reed Hospital. They had to have some medics on their team, right? Ed did what he could to motivate the team that night before releasing them to the chow hall, but to no avail. However, I could sense that he wasn't terribly concerned about the eventual outcome of the game. Instead, he was mostly irritated about their poor approach to overcoming physical discomfort, and the lack of team focus while preparing for their next contest.

Most of the boys had played against Walter Reed at least once before. Some had even played them several times, in fact. And so they apparently weren't too terribly concerned about the outcome of the game either. For me, though, it didn't seem like they weren't taking the game seriously at all. It did seem, though, as if there was a dark moodiness about them that I hadn't seen from them before, or any other team I'd ever coached. Their collective emotional highs seemed much higher than those of football teams comprised of hearing players, but shorter lasting. And their lows had much more depth and duration. Was it because, as a team of deaf players, they had a much greater dependence upon one another for emotional support and sustenance? That was my assumption.

After practices, I usually seized upon any opportunity that presented itself to converse with a player or two about their personal lives, perspectives, and goals. It not only helped me to understand my players a little better, but also helped me practice my signing. Before leaving campus that evening, I spoke in depth with JC about personal communications within the deaf community. He explained to me that his father had "learned" to talk. By that I gathered that his father had developed the ability to communicate verbally, like Josh Ofiu had done. And he, too, had probably learned to read lips. That was his way of minimizing the impact of his disability.

But JC told me that he, himself, had declined the opportunity to "learn" how to talk. He felt there was no point in learning how to talk, because doing so betrayed the deaf culture. I didn't understand his point, since from my own perspective, learning how to talk could help make life a lot easier for him. But, it was his honest opinion, and his life, and I respected that. Obviously, I think, perhaps, that his father may have felt differently. Regardless, I gained a little more insight into JC, the deaf community, and the chasms that divide people, even those who co-exist within a unique culture.

It was another bright and sunny Saturday morning on the day of the Walter Reed game and I had the car windows down as I drove into the district. A few blocks from the school, though, the whole windows down thing suddenly didn't seem like such a good idea. Police cars and streams of yellow tape blocked my usual path to the school and I was detoured a little further south than I'd ventured before. Just beyond one of the police cars I saw a white sheet on the sidewalk concealing the body of some unfortunate soul. According to the local news, it turned out that the body was just one of two murder victims found at the same location along Mt. Olivett Road.

In my opinion, putting the car windows up in a high crime area was much the same as pulling the blankets over your head while lying in bed, scared of monsters or ghosts. It just wasn't going to help a whole lot. Nonetheless, I put the windows up and again wondered in amazement about the hundreds of deaf Gallaudet students who resided in that neighborhood. And I wondered if they knew just how bad the neighborhood around their school was. Did their parents know? And I thought to myself that either ignorance was indeed bliss, or a bold sense of bravado had been born out of deafness. Perhaps it was both.

The team met on the second floor of the dining hall at 9:00 a.m. to have breakfast together. After checking in with Ed in the football office at the field house, I began my walk across campus to join the team. Justin Lathus, walking out of the training room, saw me and clapped his hands to get my attention. He joined me on my way to have breakfast. When walking alongside of me, it can be a little tough for most people to keep up with me because of my long strides. Just ask my wife. But for Justin and his bad hip it was really a challenge, but one that he embraced without complaint. Incredibly, Justin had managed to overcome his physical impediment to play the manly sport of football, and for that alone I admired him.

He wasn't a big guy at just 5'11" tall and about 215 pounds. His wasn't a sculpted 215 pounds either, but a physique of average stature and clearly some neglect. The brutal winters of Chicago must have played a part in toughening Justin up to the point that he actually enjoyed physical challenges. He was a very good natured fellow, most of the time.

As we walked by the main entrance of the stadium, we were joined by a young woman with whom Justin appeared to be familiar, and they began signing to one another. I grasped much of the niceties, but failed to keep up beyond their standard greetings. My interpreting skills were pretty weak as it was, but walking and watching them sign at the same time? Forget about it. It wasn't like chewing gum and walking at the same time. That was easy. Signing with Justin, the woman glanced over at me and smiled.

"Good morning," I signed to her.

"Good morning," she signed back and at the same time spoke the words clearly.

Huh? I didn't see that one coming, or should I say, I didn't hear that one coming. She was an immersion student residing at Gallaudet as part of the school's training program for those learning to be a translator for the deaf, and that was how Justin knew her, from the classroom. I don't remember her name, only that she was from Jacksonville, Florida and that she was studying to be a teacher at The Florida School for the Deaf. Brian Tingley's girlfriend, Mara, had gone the same route, I believe, and was currently a teacher at the Maryland School for the Deaf. Anyway, she was pretty cute and I couldn't blame Justin for being more than happy to help her hone her skills.

My surprise at the sound of her voice reminded me that I was growing used to the lack of verbal dialogue and the quiet environment at Gallaudet University. Here and there I was able to communicate verbally, but again, that was frowned upon by the administration. So those of us who worked on campus, and could hear, tried to abstain from speaking as much as possible. Mostly out of habit, though, I often spoke while signing, especially if I knew that the person I was speaking to could hear. Sometimes, though, it was out of convenience, like when asking the server at the dining hall for a western omelet. The line was long, the time was short, and she could hear me. So at the same time that I was making some lame attempt to sign the words, "western omelet," which she probably didn't understand anyway, I was also saying aloud, "I'll have a western omelet." And everyone was happy.

While waiting for my breakfast that morning, I glanced across the dining room and saw the old deaf and blind man who walked the track every day. I learned later that someone had arranged many years ago for the school to take care of this old fellow and make their facilities available to him as needed. Still, he lived off-campus and somehow made his way to the school every day. God sure has His hands full with taking care of everyone, I thought. Perhaps that's one of the reasons why He uses His people to help him out, though in this case I wasn't the one who He had tasked with taking care of the old man. Someone else had that job. And maybe that person wondered who God had tasked with working with all of the deaf football players.

The food at the dining hall was very good, as usual. After breakfast, the coaches met briefly in the football office while the players milled about the lower level of the field house. Some took the opportunity to get taped early while others sat and read or talked to one another about the game. Others lay on the floor of the hallways and napped. Eventually, the time came for their pre-game meetings and final preparations of uniforms and equipment. Just before assembling the players to exit the field house for the stadium, I walked by the wrestling room where the players had gathered. Inside, I saw a large huddle of young men wearing football uniforms on one knee, praying. I couldn't hear any words being spoken, but I recognized the silence of a prayerful moment. A few minutes later, as the team began its walk from the field house to the stadium, Fletch approached me and told me that the team had prayed before coming out of the field house.

"I know," I signed to him as he smiled broadly, "I saw!" I watched him slowly sign his reply to me so that I could understand what he was saying.

"I led the prayer," Fletch signed, putting on his helmet.

"I was very impressed," I signed. "Nice job!" Fletch nodded and joined the team as they made their entrance into the stadium before a surprisingly boisterous crowd of very supportive home team fans.

Walking across the track and toward the bench on our sideline, I looked across the field at the team from Walter Reed. Those guys were not college students by any stretch of the imagination. They were full grown men, much older than our guys, although many of our players were themselves a little older than your average college student. But many of the Walter Reed guys appeared to be in their late twenties and possibly their early thirties. They appeared to have some fast guys, too, and some pretty big ones as well. I could tell that most had played the game at some level in years past.

While some of the Walter Reed players were living out their dreams of playing college football, others were just making the most of their weekends. In either case, it gave them a break from the stress of their jobs at the medical center and something to look forward to. It was also the epitome of a team-building exercise, too, if you think about it. In any case, I had to admire them for their effort, since they only got two practices a week and had just twenty-nine players. I could only imagine just how organized and effective those practices were. And I was beginning to see why Ed wasn't particularly concerned about whether or not we would win the game. But getting out of the game with minimal injuries probably was a concern.

Prior to the start of the game, the school's president stood in front of our bench area at mid-field and addressed the team and our fans. The grunting and barking of the Walter Reed players as they warmed up on the far side of the field was all that could be heard throughout the stadium, for those who could hear.

"I attended the contest in Pennsylvania last weekend," he signed. "Now I have a taste for the game of football. And I like it."

The crowd applauded and some began to cheer wildly, which of course attracted the attention of the Walter Reed players. After the fans had calmed down a bit, three cheerleaders emerged from behind us and took a position side by side, three abreast, out at mid-field. I wasn't sure what was going on until I heard the popping of chin straps and our players removing their helmets. The cheerleaders were about to sign "The Star Spangled Banner." I removed my cap and held it across my chest as I faced the flag at the east end of the stadium, to our left. The cheerleaders began to sign the national anthem in tandem, and did so very eloquently with a fair bit of theatrics. It took some time before the Walter Reed team realized what was happening, but when they did, they too removed their helmets, and faced the flag.

I'm not sure if things have changed since my time at Gallaudet, but the school never actually "played" the national anthem for the visiting team. It was only signed. And I'm sure that the other teams always felt badly when they came to realize that they were warming up during the "playing" of The Star-Spangled Banner. But, it wasn't their fault. They didn't know what was going on and were focused on preparing for the game. Obviously, no one from Gallaudet ever gave them a "heads up" beforehand, because every visiting team that year appeared to be caught off guard. I thought that it would have been appropriate for Gallaudet to extend the courtesy of "playing" the national anthem for visiting teams. I don't know if they didn't play it because the school had no public address system in place, or a band to perform it, or if it was the expectation of the university that guests should conform to campus standards. If it were up to me, though, I'd have had someone perform the national anthem for the opposing team, like St. Vincent's had done for us. But then again, I was caught between two worlds and not in command of either.

After the cheerleaders were finished performing the anthem, I thought to myself about how much physical effort and emotion they'd put into the song. It was very artistic, and judging by the response of the people in the stadium, the song, and its meaning, were clearly inspirational, even to those who couldn't hear it.

The game itself wasn't such a thing of beauty or inspiration. We played very poorly during the first half with numerous turn-overs, penalties, and missed assignments. The team from Walter Reed would frequently call their plays aloud to expedite their set ups, knowing that our guys couldn't hear them. And while their legs were fresh they played very well, managing to keep the game competitive for the first thirty minutes. It was mostly our own mistakes, though, that kept the score close. We led at half-time by a score of 14-0.

Ed was absolutely livid in the locker room and he lit the boys up pretty good. They got the old "you will play like you practice" speech, and he reminded them of just how poorly they had practiced all week. In the second half, though, the boys managed to get their act together and simply overpowered a fatiguing Walter Reed team, who just couldn't keep up the good fight. About midway through the third quarter, the old guys ran out of gas. Their lack of conditioning and practice time had suddenly, but not surprisingly, taken its toll on them in the heat of the afternoon sun, and their will to win was suddenly gone. The final score was as lopsided as Ed had probably expected.

GALLAUDET 44 WALTER REED 0

It was during the Walter Reed game that I felt the most inadequate as a coach of deaf football players. I continued to struggle with signing quickly to players on the bench and along the sideline during the game, and it was affecting my ability to effectively coach them in real time. For that reason, I began to worry that I might lose their respect or confidence in me as their coach. And I didn't want that to happen.

But I'd also developed another inferiority complex. During this, our first home game, and with all of our fans seated behind us, I realized that everyone in the stands could see what I was attempting to sign to my quarterbacks as we stood on the sideline. If they didn't understand what I was saying in technical terms, or football terms, they surely didn't understand my poor signing, either, which would then beg the question, "Why is this guy coaching our deaf players?"

However, most of the boys had come to know me by then and were able to glean from my signing the information, or instruction, that I was attempting to convey. But to the average deaf person in the stands, my signing must have made me look like an idiot. And so I began to conceal my sideline signing in the bench area. From that day on, I kept my hands below the shoulders of the players to whom I was talking, and I always kept the players between me and the fans. And if I was addressing a bench of seated players, I took to my knee to do so. It became a conscious effort on my part to contain my signing to only the players, and no one beyond them. And I tried to do so without letting on to the team what I was doing.

The next week would be another home game and the opponent much more formidable than Walter Reed. Greensboro College, from North Carolina, was next on our schedule and the word was that they were a very good football team.

During the team meeting that Sunday, the boys were pretty embarrassed while watching their performance against Walter Reed on the game film. They acknowledged that they'd need to put forth a much better effort in order to beat Greensboro. And making that happen would require a much better week of practice.

12

Injuries and Illness: Too Bad We're Not Playing Walter Reed

During the offensive staff meeting on Monday afternoon we watched the game film of Greensboro College versus UNC Charlotte. Greensboro looked to me to be the real deal. They had good size, tons of athleticism, and speed to burn. They also appeared to be very well prepared and organized. Ed wasn't equally impressed, having taken the boys down to North Carolina as a club team to play at Greensboro in years past. He respected them, but refused to be intimidated by them. That's just the way Ed was, a pretty tough, nuts and bolts kind of guy. One could easily mistake Ed's attitude as having a lack of respect for an opponent, but that wouldn't have been the case. Ed fit the mold of a stereotypical defensive coordinator perfectly, bold and confident that his defense could stop anyone, plain and simple. And so if he thought that Greensboro wasn't all that impressive, then why should I?

Ryan introduced the offensive game plan for that weekend, and I was quite surprised to see that he'd included a few ideas that I'd suggested on Sunday. While I didn't say anything to that effect, I was definitely encouraged by the idea that he'd considered employing a little more play-action and using motion in our offense. Maybe he wasn't as hard-headed as I thought. I realized that I was kidding myself. He was hard-headed all right, just not stupid. Ryan knew he had to mix things up a bit more to open up the offense and give us a fighting chance against a quality opponent. Giving the team some new meat to chew on would not only spruce up the offensive playbook, which players always enjoyed, but the level of focus on the practice field as well. When he introduced the new plays to the team in pre-practice meetings Tuesday, the concepts were well received. In fact, the boys were eager to hit the practice field so they could begin to work on the new plays.

After the meetings, and while walking through the field house hallways among the players, I overheard, or rather saw, a few of the guys signing to one another about a particular girl on campus. Judging by their grins and facial expressions, she must have been a rather attractive young lady. When they saw me peeking into their conversation they invited me to join in on the discussion. Calvin Dought, though, had to keep me up to speed during the conversation by telling me what was going on, because in their excitement they began to sign much too quickly for my level of comprehension. Calvin, unlike his brother, Joshua, had limited hearing ability, and spoke quite well. Apparently, with the goal of becoming a model, this young woman who they were talking about had taken part in an adult entertainment production and was featured on a website called DeafBunny.com. That really was the name of the website, by the way. And so while I never got around to experiencing DeafBunny.com, I did appreciate that the guys had felt comfortable enough around me to share such a discussion with me.

Tuesday's practice had a lot more pop than usual and the team definitely had regained their enthusiasm. The pace of the practice was high tempo and upbeat and the installation of the new offensive plays went well. I think the team had a little extra motivation since the Gallaudet Football Program had been featured in that morning's edition of *The Washington Times*, a D.C. based daily newspaper. The lengthy article, written by staff writer, Jon Siegel, was very complimentary of the team and mentioned several players as well as their fearless leader, Ed Hottle. Siegel wrote about the school's football history, detailed the teams' past accomplishments, current goals and expectations, and, of course, the obvious adversity that most of the players faced as college athletes. Ed had masterfully managed to have the story published at just the right time given the team's need for a boost in morale.

Although at the end of the day it would be a good practice, it didn't quite start out that way. At the conclusion of Flex, and before we broke into small groups for the Indy segment of practice, several players jogged across the practice field toward the trainer's watering station. Suddenly, seemingly out of nowhere, Kerry, the offensive line coach, ran toward them in what appeared to be a moment of temporary insanity.

"You don't fucking need water!" screamed Kerry, his bald head glimmering in the hot sun. "You don't fucking need water!" Kerry was going off like a mad man, an eyeball-popping, screaming lunatic. Again he reminded me of the photograph of the bald guy in Ed's office.

"You don't fucking need water!" he repeated.

As he screamed, he grabbed several water bottles from the trainer's table and cast them as far away as he could. The players withdrew as if in fear, the hard-of-hearing guys at the sound and magnitude of Kerry's screaming, and the deaf players by his sudden burst of obvious angst. Needless to say, they didn't get their water, whether they needed it or not.

"What the hell is his problem?" Ryan asked out loud.

Standing next to Ryan, I glanced over at Ed about ten feet away. Ed stood nonchalantly with his arms folded across his chest.

"His wife is eight months pregnant," said Ed.

"So? Isn't your wife about eight months pregnant, too?" asked Ryan, shaking his head and looking back toward Kerry, who was escorting his linemen to the blocking sled. Ed walked toward us, slid his sunglass frames down along his nose, as he tended to do whenever he had something matter-of-fact to say, and stared intensely across them at Ryan.

"Never mind," said Ryan. "I got it. I got it."

Ed was probably referring to the fact that Kerry probably *was not getting it*, since his wife was eight months pregnant. That's how I think Ryan interpreted it, anyway.

The three quarterbacks walked up alongside me as Ryan took off across the field. They shook their heads, smiling and laughing, and shrugged their shoulders in amusement over Kerry. Jimmy pulled the footballs out of my equipment bag and they began to warm up. The remainder of the afternoon was much less eventful as both Ed and Ryan were pleased with the intensity and pace of the practice. But with the more fervent approach to practice came a few scuffles and a couple of minor injuries to players involved in the spirited effort. Rusty Nawrocki, a defensive end, was one of those players; he hobbled off the field with a lower leg injury. Jon was still tending to him when we left the field at the conclusion of practice.

Rusty's real name was Roman and he was a genuinely nice kid, a 6'2" junior out of St. Augustine, Florida. Blonde hair and thin framed, Rusty was the strong, silent type, but not afraid to smile, albeit a sheepish one. I'm pretty sure that Fletch had told Rusty that I was a Christian, because Rusty began to show me some of his favorite bible verses and passages of scripture. Just out of the blue. And he was a very cerebral guy, too. I think his field of study was Criminal Forensics. But one of the more fascinating things that I learned about Rusty was that he was a black belt of the nth degree, so accomplished in the sport that he'd earned Olympic consideration. To this day I can recall only three guys named Roman and they were all football players: Roman Gabriel, the legendary NFL quarterback; Roman Harper, a defensive back also in the NFL; and Roman Nawrocki of Gallaudet University.

Entering the lower level of the field house following practice, Kerry walked briskly ahead of the rest of us coaches. He may have been a bulky guy, but he was also pretty quick afoot. A high energy kind of coach, Kerry had worked up a good sweat out on the practice field that day.

"What's the hurry there, Phalen?" called out Ed with a smile. "Are those 7-11 chili dogs working themselves free?"

"No, man, I'm sweatin' like crazy," Kerry said without looking back, "I need some water."

"Water?" I said out loud, with just a wee bit of sarcasm, "You don't need any fucking water, Coach!"

The rest of the coaches all laughed aloud as Kerry simply fingered the universal sign of discontent back in our direction.

*

Back on the home front, my spousal support was beginning to wane. My wife, Mary-Ellen, was not eight months pregnant, but she also "wasn't loving" football season. Coming from a family of four girls and no boys, she wasn't a big fan of the game and had never been terribly excited about me coaching high school football. But, she knew that I enjoyed coaching and, considering that I didn't engage in any other time-consuming activities like golf, bowling, or playing softball with the guys, she generally tolerated me being gone every Friday night from mid-August until early November. It actually provided her some "down time," as she liked to call it.

Except for Fridays, I was usually home by six o'clock every evening when I coached at the high school. So it wasn't really any different than having a nine-to-five job with a commute. And I could help get our son, Mark, back and forth to practice. But now, with my son about to turn eleven and playing his second year of football, my wife found herself having to take him to practices, going back home to make dinner, and then going back to the field to get him, all done with our seven-year-old in tow. Getting both boys fed, bathed, and ready for school the next day was quite a chore and, unlike in previous fall seasons, I wasn't around to help much.

In retrospect, I think that that particular season of coaching football, the year 2007, was the origin of my wife's loathing of the fall. To this day she hates the fall season and the football routine that defines it. In fact, she now begins complaining about the upcoming football season somewhere between Valentine's Day and Easter.

Still, she was managing to get everything done. She just wasn't going to greet me at the door with a smile when I finally got home around nine o'clock or so. There were some nights that I'd leave campus early enough to pick Mark up from practice, which I always enjoyed. Mark liked me picking him up because he got to show dad his battle scars and ask me about how the college team was doing. Otherwise, it was usually lights out with little more than "Dad loves you. See you tomorrow, pal."

Our younger son, Tyler, was a restful little bug and would usually turn in early without even being told to do so. A lot of times, Tyler would be sound asleep when I got home. They both got on the school bus at seven o'clock in the morning so their days were pretty long, too.

Mary-Ellen usually took them to the bus stop a few miles away before beginning her own work day. A lot of moms have similar routines; it was exhausting for her and she had begun to resent my decision to coach college ball. And I was beginning to realize that the opportune time for me to coach college football had slipped by many years ago.

*

Unfortunately, Wednesday's practice wasn't nearly as brisk as the day before and the patience of both Ed and Ryan wore thin quickly. Just twenty-four hours earlier the team had been hustling about with much more enthusiasm and purpose. Now, they seemed to be wandering around and just going through the motions of practice. Some of the running backs forgot their assignments, wide receivers dropped routine passes or ran incorrect routes, and linemen jumped off-sides several times. And at quarterback, JC was now sick and simply refusing to practice at game speed, which as I've said before, had a profound effect on the rest of the team. Needless to say, Ed began to bark at a very high decibel level; I think even some of the deaf kids could hear him! And Ryan, well he began signing to the players with a whole lot of emotion, mostly anger, which just added to their lack of desire to practice.

Over the years, as both a player and a coach, I'd seen many guys try to battle their way through an illness to practice. Some just didn't want to give in for fear of losing whatever competitive edge that they had achieved. Others simply knew that if they missed a practice or two during the week that they would not be able to play in the game on Friday night. Not allowing the player to play after not practicing was usually a player safety issue, not a punitive one. But JC had just "shut it down" as a result of feeling under the weather, and I found that bemusing. Don't get me wrong, I don't think that players should practice when they're sick; that can put the player at risk of significant injury. But JC didn't really demonstrate any signs or symptoms of being ill, unlike Jimmy had with his allergies the week before. And he just would not practice. Ryan wouldn't give Jimmy any reps with the first team and Fletch continued to struggle with his proficiency under center. And so we didn't have a great couple of offensive practice days, to say the least.

*

I mentioned before that the Gallaudet campus was extraordinarily quiet, despite the all around presence of what appeared to be normal, day-to-day activities. There was one activity, though, that was conspicuously absent: people walking around talking on cell phones. Now, that did not mean that there weren't any cell phones on campus, there weren't any people walking around holding them to their ear and talking. When I first witnessed several of the boys whiling away their time on the trainer's table with, of all things, a cell phone device, I didn't realize that they were on the cutting edge of a new phenomenon: texting.

Cell phones had become very accessible by 2007 and were widely used by just about everybody, including the deaf kids at

Gallaudet. That's right, including the deaf kids at Gallaudet. But, they didn't actually use the cell phone the same way that most of us did. A new device on the market at that time, the first "all-in-one" cell phone, the T-Mobile Sidekick, was immensely popular among the deaf community because of its keyboard texting ability. Most of those kids could really hum along on the small, QWERTY keyboard of their cell phones, texting words and phrases to one another nearly as fast as I could speak them. And their messages were received in real time.

That technology really took inter-personal communication to an entirely new level for the deaf kids. They no longer had to be in sight of, or looking at, the person with whom they were communicating. Now you might think, as I did, that some of the more conservative folks within the deaf community might resist this technology, including guys like JC. But it didn't take me long to understand why texting had become so popular among them: privacy. They could now have private conversations even when seated on a crowded bus or in the school library. The deaf kids became experts in texting long before the rest of our teenagers.

*

On Thursday, September 13, 2007, Coach Hottle, Ed, informed the team that Gallaudet had been accepted into the NCAA North Atlantic Conference effective the fall of 2009. He had accomplished a major goal: taking the team from a club team status to a recognized member of an official NCAA athletic conference. That was quite a feat to have completed in just a few years at the helm. Gallaudet was a school for the deaf that everyone would soon hear from, and the boys were excited to be the flag bearers.

After our walk-thru practice on Friday afternoon, we yielded the stadium to the team from Greensboro College so they could have an opportunity to fine tune a few things before the contest on Saturday. We were not allowed to watch them practice, for obvious reasons, but I did happen to "overhear" their coaching staff talking among one another as we crossed paths outside the field house. Apparently, they'd enjoyed a day of sightseeing and local cuisine before arriving on campus. In stark contrast to our team, and the two teams that we had just defeated, most of the players on the Greensboro team appeared to be African-American. They also appeared to be very confident, very big, and very fast. I looked up at the overcast sky and impending rain. If we ever needed a little rain to slow things down a few notches, it would be tomorrow. The forecast was favorable, for us, and the rain began to fall about an hour later while on my drive home.

Sometime in the early hours of the morning, though, the misty, late, summer rain ended. When I arrived on campus around 8:30 a.m. the skies were clear, the clouds were gone, and the sun was again shining brightly upon the dew covered stadium turf. I walked across the corner of the end zone as I made my way to the Dining Hall from the parking lot. The ground was still moist, but the footing was firm and mostly solid. It wouldn't be a factor in the game after all.

The team gathered for breakfast at nine o'clock wearing their navy blue warm-up suits and white sneakers. Intimately familiar with the process by now, the boys carried their trays and visited their favorite food serving stations. One by one, and two by two, they made their way to the privacy of the second floor. Ed had instructed us to limit the conversation among the players to a minimum so as to encourage them to focus on the game. That meant keeping a watchful eye out across the room while I ate, looking for guys signing to one another. I caught a few of the guys chit-chatting about the night before and either waved to get their attention or air-mailed a few packets of sugar their way. The latter method was much more effective, of course. One of the "conversations" that I broke up, though, was one guy signing to another and asking for the salt shaker. I knew the sign for passing, but not for salt, and certainly not for shaker. My bad, as they say today. After breakfast we walked en masse to the field house for pre-game meetings, training room visits, and last minute game preparations.

A pretty good crowd was on hand for the game, just over a thousand folks, it looked like. The smell of hamburgers and hot dogs sizzling on charcoal grills wafted across the stadium from the street outside. Inside, things were beginning to cook as well. Ed seemed genuinely pleased with the team's pre-game tempo, making his way among the boys in their navy blue, white, and gold Bison uniforms. Occasionally, he'd pause for a moment and peer across the field, through his dark sunglasses, at the white and green uniformed players from Greensboro College. Then he'd resume strolling among our own guys once again.

Ryan, on the sideline in front of our bench, studied his laminated play calling sheet. Brian walked about with a broad smile on his face, pushing his shirt sleeves up over his biceps. Every once in a while I saw the two managers, Damian and Dustin, signing frantically to one another as they raced up and down the stairs from the stadium to the field. They were sometimes like a comedy act those two.

The players from Greensboro were indeed big and fast. And they appeared to be much more polished than the team from St. Vincent College. Many of their players seemed to have the size and talent to play at a much higher level of collegiate ball, but for whatever reason had made the decision to play football at the Division III level, or had the decision made for them. Our boys didn't seem to be intimidated in the least, though, having bought into Ed's assessment that the Greensboro team wasn't all that impressive. Ah, I thought, ignorance is bliss.

Things did look pretty good for us early on, though, I'll admit. After losing the coin toss to determine the opening kickoff, we contained the speedy Greensboro kick-returner to a modest return of just eleven yards. Then Ed's defense held the Greensboro offensive unit to a quick three-and-out series, bringing on the Greensboro punter. We then blocked their punt, recovering the football on the Greensboro twenty yard line. The defensive unit sprinted off the field with excitement, and much to the delight of the fans in the stadium behind us.

But Greensboro's size and athleticism kicked in. Ryan called in a run play to the left with no success. Our offensive line had no push whatsoever. He called for a run play to the right side of the line, but again, no success as the ball carrier was stuffed by a wave of green jerseys. The Greensboro defensive linemen appeared to be just too physical for our offensive linemen to move. Ryan then called for a play-action pass play to the right flats. After faking the handoff to Dima Rossoshansky, who ran toward the left side of the line, JC pivoted around and rolled out to the right. He beat the defensive end, and saw Fletch wide open in the deep flats about ten yards down the field. But JC short-armed the throw for an incomplete pass, leaving us with a fourth-and-long. Without any hesitation, Ed dispatched the field goal unit to attempt a 37 yard field goal.

Justin Wilson, our kicker, kept his head down and swung his right leg across the spot where the ball was being held in place by his quarterback. But suddenly, JC took hold of the ball and ran around the right end on a fake field goal attempt. He got by the defensive player who was trying to block the kick, and then out ran a second defender to the right hash marks. But he could not avoid the Safety along the sideline, who had run across the field to dive at JC's thighs. JC, in the grasp of the defensive player, fell forward, holding the ball out toward the yard to gain marker as he did. At first, it looked as if he'd made the line to gain, but unfortunately came up just short of the distance needed. We turned possession of the ball back over to Greensboro. It was a gutsy call by Ed and it almost worked. I liked the idea because the play probably had had a better chance of success than the actual kick attempt. And so even though we'd missed out on a golden opportunity to put a few points on the board, we were feeling pretty good about things at that point. Our defensive unit was playing with a lot of confidence and we had just pinned the Greensboro offense back on their twelve yard line.

If there was any secret as to what Greensboro was going to do on the next offensive series, the beans were spilled after just two plays. Our defensive line may have been athletic, but they were just not that big, and Greensboro figured out quickly that they could influence our boys or downright move them out of the way at will. And so they pounded the ball inside with running plays between the tackles. They ran a counter here and there, and even threw in a toss sweep just to make things interesting. But there was no doubt what they'd decided to do: drive the ball right down our throats. And they did just that. In doing so, Greensboro consumed the remainder of the time in the first quarter and scored a touchdown to take a 6–0 lead. Their kicker missed the extra point, leaving us trailing by six points. But, we still felt pretty good about things on the sideline.

Our second offensive series didn't fare any better than our first, though; we couldn't get the run game going and JC couldn't complete a pass. A big part of the problem was that the offensive line was struggling to cope, not only with the size and athleticism of the Greensboro defenders, but with a lack of focus. When running the no-huddle offense, things happen quickly, sometimes too quickly for some players. Invariably, at least one of our linemen was late getting back to the line of scrimmage following the completion of a play. This caused them to miss at least a portion of the play call from Brian. Normally, when that happens, a player will simply ask his teammate what the call is and his buddy will tell him. But for our kids, the rapid pace of the no-huddle offense didn't always allow enough time for one player to sign a complete play call to another before the snap of the ball. The result was Greensboro defensive players breeching gaps in our offensive line and defeating what should have been double-teams, but weren't because the second half of the double team had missed the sign and wasn't at the point of attack. A double-team was when two offensive players blocked one defensive player.

For the second offensive series in a row, we couldn't advance the football, and once again we turned to Kevin Alley to punt the ball back to Greensboro. Suddenly, there was quite a bit of frustration and finger pointing among the players on the offensive unit, and when JC came to the sideline he began to blame the offensive line for his errant passes.

"The line isn't giving me the time I need to pass," he signed to me in frustration.

"That's true," I signed back to him. "And that's why we're going to try the short passing game. It doesn't require the line to sustain their blocks. But you're going to have to make good pre-snap reads and start thinking 'catch and throw.'"

In other words, he needed to be like a shortstop in baseball. We wanted JC to receive the ball from the center and throw it quickly to a receiver, just as the shortstop would quickly pick up a ground ball and throw it right away to the first baseman. JC removed his helmet and reached for a Gatorade from the table behind me. He looked me in the eye, nodded his head repeatedly, and took a seat on the bench, grabbing a towel to wipe his brow.

Meanwhile, the Greensboro offense was moving the ball down the field once again, and had moved well past midfield. On third down and four yards to go, Ed called on Robin Shannon to blitz from the outside. Robin came in hard off the edge and forced the off-tackle play to bounce outside. In doing so, the Greensboro fullback reached out and actually pulled Robin to the ground as Robin attempted to tackle the runner. The running back scampered around the corner for the first down.

Ed was furious that the referee failed to throw a flag for offensive holding, and he let the whole stadium know it. When Ed went on his rampages against the referees, I often wondered if the referees had considered themselves unlucky to not be deaf. Ed could get pretty loud and so that would have been one of those times that it may have been beneficial to be deaf.

On the very next play, the Greensboro quarterback dropped back to pass and hit his receiver streaking undefended down the far sideline for an easy touchdown. The defensive backs had failed to communicate their coverage to one another and Greensboro took a 13–0 lead.

I'd like to say that things got better for the offense the next time that we had the ball, but it didn't. It actually got worse. Not only did we fail to get a first down for the third consecutive series, but our starting guard, David Morgan, a sophomore from Roanoke, Virginia, left the game with a leg injury. He hobbled off of the field and made his way to Jon's training table behind our bench. Ed began to give the offensive coaching staff the evil eye.

But just when I thought things were about to get out of hand, we got another break. On the ensuing punt, the Greensboro punt returner fumbled the ball and we recovered it inside their forty yard line. This time, though, rather than trying to run stretch plays and tosses, we began to run directly at the big Greensboro defensive linemen with dive plays and quick hitters between the tackles. Finally, we actually had a little success running the football and managed to venture deep into Greensboro territory. And then JC did what JC did best, he turned a broken play into something positive.

After the miscue of failing to hand the ball off to the running back, JC instinctively scrambled out of the backfield, avoiding several Greensboro defenders as he did. It looked as if he might take off and run, but he kept his eyes downfield, and somehow managed to see running back, Daniel Alexander, uncovered and waving his hands on the five yard line. JC lofted the ball to him for a 22 yard touchdown pass and an easy score. And just like that, the score was 13 -7, a six point deficit that would hold up after Greensboro failed to score near the end of the first half. The boys were ecstatic in the locker room at halftime, and celebrated with high fives and thumbs up from everyone, including Ed.

The second half, though, was a different story altogether, and started off poorly for us even before we returned to the field after half-time. Unbeknownst to us, Josh Doudt was flagged for a personal foul on the final play of the second quarter. We weren't aware of it, though, since in our excitement we had hurried off the field. It was a fifteen yard penalty and rather than run another play to end the half, Greensboro elected to have the penalty enforced on the second half kickoff. Thus, we had to kick off from our own 15 yard line, and that's never good. To add salt to the wound, Justin Wilson's kick-off sailed out of bounds and Greensboro opted to have us kick the ball again. The referee marched off the five yard penalty and placed the ball on our own ten yard line for the re-kick. Well, you can probably guess what happened next. The Greensboro kick returner caught the ball around midfield and made a mad dash toward his own sideline. There, he found clear sailing all the way the end zone for a touchdown.

It got worse. We received the ensuing kickoff from Greensboro and returned it to about the thirty-five yard line, down by just two scores. The game was still within reach for us, but a nice long, sustained drive was in order so that we could regain some momentum. This didn't happen, though; we fumbled the very first play of the drive. It would be just one of three fumbles that we lost during the game. Smelling blood in the water, Greensboro went on the attack and scored only two plays later.

Again, we had decent field position following the kickoff return. But after three plays, the offense just could not get any push from the offensive line and we turned the ball over on downs, giving it back to Greensboro. Their defensive players were just too big, too fast, and too good and our offensive line could neither gain any ground nor hold it. Shortly thereafter, the finger pointing began again as players tried to assign blame to someone other than themselves for our offensive woes. They could make excuses all they wanted for their poor play, but in reality we were just getting our butts whooped. Greensboro took over on our side of mid-field and quickly scored again. Less than seven minutes into the second half, Greensboro had turned a six point advantage into a very comfortable lead.

I don't want to say that our guys gave up or anything, so I'll just say that there wasn't a lot of fight left in them. Our sideline had become as quiet as a funeral home parlor, which one might think only impacted a few of us since only a few of us actually realized that our sideline was indeed quiet. But even though they couldn't hear how quiet our sideline had become, the boys could certainly sense it. And it became downright morose later in the half when defensive nose guard, Benjamin Bottoms, lay out on the field, writhing in pain. Ben was a pretty strong kid, but at just 5'10" tall and 245 pounds, he'd been worn down by the Greensboro offensive line. He was helped off of the field by two of his teammates and our trainer, Jon. Later, we learned that Ben had suffered a tear in his anterior cruciate ligament, a knee injury commonly referred to as a torn ACL. Ben was lost for the season.

Finishing out the game was almost as painful for the rest of the team as it was for Ben and David and their knee injuries. Greensboro deployed most of their bench players for the remainder of the game and, as most teams would do under such circumstances, just ran the ball. They were still able to score two more touchdowns, though, and by the end of the game they had rushed the ball an astounding fifty one times. The final score was pretty painful:

GREENSBORO 48 GALLAUDET 7

At the end of the day, our offense had managed to gain just 189 total yards, 117 on the ground and 72 through the air. The defense gave up almost 250 yards of just rushing alone, and nearly 400 total yards. And although the offensive line had officially yielded just five sacks that number could have easily been doubled had it not been for JC's elusiveness.

Following the game, Ed addressed the team in the locker room, as usual. He explained to them that Greensboro was a quality Division III football program and that if they wanted to be a quality program as well, they'd have to learn and grow from their mistakes. They'd have to make the commitment to get themselves to the same level as teams like Greensboro, and a few other teams on our schedule that we had yet to play. But that wasn't going to happen if they didn't learn to communicate. And that wasn't going to happen if they continued to make excuses for poor play rather than accept responsibility for their own performances.

Most of the boys were understandably disappointed with the outcome of the game. Some were upset and a few were angry. But none of them were as angry as Ed, though, who called the coaches into the football office after leaving the locker room. There, he lost his cool.

"What...the....fuck...just...happened...out...there?"   he yelled across the desk and directly into Ryan's expressionless face. "That was fucking pathetic! That was fucking embarrassing!"

None of us dared to speak as the veins in the side of Ed's neck pulsed to the point that I thought I was about to witness an aneurism firsthand. Ryan, his cheeks reddened, and jaw clenched tight, just stared down at the desk in front of him. He never once looked up at Ed across the desk. Seated along the cinder block wall of the small room, I kept my mouth shut and looked intently at Ed. He never spoke directly at or to me, though, only Ryan. Brian, sat on the floor directly across from me, indiscreetly popped his hearing aids off, and looked up at Ed.

"Will somebody answer my damn question?" Ed bellowed out, pressing his visor into the corner of the desk and leaning over it toward Ryan. "What the fuck kind of offense was that that I just saw out there on the field, Hite?"

"I don't know," said Ryan, shaking his head, still looking down at his desk.

"You're damn right you don't know. Clearly, you don't know. Clearly, the fucking players don't know. Clearly, nobody knows what the fuck was going on with the offense today!"

He was spitting mad. Red in the face, head about to explode mad.

"Well I want it fixed. Do you hear me, Hite?" he said as he pounded his knuckles onto the surface of the desk. "I want it fixed, and I want it fixed now!" Ed pulled the visor back down onto his head and walked to the door.

"I'll fix it," murmured Ryan, sitting back into his chair, still looking downward.

"You're damn right you'll fix it," Ed scowled, "and you better get it fixed before you leave here tonight!" He opened the door. "Don't even think about leaving until it's fixed, Hite." And with that he departed, slamming the door behind him.

Obviously, there was silence throughout the room in the wake of Ed's fury. Kerry just sat and shook his bald head, and Ron Luczak, grimacing, let out a sigh. Ryan looked befuddled and continued to stare blankly at his desk. I looked out from under the brim of my cap, briefly glancing at each of the coaches seated around me. Not a word was said. Harold stood up, smiled, threw his arms up in resignation, and left, waving goodbye as he approached the door.

"Where are you going?" called out Ryan. But of course, Harold couldn't hear him and continued to walk right out of the room. "Where does he think he's going?" Ryan asked out loud.

"It's Saturday night," said Brian, putting the hearing aids back into his ears, "where do you think he's going? He's going out."

Kerry laughed.

"Hey? I have a long ride," Ron said as he grabbed his motorcycle helmet. "I'll see everyone on Monday."

And then he left. Brian had to prepare the game film and download it onto the computer as he usually did after each game. There was never going to be a good day *to not* have the film ready for Ed, but tomorrow was definitely *not* the day to have it happen for the first time. And so off went Brian to work on the film.

"Hey, I'd love to stay, but with the kids and stuff…" Kerry gathered his bags, preparing to leave as well, "…I really can't hang around."

I looked at Ryan, slumped back in his chair and frowning at the dry erase board on the wall where he'd diagrammed several plays that he thought would work against Greensboro.

"What do you need, Ryan?" I asked him. "What's the plan?"

"Just go," he said, waving me off. "I'll take care of it."

I didn't say anything. I just looked at Kerry, who raised his eyebrows as he walked by me on his way to the door. I then looked back at Ryan.

"Just go," he said again, this time angrily as he placed a pinch of chew inside his cheek.

And so, I went.

13

The Edges Become a Little Frayed

The loss to Greensboro stung our team and it hurt our kids both physically as well as emotionally. If anyone's head had started to swell after the two season-opening wins, it was now back to its normal size, maybe even a little smaller. As for me, I thought it was quite an accomplishment for us to do as well as we had in the first half of the game against Greensboro. Although Ed maintained that he thought we could have won the game, I think he pretty much felt the same as me. Greensboro was a well-organized, athletic college football team and we just weren't ready to play at their level. Not yet, anyway.

At the field house for Sunday's film review, Ed tried to lift the boys up, but also addressed the issue of players coming up with excuses for their poor play. "That guy did this," and "this guy didn't do that," just wasn't going to cut it. He didn't point any fingers or call out any particular player, position, or group of guys. He just put it out there to them that we needed to manage the game better, focus on individual assignments, and do more than just learn from our mistakes. If they wanted to be competitive as college football players, they'd have to actually grow from their mistakes. And his talk was pretty well received, although there were a lot of frowns and sour faces during the conditioning portion of Sunday afternoon's agenda.

Following the team's workout, I came across Kevin Alley and Fletch in the foyer outside the weight room. They were waiting for the rest of the team to finish up. Both of the players were a bit discouraged following the game, and disappointed. They were seasoned athletes and had surely experienced disappointing losses in the past at some point. I was very confident that they'd be back on the field and working hard on Tuesday. But considering their lowly spirits at the time, it seemed like a good opportunity for me to give them a little something that I'd picked up in church earlier that morning. I pulled a couple of booklets out of my shoulder bag titled, "What on Earth Am I Here For?" by Pastor Rick Warren, and handed one to each of them.

Rick Warren was mostly well known for his book, *The Purpose Driven Life*. He was also the pastor of a mega-church in California called, Saddleback Church, and made frequent appearances on numerous television shows. The booklet was basically an introduction to his best seller. The book provided a guide to prayer and a pathway to understanding what God's plan for each of us is. And He does have a plan for each and every one of us. We just don't always know what that plan is. You see, we don't usually pray in a way that opens our heart to hearing God's instruction or recognize the work that He is actually doing through us. Both Kevin and Fletch smiled and took the booklets as they departed for the dining hall. As they walked away, I thought about how God had put those booklets, His word, into the hands of those two particular boys, and the people, including me, who had He used to do so. It was one of those mini awe-inspiring moments for me, if you know what I mean.

Monday afternoon's staff meeting didn't bring much good news in the way of an injury report. As expected, both Benjamin Bottoms and David Morgan were lost indefinitely with knee injuries. Ed also notified us that a football player had been dismissed from the team. At first I was somewhat stunned at the thought, but then I realized that not only did I not recognize the kid's name, in fact I can't even remember it to this day, but I didn't even know that we had a number 44 on the team. He must have been a defensive player. He'd been caught by the police after drinking at a dorm party, driving his car 70 miles per hour on campus, and then crashing into a fence somewhere in the city.

As if Ed and Ryan weren't already high strung guys, the idea of playing our next game against Denison University ratcheted up their intensity a few extra notches. You see, Ed's first big coaching assignment had been that of defensive coordinator at Denison several years earlier. In fact, he'd moved his entire family out to Granville, Ohio to do so. And Ryan had a connection to the school as well, having graduated from Denison and playing wide receiver for their football team. He must have been pretty good, too, because I think he set several school receiving records. So it was definitely a homecoming for Ryan, and for Ed it was a chance to strut his stuff across the field from his former employers. Both were highly motivated to do well that weekend.

For the first time, and maybe the only time all season, Ed injected himself into the process of developing the week's offensive practice plan, and made clear his opinion on how we should approach the game offensively. He wanted Ryan to cut down the play list and simplify the offense. And so Ryan modified the passing game to reflect quicker, more efficient routes, and easier defensive reads for the quarterbacks. The plan for the upcoming game against Denison University was to get JC out of the pocket so that he could see the field better and take advantage of his play-making abilities. That seemed like a good plan since we'd suffered some injuries on the offensive line and protection could perhaps be an issue once again. Ryan felt that we had to further incorporate some of our more talented offensive players, as well as work on ball control, so that we could take some of the pressure off of the defensive unit. That was the plan.

On my way from the coach's office to the practice field on Tuesday afternoon, I glanced into the training room. Rusty Nawrocki was lying atop a training table, propped up on his elbows. He was having his injured leg worked on by Jon. When he noticed me in the doorway, he smiled and waved.

"What happened?" I signed. "Are you alright?"

"I'll be okay," he signed back.

While he continued to sign across the room to me, Jon peeked over his shoulder to see who Rusty was signing to. Jon nodded in my direction. Although I was getting better with my signing, I still struggled to interpret it. I had a pretty good idea what Rusty was saying just by watching the expressions on his face. But Jon would often fill me in as he worked on a player. And with his hands already busy, he usually just spoke to me.

"Looks like a high ankle sprain, a fairly mild one," John said without turning around. "We're going to try to get him back onto the field for this weekend, but I don't have a whole lot of confidence that it's going to happen."

"Well, I'm sure you'll do your best, Jon," I replied.

Interestingly, Rusty went on to tell me that he read the bible daily and asked me if I did the same. And my suspicions were confirmed when he said that Fletch had told him that I was a Christian, too. Apparently, both he and Fletch had come up with the idea for a team prayer; it was Fletch, though, who took the bull by the horns and made it happen. That's a Texan for you, I thought. Rusty also hoped to begin a bible study. And so it seemed only fitting that Rusty receive a copy of the "What on Earth Am I Here For?" booklet. I pulled one out of my bag and flipped it to him.

"That's for you," I signed.

"Thanks, Coach," he signed and smiled.

Jon looked at the cover of the booklet as Rusty began to thumb through it. He then turned and looked at me as I began to leave the doorway, his hands still at work on Rusty lower calf. He smiled his approval of the booklet and nodded toward me once again.

"See you guys," I said as I left the room.

"See you, Coach," said Jon.

Out on the practice field, and at several points around the stadium, there were what appeared to be television cameras on stands and a few sound booms here and there, apparently strategically placed by a film crew. This time, it was a French television station producing a documentary about Gallaudet University. I guess today was the day they wanted to profile the athletic programs at the school, football being the flagship sport. Not that I could understand French any better than I did ASL, but I never saw the documentary. I doubt, though, that the pronunciation of my last name was of much concern to the French film-makers.

I saw Damian working frantically with our own filming equipment in the end zone as I made my way across the stadium turf to the practice field. He seemed perplexed, but at least making progress toward erecting the telescopic camera.

"How's it going?" I signed to him.

"On my own today," he replied, and then threw his hands up into the air seemingly in despair, "Dustin is gone." Damian frowned.

"You want some help?" I asked.

"Brian is coming over to help me," he smiled. "Thanks."

Damian would be by himself for the rest of the season as Dustin was no longer a team manager. Although I never found out exactly what happened to Dustin, I guessed that he struggled with handling routine assignments. I wasn't sure if he quit, or was relieved of his duties. I never found out. Damian eventually became pretty good at setting up the film equipment for both games and practices.

It was no secret that I didn't enjoy the 'inside run' portion of our offensive practices. And it wasn't because I didn't value that particular practice routine, because I did. During 'inside run,' Ryan took charge of the offense and worked on running plays. On the other side of the line, Ed took charge of the defense and worked on stopping the run. The other assistant coaches coached their position players throughout the drill. Me, I was dispatched to work with the wide receivers and defensive backs, which was fine except that we were limited to stalk blocking and cut blocking, which could easily become a bit mundane. Okay, very mundane.

The segment allowed the receivers to practice their blocking techniques and the defensive backs an opportunity to work on protecting themselves and getting off of those blocks. It was a valuable work period, but only required about ten minutes of time since I only had four receivers to work with and about a half-dozen defensive backs. Unfortunately, Ed and Ryan had a tendency to work the 'inside run' segment of practice well past twenty minutes, as the practice schedule dictated.

After about twenty minutes had passed, I dispatched the players to the water station for a short break. I hoped that 'inside run' would wrap up within the next few minutes. When it didn't though, I received a special visit from Ed, who briefly left the 'inside run' drill to approach me.

"What the fuck is going on, Coach?" he asked.

"What do you mean?" I asked.

"What the hell are those guys doing?" he asked with a clenched jaw and pointed toward my group of players as they neared the water table. "Get over here," he yelled toward them, though they obviously couldn't hear him. "Get the hell back over here!"

Cole Johnson looked over his shoulder and was the first to catch sight of Ed waving them back to the drill area. He quickly reversed course and headed back toward us.

"Get those guys," Ed signed with his hands above his head.

Some of the players who were still working on 'inside run' saw what was happening and took an interest in our plight. They were pointing and waving to my backs and receivers, trying to get their attention as well.

"Bring those guys with you," Ed yelled and signed to Cole.

By now, Kevin Alley had become aware of what was going

on, too, and helped Cole corral the others and lead them back to where we'd been working.

"They don't get any fucking water until the rest of the team gets water," Ed said. "Is that understood, Coach?"

"Understood," I said, calmly.

Ed walked away and returned to the 'inside run' drill, about forty yards away from us. I waited for him to get about twenty yards away and then turned to the guys that I'd been working with. At first, they were just looked back at me, expressionless behind their assorted facemasks, their eyes as wide as saucers. Then Kevin Alley smiled.

"Uh oh," he uttered in a low voice.

I chuckled. The players begin to smile and giggle a bit as they watched Ed walk away. I shrugged my shoulders and signed to them that I was sorry.

"My bad," I signed. They laughed.

So, not knowing just how much longer 'inside run' was actually going to go, I decided to change things up a bit, and make the time more productive. My idea was to utilize Jimmy by having him throw different passes to the receivers. Jimmy could work on his passing, the receivers could work on getting off the line and into their routes, and the defensive backs could work on their man coverage skills. The receivers included Cole Johnson, Kevin Alley, Chester Kuschmider, and Shawn Shannon. The six defensive backs included starting safety, Rantz Teeters, as well as Justin Wilson, Chris Green, Willis Cook, Marty Blomquist, and Paul Donets, or as the guys frequently called him, "Doughnuts".

We began by first running and defending slant routes, and then fade patterns. Slant routes involved taking two steps forward and then cutting back across the field, just a few yards from the line of scrimmage. A fade began with the same first two steps as a slant, but rather than cutting across the field, instead required that the receiver run vertically along the sideline. The guys enjoyed the change of pace and embraced the man-to-man competition. It became quite spirited.

"Uh oh," Kevin Alley said again.

"What?" I said.

Kevin pointed behind me toward the area of the field where they were practicing 'inside run.' I looked over my shoulder and Ed was again on his way over for a visit. From a distance I could hear Ryan complaining out loud to him.

"I don't know what that shit is they're doing, but that's not stalk blocking," Ryan shouted as Ed made his way once again toward us, "Jesus!"

Ed walked up to me and pulled a copy of the practice schedule from the waistline of his shorts. He looked down at it and then up at me from under the brim of his white visor.

"The schedule says stalk blocking," he said. "This doesn't look like stalk blocking to me. I want stalk blocking, do you understand? Stop doing your own shit and do as the schedule says."

"We stalked for twenty minutes, Coach. That's a long time to stalk," I explained, "especially with only four receivers."

"I don't give a shit, Coach. If we go twenty minutes on 'inside run', then you stalk for twenty minutes. If we go forty minutes on 'inside run' then you stalk for forty minutes," he continued, "Do what the schedule says. Do you understand?"

I nodded again that I understood.

"Good," he barked, "because, clearly you didn't understand up until this point."

Ed stared at me for a few more moments, tucked the practice schedule back into his shorts, and left. I glanced down at my own copy of the practice schedule. It *clearly* showed a twenty minute segment for inside run. By this time, though, we were almost thirty minutes into the segment, an over-run of about ten minutes. We returned to stalk blocking, but I didn't allow the receivers to cut the defensive backs out of concern for player safety. By the time the practice segment had ended, 'inside run' had lasted nearly forty minutes. That's really placing an emphasis on ball control,

I thought. And as a result, we'd worked on our stalk blocking for nearly forty minutes. That's too long. We finally broke for water and then finished the practice with a conditioning period.

On the drive home that night, listening to the car radio, I thought about all the little things that those of us who can hear take for granted, like listening to the radio while driving. I'm told by the boys that they enjoy the vibration of a base guitar and will crank their car stereos up just for that purpose. A few of them admitted, though, that the rumbling of their tires over highway seams and potholes greatly diminished any recognizable beat of the music. I can also choose to turn off the radio, put the windows down, and listen to the sound of the rushing air, which I often do. Like the beat of the base guitar, deaf folks could feel the rushing air, but not hear it.

Of course, one also has to consider the peril of not hearing emergency vehicle sirens and horns while driving; that's probably cause for concern for parents of deaf, teenaged drivers, I'm sure. And, of course, so would texting while driving, which the deaf community had been doing long before it became known as "distracted driving." And so that was my revelation about the deaf community that day.

Before practice on Wednesday afternoon, I walked across the campus to College Hall. That's where I picked up my first bi-weekly paycheck from the Finance Office. The hallways were quiet, but for the sound of sandals and shoes clapping or sliding across the tile floors. Each of the offices I passed was filled with people busy about their jobs, but no phones ringing or cross-counter conversations. I could hear heavy strokes on computer keyboards and the humming of copy machines, but otherwise nothing but silence.

I made my way to the clerk's counter at the Finance Office and signed to the young woman behind the glass partition that I was there to pick up my paycheck. She asked for my identification and instructed me on where to sign for receipt of the check. After doing so, we engaged in a little "small talk" about how football was

going, and then I was back on my way to the field house. Somewhat confident that I'd just used signing in a practical manner, I
was secure in my thinking that if I was immersed completely in a
deaf environment, I'd become proficient at interpreting sign language in a very short period of time. Having to sign, though, still
seemed to be a very cumbersome form of communication.

Wednesday's practice found most of the team in good spirits, an indication that they'd gotten over the disappointment of the
Greensboro loss. But then, about a third of the way into the practice, just after the special teams segment, Ed called for 'inside run.'
I pulled out my copy of the practice plan and put my finger on that
portion of the column dedicated to the 'inside run' drill, to see how
much time Ryan had allotted for the segment. Twenty minutes. I
was hoping that Ryan had split the segment up for us so that we
might work on a few skills other than stalk blocking and cutting.
No such luck, though. I could tell by their facial expressions that
the boys weren't any more thrilled about it than I was. But, they
resigned themselves to getting it done and approached the period
with a very good attitude, as usual.

After about fifteen minutes had passed, we progressed from
stalking to cut blocking. On the very first repetition, Kevin Alley
was working on Paul Donets when Paul stumbled and dropped
onto his side, grimacing and grunting. I could tell right away that
he had rolled his ankle, a very common injury among most athletes.

Paul was a junior from the Chicago area, about 5'9" and 175
pounds. He was a veteran player, but not a starter, and willing to
do whatever his team needed of him in a reserve capacity. That
selflessness made him a popular guy among his teammates. After
a few minutes, when he was able to gather himself together, I sent
him over to Jon with the help of two other defensive backs.

"Do you want to continue cut blocking?" Kevin Alley signed
to me.

I looked at my watch and then over to the opposite side of

the field where Ed and Ryan were working on 'inside run.' Twenty minutes had passed, but 'inside run' didn't appear to be ending anytime soon.

"Yes," I signed, "but let's slow the pace a bit, okay?"

"Okay," signed Kevin.

The boys went back to work as I observed their blocking techniques and offered light-hearted commentary to break up the monotony of the drill. At the twenty-five minute mark I glanced again over toward the 'inside run' drill. For a moment, I considered giving the boys a break, but then thought about the three additional paychecks that I had coming to me over the course of the next month and a half. I might not ever see those checks if Ed had to make another trip over to visit us. And so we trudged on. In retrospect, I should have taken my chances with Ed and given the boys a water break, especially since we were well past our scheduled break time according to the practice plan. Not doing so led to an unfortunate incident not two minutes later in the drill. And although unforeseeable, it was regrettable.

I can't remember who the receiver was that he was working with, but while engaged with that receiver, defensive back Justin Wilson fell awkwardly to the ground without hardly any contact. It was the oddest thing to see Justin just twist a little and then collapse. When he didn't immediately get up, I jogged over to where he lay motionless on his back, gazing up into the sky. I noticed he was digging his fingers into the soil along his sides.

"You okay, Justin?" I signed as I kneeled beside him.

"Something's wrong," he signed, but hardly lifted his hands off the ground.

Through his face mask, Justin's eyes fixed upon mine and he stared at me while gritting his teeth and making slight, whining sounds, sounds that clearly indicated to me that Justin was scared. And he wasn't moving any part of his body either, except his hands. It was as if his back was glued to the ground. He managed to continue signing and I watched his hands, although I couldn't quite understand what it was that he was signing since I could only watch one hand at a time. I felt a tapping on my shoulder and I turned to see Marty Blomquist, a defensive back. Marty was shaking his head and running his thumbs across the other fingers of his hands.

"He can't feel?" I asked aloud, "Numbness?"

Marty pointed repeatedly to his own right arm.

"Go get Jon," I signed to the group. Two players ran toward the trainer's station.

I put my hand on Justin's chest and tried to calm him while we waited for Jon, but instinctively used the spoken word instead of signing. But, Justin seemed to understand me, or at least got the gist of what I was saying anyway, as he began to breathe a little easier. I'd been the first responder to many injuries on the football field over the years, and wasn't nervous about handling such a situation. But I'd always been able to communicate quickly and effectively with the player in order to determine what his problem was and how best to handle the situation. I knew not to move Justin, or try to take his helmet off. And since I didn't want my poor signing to inadvertently give him bad advice, I merely kept him as calm as I could until Jon arrived. And so for the first time, I was really bothered by my inability to sign fluently, because this was critical communication in real time and I felt as if I was letting Justin down.

"What's the problem?" Jon asked as he arrived and took a knee on the opposite side of Justin. He began signing to him while talking with me at the same time.

"Justin just collapsed while working on blocking drills," I said.

"Did he get hit in the head?" John asked.

"No."

"Fall on his head?"

"No."

"He just collapsed?"

"That's it," I said as I rose to my feet. "He was being stalk blocked by a receiver when he suddenly twisted, fell to his knees, and then onto his back. He hasn't moved since."

"Hmm," murmured Jon, "he has numbness in his shoulder and arm."

By that time, Ed had rushed across the field as well, moving the rest of the players away from Justin as he arrived.

"What's the problem, Jon?" Ed asked.

"He's got numbness in his shoulder and arm," Jon said without looking up. "He seems to have feeling everywhere else though."

"It's a stinger, maybe?" suggested Ed.

"I don't know, but I don't want to take any chances," said Jon. "Let's get an ambulance over here so we can get him checked out."

Ed took Jon's cell phone and called for an ambulance as I began to direct the rest of the players away from Justin.

"Give them a break, Coach," Ed said as he waited to speak to 911.

Within a few minutes, the ambulance had arrived. While they attended to Justin, the rest of the team eventually resumed practicing, though with limited focus, of course, as everyone was worried about their injured teammate. Brian accompanied Justin to the hospital to act as an interpreter between him and the medical staff. Later, we found out that Justin had suffered a minor neck injury, a contortion of some kind, but that he'd be okay. He wasn't going to be able to play against Denison that weekend. And so, we spent much of our light practice on Thursday looking for a replacement kicker.

*

Our buses were scheduled to depart Gallaudet at 7:00 a.m. on Friday morning, and at 7:01 a.m. Ed told Ryan and I to get onto our bus, while he headed back to board his own.

"To hell with them," he said as he turned away. "I'm leaving their asses behind!"

We were missing three guys: Eric Jindra, Ricky Bailey, and Josh Ofiu. Ryan glanced down, his lips compressed, then back up at Ed who was walking away from us. Then he raised his eyebrows and motioned for me to board the bus ahead of him. At 7:02 a.m. we saw Chris Burke jog past our bus and toward the player's dormitory. Ed had had a change of heart and dispatched Chris to go and find the missing players.

On any other weekend, Eric probably would have had the opportunity to continue his hibernation. But with our offensive line thinned by injuries, we needed his 280 pound body at the tackle position. Eric's short, bleached blond hair was unmistakably Californian. A junior from San Mateo, he wasn't nearly the best player on the team, but he did give us options along the offensive line. His eyes were crossed, which could be a bit of a distraction when talking with a cross-eyed person face to face. But that was never really an issue for me with Eric, because when we conversed, I didn't look him in the eye, but rather at his hands.

And Ed wasn't going to leave without Josh and Ricky, no matter how angry he was. They were the two most physical players on the defensive side of the ball for us. Several minutes later, Chris and the three ball players appeared on the sidewalks in front of the buses. Eric boarded our bus and the other two were warmly welcomed by Ed onto the defensive bus, I say that tongue and cheek, of course. The buses departed the campus for Ohio thirty minutes later than planned.

After seeing the faces of the three latecomers, I was convinced that none of the boys on the team ever looked into a mirror before leaving their dorm rooms. They didn't appear to be any less groomed than any of the guys who were on time. I know that deaf guys had a tendency to oversleep, and therefore might be pressed for time before leaving in the morning, but they almost all had terrible cases of "bed head" on a regular basis. And they never seemed to care about it.

The bus ride to Granville, Ohio took longer than one might expect. If you were to plot it out you'd probably plan on about a seven hour trip. But, because of rush hour traffic delays in Washington, a walk-through practice at Frostburg University in Western Maryland, and a couple of charter buses again in need of repair, it took us a little over ten hours.

The large crack in the right side of our windshield should have been the first clue that we didn't exactly have top of the line chartered buses. But then again, we were a small Division III college football team working on a shoestring budget. We might expect to get a flat tire, but not one *per* bus! And how bad was our luck when our bus engine overheated for the second consecutive trip through the mountains of Southwestern Pennsylvania? Except for when going downhill, the buses again crept along at about forty miles per hour. And so we sat on those buses a lot longer than we would have liked to that day.

Besides being able to watch an extra movie, or two, the lengthened trip gave me the opportunity to learn a little more about our players, and practice my ASL while doing so. I made my way around the bus, sat amongst the players, and engaged them in small talk, or "little signing," as I jokingly called it. I discovered that the overwhelming majority of the boys on the team were but the latest in a line of generational deaf. In other words they had at least one deaf parent. Conversely, they also had a parent who could hear. According to the U.S. Department of Health, only about 7 per cent of children born deaf are actually born into deaf families. I thought that to be pretty interesting.

When our buses finally rolled into the parking lot of the Quality Inn in Heath, Ohio, it was five o'clock in the evening, and the boys were understandably anxious to get off of the bus. Rather than having the guys mill about the lobby, Ed had us wait on the buses outside while he and Ryan went in to the front desk to get everyone's room keys. As we had done two weeks prior, the buses drove us to the rear of the hotel where the Dynamic Duo met us in the parking lot and handed out keys according to our room assignments. Ed gave the team thirty minutes to take their bags up to their rooms, get freshened up, and return to the buses. We were going out to dinner this time.

It was a short bus ride to Stacy's Restaurant, a small, buffet style eatery just a few miles or so from the hotel. Stacy's was a mom and pop type of place with hearty, home style cooking, a very relaxed atmosphere, and Early American decor. There were no big screen televisions or piped in music, only the clanking sound of porcelain plates and silverware and the murmur of friendly conversations across the dinner table. The food was fairly good, though, and buffet style serving again was perfect for our football team. We were seated quickly, had a dining section to ourselves, and everyone finished eating at about the same time. They were so efficient and accommodating that Ed took us back there for breakfast in the morning.

While we didn't have an opportunity to actually visit Granville, Ohio, we did get a pretty good look at it from our buses as we traveled through the town to the campus of Denison University. Granville was a very charming community about forty-five minutes due east of Columbus, Ohio, which of course is the home of the Ohio State Buckeyes, one of the most successful college football programs in the country. Granville's tree lined streets, historic homes, and cozy shopping district was reminiscent of an old New England township, and there was an air of dignity about the town. It appeared to be a postcard perfect place to live and raise a family.

The campus of Denison University was quite impressive, as well, and immediately upon arrival I knew that the school was an unlikely destination for my offspring. Tuition at Denison was well beyond our family's financial means at the time. In fact, it was probably well beyond the financial means of most families. The campus felt more like a country club setting than it did a college. But there would be no valet parking for us, of course, as we arrived in the two, older charter buses, both in need of mechanical repair. Something about that just didn't feel right, like showing up in jeans and a sweatshirt for a formal dinner event. Regardless, we were on campus and ready to play the Big Red of Denison University.

Centrally located on the campus, Deeds Field-Piper Stadium

had been newly renovated just a year earlier, although the field itself had existed since the early nineteen twenties. The renovations
had been so recent that the playing surface seemed to still have
that brand new smell, like a room with new carpeting or a car that
you test drive for the first time. On the north side of the stadium
was a small area of bleacher seating near mid-field for supporters
of the visiting team. Across the field, and behind the home team
sideline, was the seating area for the home team. It extended from
the end zone nearest the field house to about the twenty yard line
at the far end of the field. The press box, which housed the public
address announcer and members of both coaching staffs, rested in
the shade of the nearby oak trees, and along the upper level of the
home team's seating area. The stadium was heralded as one of the
premier small college athletic venues in the country.

The field house was directly adjacent to the field and at the
east end of the stadium. It was a much older facility, but pristinely
maintained, and housed both the home and visiting team's locker
rooms on its lower level. Our buses arrived and parked at the front
of the field house where we disembarked, gathered our gear, and
assembled at the main entrance. A representative from Denison
greeted Ed and Ryan, and then guided our team through the field
house to our locker rooms. The exit from our locker room to the
stadium was on the opposite side of the field house, and just about
fifty yards from the access point that lead into the stadium itself.
The field house was indeed old, but very nice, with clean locker
rooms and plenty of space for our trainers and managers to work
while the team dressed for the game.

The weather was perfect. It was bright, it was sunny, and it was
warm. Although the shade on the home team side of the field was
awfully inviting at first, the heat of the sun had somewhat lost its
mid-summer sting and after a few short minutes felt quite comfortable.

As our team took to the field for warm-ups, I strolled over
toward the seating area behind our bench, where we had a very

large showing of fans and supporters. There were quite a number of local Gallaudet alumni on hand, as well as players' friends and families from throughout Ohio. And just as they had been at the St. Vincent's game, were very fervent in their support of the team. I signed to them as a group, emboldened to do so by their enthusiasm.

"It's great to see you all. Thank you for coming to watch us play." I signed.

Unfortunately, I might have actually signed, "Great to be able to see. Thanks for being players!" Oh well, it didn't seem to matter to them; they all cheered at my remarks, whatever they actually were. I just wanted to acknowledge them for being at the game and to let them know that we appreciated their support. And even though they knew that most of our kids couldn't hear them, they were quite loud anyway. Many of the friends and relatives at the game were not deaf, like the families of Josh and Calvin Doudt.

Also among those supporters was Ryan's wife, who I think might have been a local school teacher. Obviously, it was a perfect opportunity for those two to spend a little time together, maybe begin to patch things up a bit. Although she would occasionally visit him at his apartment in Annapolis, she continued to reside in Ohio, which as I mentioned earlier, did not seem to bode well for their chances of reconciling their differences. Maybe that was part of the reason that Ryan always had such a sour disposition, or maybe his disposition was part of the reason that his marriage was in trouble. Either way, I'd been in a similar situation myself when I was his age, and I told him on several occasions throughout the season that if he needed to talk about such things, I'd be happy to do so. He never took me up on my offer.

The game got underway at two o'clock sharp, as scheduled. At ten minutes past two o'clock, we were already in trouble. While at first glance it would have appeared that we matched up well with the team in the bright red jerseys, the fact of the matter was that we didn't. They weren't bigger or faster than us, they were just better football players.

For a little while, though, we were able to keep the game close, largely because Denison was intent on trying to pass the ball during their first several offensive possessions. They weren't very good at passing the ball, though, as their quarterback threw three interceptions in twelve attempts. That was good news and bad news for us. The good news was that we were hanging with them on the scoreboard due to their mistakes. The bad news was that they corrected their mistakes by abandoning their passing game and running the football instead.

Once they discovered that we couldn't stop the inside run, they just ran the ball right down our throats, over and over again. They must have watched our Greensboro game film. It was just brutal, and when the final whistle blew, Denison had racked up a whopping 470 yards of rushing offense, and six touchdowns. It would be a season lowlight for our defense. Fifty eight times they ran the ball for an average of over eight yards per carry. That's a lot! Our leading tackler that day was our Safety, Rance Teeters. And when your safety is making tackles it means that your linebackers are not. Needless to say, Ed wasn't a happy camper.

Our offense didn't fare any better than the defense, and failed to put a single point on the board. The run game managed to gain just seventy-seven yards; the passing game a mere eighty-four. Once again the offensive line played poorly, missing numerous assignments and yielding another five sacks. Denison penetrated our line with such ease that our ball carriers were tackled for a loss thirteen times. JC was scrambling all day long. He had a few good looks downfield, but managed to complete just eight passes in twenty five attempts. Kevin Alley punted the ball ten times, which was another season high. He did a great job, though, averaging nearly forty one yards per punt. And so Ryan wasn't a happy camper, either.

There was one other bright spot, too, sophomore Cole Johnson. He emerged as a quality player, hauling in several nice catches and making a couple of very big hits while blocking downfield. But that was of little solace to Ed as he walked across the field at the end of the game to shake hands and mingle for a few minutes with his former coaching staff. And the scoreboard didn't make him feel any better either. We had to walk by it on our way to the field house:

DENISON 42 GALLAUDET 0

It was easy to see that Ed was angry, and quite embarrassed, and who could blame him? What a dismal performance his football team had just turned in against his former colleagues. That had to sting. But, to his credit, he didn't lose his temper in the locker room like I thought he might. Some of the players did, though, and acted out angrily in frustration. Just like the bottom of the pant legs on your best old jeans, the edges were beginning to fray for our team.

Justin Lathus, like many of the old vets, had become comfortable in those old jeans, playing club ball against inferior opponents and winning games on a regular basis. The game had been fun for him then. But now, this losing thing didn't feel so good to him and it challenged his integrity. Everything that he'd thought to be true appeared to be failing him: work hard and good things will happen, there's nothing that you can't accomplish if you set your mind to it, and other inspirational devices. Being deaf and having already overcome so much, it was really hard for him to understand why winning college football games was so difficult, and I think that hurt his psyche.

The emotional guy that he was, Justin refused to sit in on Ed's post game talk in the locker room. Instead, he wrapped a towel around himself and headed off to the showers. Ed called out to him, and then he screamed out to him, but Justin didn't turn around. Justin obviously could not hear Ed, and I doubted that he would turn around even if he did. Ed didn't pursue him.

Like several other older players on the team, Justin thought that the other teams were able to read our signs and gain the upper hand on us by doing so. He didn't think that was fair and that we couldn't expect to win football games if the opponent knew what play we were going to run beforehand. Now, none of that was true, of course, but it gave Justin and those guys an excuse for why the team was losing games. Of course an opponent would have a huge advantage if it knew the other team's plays, but that's not what was happening with our team. We were just competing against a much more competitive opponent than the boys were used to. They were no longer playing club teams on Friday afternoons, but rather much more efficient, prepared, and physically capable athletes.

Ed knew this to be true, for he'd been around the college game for some time. And he knew that stepping up to play Division III college football wasn't going to be a cakewalk, and that the time would come when some of his core players would struggle with their deficits. That time had come and Ed was prepared to deal with it. He was calm, but firm in his talk, because he didn't want to lose the boys. He needed to motivate them rather than tear them down. It wasn't like they weren't playing hard or that they were giving up out on the field. They were just losing to teams that were better than us. And so again, just like he'd done the previous weekend, he spoke to them about the importance of individual responsibility, accepting the personal challenge to physically improve themselves as athletes, and being supportive of one another rather trying to place blame.

About halfway through Ed's talk, Justin returned from the showers. The towel was still wrapped around his mid-section, but neither Justin nor the towel was wet. With an open hand, and without comment, Ed welcomed Justin's return to the fold, just like a good shepherd would. Soon after Ed's talk, the players who were upset settled down, resigned in spirit, but not broken.

*

While we were in the locker room after the game, several local families of players on the team put together a nice post-game meal for us to eat before our long journey home. The Doudt family, of northern Ohio, was one of those families. In the emptied parking lot outside of the main entrance to the field house, they had set up several tents, complete with portable tables and chairs. Under the main tent, some of the mothers on hand served lasagna, salads, pizza, and sandwiches. Under another tent they had a variety of desserts, chips, and soft drinks.

While I waited for the players to proceed through the serving line before me, I met with family members, former players, and Gallaudet alumni who now lived in the Ohio area. Ed and the other coaches did the same. Quite a few of those folks were deaf and I communicated with them via sign language. But there were just as many who heard perfectly well. With them I spoke freely and without simultaneously signing, as did they. I found them all to be very warm and caring people, very supportive not only of their own deaf family members, but other families with deaf children and parents as well.

I also found it interesting that many of the family members and friends, who were not deaf, worked as teachers of the deaf, including the aunt of Josh and Calvin Doudt. An attractive young woman, probably several years younger than me, she spoke and heard perfectly well. A teacher by profession, she decided to become a teacher for the deaf after witnessing the difficulty that her sister endured while educating her hearing impaired sons. And like many teachers, she was very passionate about her work, and was especially appreciative of our coaching staff and our commitment to working with the boys on the team.

Following the meal, we boarded the buses for our long ride home while the folks from Ohio took down the tents and cleaned the area. It had been a pleasant departure from the brutality of the football game, and I think made most of the boys feel a good bit better about themselves. Having a loving and supportive family always seems to help heal our emotional wounds, even football players.

Most of the boys dozed off shortly after leaving the campus

and so the bus was relatively quiet. I too sat quietly and gazed out the window at the starry sky above, appreciating the peace and serenity of the night. Having watched the boys on the team interact with their families that evening, I thought of my own family back home. I wondered what they were doing and how my own son had fared in his football game that afternoon.

Was I doing the right thing by coaching college football? That question began to haunt me more and more and I tried to justify my decision to so, but not with much success. I didn't earn much money doing it, and yet I spent more time coaching than I did running my business, Coach & Courier. Coaching also kept me from my family at critical times of the day, leaving my working wife to almost raise our seven and ten year old boys alone, at least for several months. And then I finally came upon the question that I tried not to address, "Was I doing what The Lord really needed me to do or was I doing *what I wanted to do for myself*?"

I looked across the bus at Brian Tingley, seated across the aisle from me. He was just staring through the windshield of the bus, expressionless. I waved my hand up and down to get his attention, not knowing if he had his hearing aids in.

"Brian?" I asked and he turned his face toward me.

"What's up?" he asked.

"Are you all right over there? You seem to be in deep thought," I asked.

"Yeah," he said. "I'm all right. I'm just a little worried about my mom. She has cancer."

Whoa! That's a bombshell of a response, I thought. I looked blankly at him for just a moment, unsure about what, if anything, I should say in response. And then it just blurted out.

"Are you believers? Have you prayed about it?"

"Yeah, well, she is now," he said. "And I've prayed about it, yes."

"What do you mean?"

"When she was first diagnosed with breast cancer a few years ago, some of my friends prayed with me about the whole situation. I started going to church with them and later became a Christian. When her cancer went into remission, I told her that my friends and I had been praying for her recovery. She decided to follow The Lord as well."

"That's a great testimony," I said to him. "And so what are you worried about now?"

"We think it may be coming back."

"I'm sorry to hear that." I winced. "Are you sure?"

"No, not at all," he said. "I'm just always worried about it. She goes in for a checkup next week, that's all."

"I understand," I nodded, "But you have to leave these worries to The Lord, Brian. I know that's very hard to do, but He can handle that stress a whole lot better than we can, you know?" Brian nodded his head but he didn't seem willing to surrender his cares. "I mean, you do know that God loves your mom?" I said.

"Of course," said Brian, nodding.

"He's probably not too worried about her cancer. What do you think?" I went on.

"Probably not," he said.

"I mean, He knows how the story ends," I said and then paused as Brian stared at me through the dimly lit cabin of the bus. "Now that she's a Christian, she's going home to Him eventually, cancer or otherwise. We all are."

Brian nodded as he sank back into his seat a little more.

"Maybe He was a little worried about her *before* she became a Christian. And that's why He sent your friends and eventually used you to show her 'the way home.' But He's not worried now," I assured him. "He's not up there wringing his hands worrying about what happens next, I guarantee you. And He *knows* what's going to happen next."

Brian smiled as if something I said was finally making sense to him.

"I mean, really?" I concluded.

"Thanks," Brian said with a slight grin on his face. "You're right."

"No problem," I said as I reclined my seat and returned my gaze to the night sky above. That's what I'm here for, I said to myself. That's what I'm here for. In the window, I could see the reflection of Brian behind me as he tilted his head back and reclined his seat. It's hard not to worry, no matter how strong we are in our faith.

A short time later, I heard the bus engine downshift and begin to slow. We were exiting the expressway, but I didn't know where or why, although I'd seen the exit for Wheeling, West Virginia about twenty minutes earlier. Bright white lights shattered the darkness from the port side of the coach and as the driver came about it was clear to see through the windshield that we had arrived at a truck stop in Claysville, Pennsylvania. Now this was going to be interesting, I thought, chaperoning 55 deaf guys at a truck stop in western Pennsylvania late on a Saturday night. Yeah, that happens every day.

But, it wasn't so bad. Most of the guys made a dash for the restrooms while others went for sodas and candy. Some of the players were trying to order sandwiches at the café grill. The players who were hard of hearing were helping the deaf players place their orders for pizza, burgers, and hot dogs, but you can imagine the manner in which so many hungry, young college boys conducted themselves, deaf or not. It was a little chaotic. The old woman behind the counter had probably dealt with a lot worse. I imagine that this was a nice break in the routine for her. Ed and Ryan were keeping their distance and stood out in the breezeway. I milled about, looking at some of the novelty items for sale, as did a lot of the boys, and eventually bought myself a Coke.

"Are you boys a football team?" I heard a man ask.

I turned and looked to see an old man a few feet away wearing a red baseball cap and blue jeans. The sleeves of his white, short sleeved shirt were rolled up over his sagging biceps, revealing his farmer's tan. He had a carton of cigarettes in his right hand and a two-liter bottle of Mountain Dew in the left.

"Are you boys a part of a football team?" he asked again.

But the players nearest him, wearing their dark blue warm-up outfits, were all deaf and couldn't hear the man. They laughed and chuckled aloud as they played around with some flying monkeys and clattering teeth on the shelf in front of them. The old man had no idea that they were deaf and wasn't about to figure it out on his own. Unlike a blind person with a walking stick, it's impossible to tell that someone is deaf, unless you see them signing to one another, which the boys were not.

"I said, are you boys part of a football team? What team are you boys?" he asked again with a growing frustration in his voice. He straightened up and his chest stuck out slightly. He set his soft drink on the counter and put his hand on Jimmy Gardner's shoulder. Jimmy turned around quickly and in doing so startled the old man, who took a slight step back.

"Are you boys some kind of idiots?" He began to get angry. "I asked you a damn question and you just ignore me? You got no damn respect, I tell you that!"

Jimmy could tell that the old man was angry, and I could tell by the look on Jimmy's face that he feared that he'd done something wrong. He looked over at me, quizzically, and with what appeared to be a sense of relief when he saw that I was quickly approaching them. Marty Blomquist and Robin Shannon were both standing next to Jimmy. They sensed a disturbance and looked up at their teammate and then at the old man. And then they looked at me, and back to the old man. They realized that something was not right.

"Sir," I said to the old fellow.

He turned and looked up at me as I approached. I was a good half a foot taller than the old guy, so his jaw dropped a little bit as he lifted the brim of his hat up to see me.

"They can't hear you, sir. They're deaf," I smiled.

"Deaf?" he asked loudly as if I was hard of hearing myself.

"Yes, sir, they're deaf. They're football players from Gallaudet

University," I told him. "They mean you no disrespect, they just can't hear you."

"Oh, oh, okay," he said as he picked up his bottle of Mountain Dew. "I'm sorry. I, uh, didn't know they were deaf. I thought they looked like a football team, you know? I just wanted to talk to 'em a bit, that's all."

"No problem, I understand." I smiled at him as he began to walk away.

"Ok, well, tell them I said 'good luck,'" he said.

I signed to Jimmy and the boys that the old man had said 'good luck' to them. They all signed a 'thank you' to the old man.

"They said, thank you, sir," I said.

"They're welcome, tell 'em I said they're welcome," he added as he approached the checkout clerk. "Thank you. You all have a good night."

He was obviously a little embarrassed, but who could hold it against him? I mean, think about it. He was old, a truck driver, probably a little bit excited for some small talk after a long, lonely drive, and who does he come across but a bunch of deaf guys who can't hear him, at a truck stop, on a Saturday night, no less. What are the odds? I'm sure the old man will tell that story a time or two.

"Everything okay?" asked the familiar voice of Chris Burke. I turned to him and smiled.

"He just tried to talk to the boys and got a little upset when they didn't answer him, that's all. He didn't know that they couldn't hear him," I explained.

"That happens. What are you going to do?" said Chris as he shrugged his shoulders.

"It doesn't happen to me too often," I smiled. Chris smiled back and gave me a light punch on the arm as he nodded toward the exit.

"Time to go," he mouthed. "Let's go!" he said loudly as he signed to the remaining players in the shop. And with that we returned to the bus, no harm, no foul.

Our buses finally arrived back at Gallaudet at 2:30 in the morning and as we approached the school, I was surprised to see so many young college students wandering about on the streets outside the campus, both boys and girls. They were heading back to their apartments, I guess, maybe after a few dorm parties or the like. Or, maybe they were leaving campus and going to a party, I didn't know. I just couldn't imagine being in that part of town, walking around at that time of night, and not being fearful of what danger might be lurking nearby. Whether it was the bliss of ignorance or the bravado of youth, I thought it unwise for them to be out on the streets, tempting fate. Obviously, poor judgment was not limited to the hearing.

14

R-E-S-P-E-C-T

R espect; that was the objective of our coaching staff for the next game; that our team would earn a little respect against Case Western University. After crushing losses in consecutive weeks to Greensboro College and Denison University, we now faced perhaps the toughest opponent on our schedule, a Top 25 team looking to break into the Top 10 of college football's Division III teams. Winning the game wasn't a realistic goal for us, but making it a competitive contest was. But in order to attain that goal we'd need a positive attitude during our practices that week, both from the players as well as the coaching staff. Without that positive attitude, we would get very little accomplished toward achieving our goal.

I wasn't at Sunday's staff meeting at the field house. I'd told Ed long before that I'd made a commitment to take my oldest son to Dover, Delaware to experience a NASCAR Sprint Cup Race for his birthday. Mark had become a big Jimmie Johnson fan so I'd promised him that I'd take him to watch Johnson and his Number 48 Lowe's Chevrolet at the nearby speedway. I was intent on keeping that promise. I was dog tired, though, since I hadn't gotten home from our game against Denison until well after 3:00

a.m. that morning. It seemed as if I'd barely fallen asleep when the alarm clock went off at 7:00 a.m.

Although exhausted, I was very happy to spend some time with Mark, especially since I'd missed most of his youth league football games. My father and brother joined us as well, which was the first time, in what seemed like forever, that we'd all done something together. You see, there were quite a few people in my life who saw very little of me from the middle of the summer until late fall. Coaching football tends to have that effect on families.

When the alarm clock sounded, I slid out of bed, and took a quick shower, which brought me back to a somewhat semi-conscious state. Still, I had to shuffle my way down the hallway to the kitchen, dressed only in a tee shirt and jeans. I expected to see Mark asleep in his bedroom when I walked by, but his bed was empty. Instead, he was seated at the kitchen table wearing a navy blue, Number 48 baseball cap and eating a banana.

"You ready to go, Dad?" he smiled broadly.

"Almost, buddy," I said, "I have to grab a few things first, okay?"

"Yep," he said as he continued to eat his banana.

He watched me as I made my way around the kitchen looking for snacks and drinks to take with us to the race, especially the kid stuff, like fruit roll-ups and cheddar fish. But I was not having much success in my state of fatigue, and was growing a little more irritated than I otherwise might have.

"What are you looking for, Dad?" asked Mark as he threw his banana peel into the kitchen trash can.

"Something for us to eat at the race later on," I told him.

"Oh," he said as he washed his hands at the sink. "Mom already packed us a cooler of food. She went to the store last night and made sandwiches for you, me, Pop Pop, and Uncle Danny."

"She did?"

"Yea, it's on the stoop out front," he said as he skipped toward the front door and walked outside. My wife appeared from the hallway as Mark walked by; she gave him a kiss as he did.

"Thanks for making us lunches," I said to her.

"Yeah, yeah," she said, folding her arms across her chest, still dressed in her pajamas. "Your dad has a cooler of soft drinks, too."

"Alright," I smiled and gave her a kiss on the forehead. "We're good to go then."

I finished dressing and grabbed a couple of jackets for us, just in case it rained. I kissed Mary-Ellen again before walking out to the car, where Mark was waiting for me.

"You guys have a great time," she called out.

"We will, Mom!" Mark smiled as he opened the car door and jumped inside.

She waved to us as we backed out of the driveway and pulled off. When we got to the end of our street, I stopped at the stop sign and took a good look at Mark sitting next to me in the passenger seat. He was smiling ear to ear as he looked out the passenger side window. He then turned and looked up at me.

"Are we picking up Pop Pop and Uncle Danny at Pop Pop's house?" he asked.

"Yep."

"This is going to be great, Dad!"

"It sure is, buddy. It sure is!"

And it was a great day, for all of us, including Jimmie Johnson, who won the race.

*

At Gallaudet on Monday, the week hadn't started out too well for us, related to our goal of earning respect, anyway. Ed received more than two dozen emails over the course of the weekend asking whether or not the boys had "quit on us yet?" Our two consecutive bad losses had people from both inside and outside of the deaf community beginning to question the commitment of our players. We also learned that we'd lost two more players to injury following the Denison game. Freshman players Scott Lehmann, number 28, a running back from Frederick, Maryland sustained a high ankle sprain, and linebacker Mike Harper, number 50, from Wichita, Kansas suffered a torn ACL. Scott would eventually work his way back onto the field by the end of the season, but Mike was done.

Tuesday's practice was terrible. Dissention reared its ugly head, even before practice actually started, as many of the players started questioning one another's ability to just play the game, much less at the collegiate level. Once out on the field, they became even more frustrated with one another, especially the offensive linemen. Kerry, at Ryan's direction, collected the linemen and revisited their primary techniques and assignments. But even that became quite a challenge because of players blaming one another for miscues, and overly critiquing their teammates. And so Ryan shuffled the line personnel each day in search of the right chemistry among the players. However, he quickly grew impatient with them, which drew a reprimand from Ed for not maintaining a positive attitude in front of the players.

Ed and Ryan were obviously upset with the team and the quality of our practices. They tried to maintain their composure, however, and demonstrate a positive attitude as planned. But Ryan was just too impatient and struggled to do so. I tried to maintain a positive approach as well, but used a different tactic than those guys. I would frequently visit the players throughout drills and conditioning segments of practice. Occasionally, I would pat a player on the back of his shoulder pads, or give a "thumbs up" sign here and there; whatever I could do to acknowledge a player's positive attitude whenever I saw one. Of course, when Ryan saw me doing those things, it just reinforced his opinion of me that I wasn't college coaching material.

During the offensive team segment of practice that day, I heard Kevin Alley actually mouth and say the word, "C'mon!" He didn't say it loudly, but he did say it repeatedly, since his teammates just couldn't seem to get their act together as a unit. Ryan had extended the snap count as a means of slowing the game down against Case Western, and our guys kept jumping off-sides and committing false-starts. And with each miscue Kevin would say, "C'mon!"

Oddly enough, I came to know the unique sound of Kevin's voice for no other reason than the way that he pronounced the phrase, "C'mon." It sounded more like, "Come, Awn," and almost seemed like the "c" was silent. Maybe like, "Ummm awn?" I guess that's the way that he had taught himself to utter the word. Whenever it was that he first started to say it, he'd probably drawn a response from those around him who could hear his plea. And that must have validated his use of the phrase and given him the confidence to say it out loud.

Kevin was a Physical Education major from Lebanon, Oregon and one of the best athletes on the team. He played both football and baseball at Gallaudet and excelled at both. I don't ever remember Kevin's performance or attitude, at practice or in a game, being anything but exemplary. He was a player that we could always count on. And we sure could have used a few more Kevin Alleys, albeit bigger Kevin Alleys, on the offensive line.

By the end of practice on Wednesday, Ryan had shuffled the entire offensive line several times, and it finally appeared that he'd found a group that played well together. And with that chemistry came improved execution at the line of scrimmage, and hence, better production from the entire offensive unit. Once the offense started to show improvement, the overall attitude of the whole team began to change for the better, which rekindled the team's spirit and energy. As such, the tempo and pace had pick up significantly, and our time on the field had become much more productive. And that, of course, brought about a much better mood from both Ed and Ryan.

In a post-practice, coaches meeting, Ed informed us that he'd decided to have Ryan call the plays from the press box instead of from the sidelines. He felt that the change might improve communication among the offensive players out on the field, most importantly, the linemen. Brian was going to wear a headset on the sideline and relay Ryan's play calls to the offensive unit on the field via ASL.

Think about the irony in having a hard-of-hearing graduate assistant use headsets to relay play calls to a deaf football team. That's kind of the opposite of amplification isn't it? Some things you just can't make up. Anyway, Brian was much more proficient at signing than Ryan, so that just had to help. Ed's only concern was that Brian might not be able to hear Ryan via the headset. But who else was there? Neither Kerry nor I signed better than Ryan, and it didn't make sense to have either of us relay the play call to Brian, who'd then have to relay it to the team on the field. That wasn't keeping things simple at all. Plus, Kerry had a tendency to get a little too excited during a game, and that worried Ed. Eager for the opportunity to relay the play calls to the players on the field, Brian assured Ed that he'd be able to hear Ryan, especially if he wore a double headset. He also said that he would carry an extra earpiece and batteries in his pocket. He really wanted that job. And so during the team segment of Thursday's practice, the plan was put into action. The new system worked just fine.

While the team was stretching before its walk-through on Friday afternoon, Ed met with the coaching staff of Case Western. Their team had arrived early from Cleveland and was checking in at a hotel just outside of town. We would yield the field to them after completing our short pre-game practice. I strolled about the formation of players as they stretched. I'd always made a point of making small talk with players during such segments of practice, regardless of my position on the staff, whether it was as head coach or an assistant. It was just how I got to know them a little better, always working on building a stronger rapport with them, developing a trust.

It was also just another facet of my coaching style that clearly separated me from coaches like Ryan. Maybe there were better technical coaches, but not many as capable of understanding their players as I did, nor able to develop a positive team chemistry by weaving together so many different personalities. And the fact that they couldn't actually hear my voice hadn't gotten in the way of me doing the same with the players at Gallaudet. The fact that I had a tendency to smile a lot had actually enhanced my ability to relate to the deaf kids, since facial expressions were such a vital part of the deaf communication process.

Near the front of the formation I came across number 7, Cole Johnson. Cole was another handsome, young man with dark hair and a strong jaw line. His thin framed physique belied the competitiveness of his athletic abilities. Cole generally seemed to be a little short on confidence, although I thought he was a terrific player, much better than he actually thought he was.

"Nice game last week, Cole," I signed to him.

"Thank you," he signed back as he looked up at me.

"I've been to Minnesota quite a few times, you know?" I said to him. "Nice place."

He smiled. During my fourteen years in the military as a C-130 navigator, I'd been on many training missions to Camp Ripley and Duluth in support of local Army National Guard units there. Camp Ripley was an Army Base located a good bit northwest of Minneapolis-St. Paul and pretty much out in the boonies. And so I told Cole about my times in Minnesota and how I'd had my first, and only, one pound hamburger while in a small town named Brainerd, Minnesota. I believe that the airfield there was called Brainerd-Crow Wing, or something to that effect, and the little restaurant was but a short walk from the airport. He smiled broadly as I told him of the burger.

"You know where Brainerd is?" I asked.

"Yes," he said, raising his eyebrows and nodding his head. "My family has a fishing cabin in Brainerd."

"With all of the lakes up there, doesn't everyone having a fishing cabin?" I said.

Cole laughed.

"And how come you don't shrug your shoulders after everything that you sign?"

"What?" he said, confused by the question.

"When people from Minnesota speak," I said, "they always finish a sentence or comment with an "eh?" I shrugged my shoulders and mouthed the words for him, "Like, nice weather, eh? Good day, eh? Now that's a burger, eh?"

He shook his head and laughed again.

I'm pretty sure that Cole never thought that one of his football coaches at Gallaudet University in Washington, D.C. would know anything about Brainerd, Minnesota, or been there, for sure. And I'm also pretty sure that he thought I was a little crazy to assume that deaf Minnesotans might actually sign with a dialect similar to Minnesotans who spoke normally. I might have been a little crazy, but thinking that way was more like ignorance than idiotic. Cole and I got along very well from that day on, and talked frequently thereafter. It was a pleasure to watch him develop as a collegiate football player.

While the team went through its customary Friday walkthrough, I saw Ron Cheek working on the stadium turf. It was part of his grounds maintenance responsibilities, so what better time to work on it than while at practice, eh? Sorry, I'm still thinkin' Minnesota.

Ron was applying pre-germinated grass seed to the field. It grew faster than normal grass seed and therefore was much quicker to take hold and withstand the wear and tear of athletic cleats and such. Afterward, Ron was in the end zone, this time utilizing his artistic skills by painting onto the surface what appeared to be some form of an alien blob. Actually, it turns out that he was trying to paint a blue bison.

When Ed gathered the team following practice, he told them that the Case Western coaches had commented on how nice it was that deaf kids were trying to play football. Now I'm pretty sure that they'd meant it in a complimentary and respectful way, but you know darn well that Ed presented it to the team just a bit differently. And the boys received it as such by responding with a post huddle exclamation, "FU!" Well, they certainly knew how to use their vocal chords to say that loud and clear. We yielded the stadium to Case Western as protocol dictated. The boys showered and headed off to the dining hall. I headed home.

*

During the team breakfast the following morning, I had the opportunity to speak with Michael Daze. Mike wore the number 32 jersey and played defensive end, so I hadn't had many opportunities to speak with him since most of my time was spent working with players on the offense. At 6'3" tall and just 210 pounds, he too was a little undersized for a collegiate defensive end, but he was smart and he was tough, and since it was Division III football, he was able to make it work for him.

Mike told me that he'd been born hard of hearing and not completely deaf like most of the boys. From Frederick, Maryland, he was the son of two deaf parents, though, both of whom were teachers with psychology backgrounds. Mike was a sincere guy, very engaging, and very well spoken. But, he was also another kid who could have used a little more self-confidence.

"I have quite a standard to live up to, Coach," he commented as he stood next to me waiting for an omelet to be cooked. "My brother went to Towson University."

"Hey? That's my alma mater," I said. "Did he play football, too?"

"No, sir, he didn't play football there," he smiled as he reached for the plate being handed to him by the cook behind the omelet bar. "But like my parents, he graduated with a degree in Psychology."

"Hmm," I said. I pursed my lips and nodded.

"He also earned a degree in Chemistry. And neither happens to be my strong suit," he said as he took his tray and headed for a nearby table. "Have a good breakfast, Coach."

"You, too, Mike." I smiled and remained in line waiting for my own omelet.

I wondered why he'd attended The Maryland School for the

Deaf when he seemed to be able to hear pretty well. Perhaps it was a sort of safety net for his parents, one that allowed them to be much more involved with his education. It likely would have been much more difficult for them to communicate freely with teachers and administrators from a regular high school, public or private, than a school for the deaf. But on the other hand, did studying at a school for the deaf inhibit Michael's capacity to learn? And I wondered how it came to be that his brother went to Towson instead of Gallaudet. Why the different path? Perhaps it was Michael's choice, but I realized that deaf parents are confronted with many of the same decisions about their children's college education as the rest of us.

After returning to the field house and attending their pre-game meetings, the players were released to go about their business of getting ready to play a football game. Some went to the locker room, some went to see the trainer, and some went to find a dark hallway where they could lay down on the floor and take a nap. Believe me when I say that I stumbled over more than a few of them during the season. They'd lie down in the craziest places, too. I'd never seen such a thing. I'm not sure why the lights weren't on while the building was occupied, but they weren't. And remember, not only was I was unable to see them lying on the floor, but they couldn't hear me coming. Thankfully, we never had any serious injuries, to either me or them.

When the time came for the team to depart the field house for the stadium, those hallways became anything but quiet. Their raucous hollering, and the sound of their cleats upon the tiled floors of the building, echoed loudly as they made their way toward the exit. Chris Burke and I'd positioned ourselves at the exit to restrain our boys from leaving the building until the players from Case Western had first departed. The Spartans were just beginning to assemble at the exit when our boys arrived. There was no taunting or smack talking, but the boys in Blue and White were exhibiting an awful lot of Bison confidence in that hallway.

The team from Case Western finally departed the field house. We were not far behind. We waited for them to cross the track onto the grass playing surface before we, too, entered the stadium. When we did, we did so with as positive an attitude as I'd seen since week one back at St. Vincent College. I think the boys had figured out that playing well against a top team like Case Western would go a long way toward earning them the respect they desired, which in turn would validate them as a credible collegiate football team, and legitimate college football players.

As advertised, Case Western was the real deal, a very good football team, and they executed their offensive plays with coordinated precision. They ran the ball extremely well during the early stages of the game, moving up and down the field against our defense with ease. They made a few mistakes in the first quarter, including a red zone fumble deep in our territory that stalled what surely would have been a scoring drive. Later, a holding penalty nullified an exciting, long touchdown run, killing yet another drive. And when their coaches decided to pass the ball, they did so with a great deal of competency as well. That, too, was done with precision as Case Western simply put on a clinic, scoring twice by air in the first half. But again, mistakes along their offensive line cost them a few sacks and an opportunity to score a few more points.

Now whether or not it was our new play calling system, I don't know, but our offense was playing quite well, giving the boys from Cleveland all they could handle. And, for a change, the offensive line was leading the charge, playing much more up to their potential than they had in the previous two weeks. Our running game still wasn't doing as well we would have liked, but the passing game was doing just fine, largely due in part to the much improved pass protection from the line. As a result, JC was able to compile pretty substantial amounts of yardage in the first half of play, including a long touchdown pass to Kevin Alley that kept the game surprisingly close. Only a last minute score by the Spartans near the end of the second quarter made the game appear to be one-sided at halftime as Case Western lead 24-7.

On the way into the field house at halftime, I happened to jog alongside the coaches from Case Western as the two teams merged to enter the building. Obviously, they didn't know that I could hear, or they might have been a little less harsh in their assessment of our guys.

"I can't believe we're not pummeling a team like this," said one coach to another.

I remained expressionless, my eyes cast downward, as they voiced their frustration among themselves about how poorly their team had played during the first half, and the mistakes that they'd committed. But there was no strategic information gleaned from the Spartan coaches that I could pass on to Ed and Ryan. Not that it would have mattered, because Case Western played like a Top 10 team in the second half.

With their first possession of the third quarter, Case took to the air again and just picked our defensive secondary apart. We couldn't get any pressure on their quarterback, their offensive line was just too good, and he had all day to find his receivers. Had it not been for building such an insurmountable lead, I think they could have thrown for seven or eight touchdowns. Instead, after throwing their third touchdown pass, the Spartans went back to their ground game for three more scores. It would be the most yards allowed by Ed's defense all season long, a combined 589 yards of total offense for Case Western, 340 of it through the air. Their primary receiver had a heck of a day, hauling in ten catches for 211 yards, another season high against us. At the end of the game the scoreboard looked pretty grim for the home team:

CASE WESTERN 52 GALLAUDET 13

But all wasn't lost for our Bison. The offense had performed pretty darn well against a quality opponent. JC easily had his best performance of the year, completing 23 of his 35 pass attempts for 317 yards, including two touchdowns. Kevin Alley posted his best numbers of the season, as well, catching eight passes for 172 yards. And both players were congratulated by the Spartan coaching staff following the game, accolades they justly deserved.

What I was most pleased with, though, was the vastly improved attitude among the players, despite losing their third game in a row. And I couldn't imagine anyone sending Ed another derogatory email questioning our players' integrity now. I didn't see any quitters on the field that day, nor did I expect there would be. In fact, the players were feeling pretty good about themselves in the field house after the game. Despite the loss, I thought that things were looking up for the team. And for a change, only the usual suspects took up residence in Jon's training room that afternoon; there were no new injuries.

When the head coach of Case Western shook Ed's hand at mid-field, he told him that his team was very impressed with how competitive our boys played the game, and the fact that they didn't quit despite the deficit on the scoreboard. And so, although we'd lost the game by a large margin, Ed had achieved his goal of having the team earn the respect of an opponent, a quality opponent. Case Western became a Top 10 team later that season.

15

Bad Day at Black Rock

Have you ever heard of the movie, *Bad Day at Black Rock*? It was filmed in 1955 and starred Spencer Tracy as a one-handed stranger who visits a nearly deserted town out in the middle of nowhere. In fact, when the train stops at the town's depot to let Tracy off, it's the first time in four years that the train has actually stopped in Black Rock. Tracy's character is in search of another man whom he believes now lives in the town. The few residents are strangely hostile toward him and he finds peril at nearly every corner. In other words, they give Tracy a pretty rough go of it. Indeed, he was having a bad day and hence, the name of the movie.

We were about to have our own bad day as well. Make that bad days. No, make that a bad week, "Bad Week at Gally."

The previous year's narrow defeat at the hands of Becker College had given Ed some confidence that we could pull off the win in week six. Becker had been playing Division III football for three years now and didn't yet have a victory. Located about one hour's drive west of Boston, Becker's football program had been successful recruiting a good bit of talent from the southern states, namely Florida. But the team wasn't particularly well coached, nor was it very disciplined. So Ed had good reason to be optimistic about our chances of defeating them.

When I arrived at the field house on Tuesday afternoon, I was surprised to hear yelling, screaming, and the slamming of doors. The yelling and screaming was coming from the football office, as was the slamming door. I'd just exited the stairwell around the corner from Ryan's office when I heard the ruckus. Two girls from the volleyball team passed by me on their way to the gym for practice, smiling and signing to one another, unfazed by all of the commotion behind them. They obviously had no idea that something was astir. Suddenly, from around the corner stormed Brian, chest puffed out and shaking his head back and forth as he rumbled down the hallway toward me.

"They think I'm incompetent," he said in a loud voice. "I'm not!"

"What's wrong?" I asked him.

"They said I fucked up the video clip storage on the computer," Brian said, stopping in front of me. "And I didn't."

"Who's that, Ryan and Ed?"

"Yeah," he said as he took a deep breath, smacked the wall with his open palm and then continued on his way.

Brian took the heat for a lot of things, so I could understand his frustration. Obviously, things weren't always his fault, but he usually got the blame. Since he was a graduate assistant, Ed and Ryan felt it perfectly appropriate to over-task and under-appreciate their indentured servant. That's just the way they'd learned the ropes themselves, and that's the way they were going to utilize the free labor. Right or wrong, I'd become pretty sympathetic to Brian's cause. I'd never been a GA, only a fraternity pledge, so I really didn't have an ax to grind.

Whatever it was that Brian was off to do it took him a long while. In fact, he didn't get out onto the practice field until about a third of the way through practice. By then, Ryan, too, was grumbling and had grown very impatient with the team's laissez-faire attitude.

"Mother of God!" he screamed aloud to the offensive linemen.

"Mary, Coach," I said looking out onto the field without as much as a tiny smirk.

"What?" he grimaced and glanced over his shoulder at me.

"The Mother of God would be Mary," I said without expression, knowing that it might get his goat. Of course, I was being a smartass.

"What the fuck?" He shook his head at me and stomped off toward the offensive linemen who were milling about almost aimlessly. I guess he didn't think my comment was funny, but I thought it pretty amusing, albeit a bit immature.

Ed remained in the distance for much of the practice. He was at the far end of the stadium entertaining a gentleman from the Board of Trustees, a man who also was a former congressman from Wisconsin. He was a big football fan, who liked what Ed was doing with the team and had come to watch us practice. Ed, the consummate opportunist, was trying to figure out a way to appropriate more funding for the football program. He had the congressman's ear and even managed to get a follow-up meeting with him to discuss more money for the team. But, it wasn't a good practice for us, by any definition of the words, "good practice."

Things didn't improve any on Wednesday either. Our pre-practice meetings had to be cancelled when the field house was evacuated following a bomb threat called into the school.

Chris Burke said that the threat was made on the one year anniversary of a big protest that shut the school down for a while. The protest had centered on the appointment of a University President who many students had felt wasn't "deaf enough." In the opinion of the protesters, the appointee, Jane Fernandes, wasn't fluent enough in ASL and they feared she'd diminish the importance of ASL within the deaf community. It became an issue of "what it means to be deaf." Fernandes was eventually replaced by the current President, Robert Davila, shortly after those protests.

Not surprisingly, football practice, on a campus disrupted by a bomb threat, was highly unproductive. The players on the team were distracted, not focused, and for whatever reason, very lethargic. By the end of Wednesday's practice, Ed had become very impatient and short tempered with both the players and the coaching staff. He was just not handling matters well. And when the poor practice regiment carried over to Thursday afternoon's practice, Ed kicked the entire team off the field and sent them back to the locker room, disgusted with their lack of effort and, in his opinion, commitment. He also dismissed the coaching staff as well. Without a single word spoken to one another, we each left the field and the campus.

On my way to the field house, I heard Ed say out loud, "I've got to get out of this place." I knew then that Ed had grown weary under the stress of trying to develop the kids into a college football team. Besides all of the NCAA hurdles that he had to clear, trying to straddle the two cultures was exhausting, especially when trying to navigate one within the other. It wouldn't be long, I thought, before Ed would be in search of a coaching vacancy somewhere else.

That evening, the deaf community got a real black eye from the media, which of course prompted lots of questions of me from my family, friends, and employees. CNN reported that several white students at Gallaudet had held a black student against his will over the previous weekend, and used Sharpies to inscribe swastikas and the letters KKK all across his body. The assault did indeed occur in the general area of the Gallaudet campus, but it neither involved Gallaudet students, nor any Gallaudet football players, thank God. The incident took place at the Model School, the deaf high school campus located adjacent to Gallaudet, and all of those involved were Model students. How do you like that for a play on words? The kids who assaulted their classmate were "Model" students. Although it wasn't actually a Gallaudet incident, it certainly tainted the image of the university, at least for a little while.

The next day, as I sat at the traffic light on Florida Avenue waiting to enter the Gallaudet campus, I heard a man's voice counting down out loud, "Four, three, two, one…" and I thought to myself, "What is that?" It sounded like a recorded message. I looked about, but there were no car radios, no loud speakers, or anyone even near my car. And although the countdown coincided with the traffic light changing to give me the right away, I knew it wasn't the voice of God as my co-pilot. I was a little perplexed, and a bit amused, I must admit. I thought about the strange voice several times during our walk through practice.

Later, when I left for home, I stopped at the same gate and was waiting for traffic to ease so that I could make the right hand turn onto Florida Avenue. It was a mild, pleasant evening and so my car window was down. Once again I heard the voice, loud and clear. However, this time something caught my eye as the voice continued to count down. Just to the side of the roadway was a little yellow box affixed to a light pole. On the box was an orange-red LED display with a crescent shaped cover that shielded the display from the sun so that it could be seen brightly in the glare of the day. But in order to see it, one had to be directly in front of it, either nearby or afar. And simultaneous to the display of descending numerals was a man's voice counting down. When the countdown concluded, the traffic light changed. It was a pedestrian crossing signal for handicapped folks who needed assistance crossing Florida Avenue safely. The "Walk; Don't Walk" sign also counted down out loud. It was pretty cool; I'd never seen one before. The signal was newly installed, which explained why I didn't recall seeing, or hearing, it over the past several months. And it prompted to me to wonder if the District of Columbia Department of Public Works had confused Gallaudet with a school for the blind instead of a school for the deaf.

The bad week continued on into Friday afternoon. Eric Jindra, our big offensive lineman from California, who had injured his shoulder in practice several weeks ago, quit, although he hadn't bother to tell anyone. He just turned in all of his gear at the cage and left. Ed and Ryan had hoped that he'd soon return to shore up the unit, but it wasn't to be. I think they'd somewhat figured that Eric was done, though, since he hadn't seen a physician or shown up for any rehab with Jon's crew in the training room. It was just a matter of not having the heart to play the game, according to Brian, who knew Eric better than any other member of the coaching staff.

That brought us down to fewer than a dozen and a half players wearing jersey numbers greater than the number 50. Players who wear those jerseys are typically linemen of some sort, and linebackers.

After the walk-through on Friday, I stopped by Ryan's office to pick up the play sheet for the next day. He was very melancholy, for a change, almost approachable.

"Just came by for the play sheet, Ryan. Is everything okay?" I asked.

"Yep," he said as he picked the sheet up from his desk and handed it to me. Not being his normal self, I couldn't tell whether or not he expected any conversation. Since I was eager to get home a little earlier than usual, I just started to go on about my way.

"Okay," I said. "Thanks." I took the sheet, glanced quickly at it, and then back to him, "I guess I'll see you in the morning?"

"Yeah, sorry," he said. "I've got a little bit on my mind."

Ok, so it seemed like he wanted to get something off his chest. After a few moments of small talk, he spilled out his thoughts. His estranged wife was in from Ohio for the weekend and he obviously had some thinking to do. I guess things hadn't gone so well with him and his wife during the team's visit to Ohio, or maybe they had. He was a tough one to read at times. I was surprised, though, by something he voluntarily disclosed. He told me that he'd actually attended a seminary school for a time and had been studying to be a youth pastor back home before coming to Gallaudet.

I was a little bit floored by that revelation, I must admit. He certainly hadn't impressed me as a man of faith, and definitely not as a man of the cloth. And I wondered how it had come to be that he would stand here before me at this place and time. Was it marital conflict? Was it a personal struggle with faith? I didn't know, nor was it my goal to find out. But, I thought to myself, that perhaps God had planted me at the school to redirect Ryan, or in some way let him know that God still needed him, because he surely appeared to have walked away from God. However it came to be, I suddenly felt badly that I'd not made a better effort to work more closely with Ryan, or even be his ally. He seemed to be a sad soul in search of his way and if God had indeed sent me here to help, well, then I wasn't getting the job done. And so I, too, had a little bit on my mind that night.

*

Game Day was upon us once again, but unlike the previous five games, on this day we would face an exceptionally "confident" football team from Becker College. You see, to merely say that the Becker football team was confident would be a tremendous understatement. Wearing royal blue and white uniforms, players from Becker literally danced in the end zone before the game. Obviously, their sideline demeanor was the diametric opposite of ours. For as quiet and measured as we were, Becker was equally as loud, brazen, and seemingly just downright nasty. They appeared to be genuinely eager to get out onto the field to "bang heads." Whether or not this was just their game persona, I didn't know. What I did know, however, was that they had a roster full of impressive athletes. And that roster had quite a few kids from Florida and, oddly enough, the Washington D.C. area. According to Ed, the coach of Becker had recruited heavily from the south. I could see that by looking at their home towns listed in the game program. He also said that Becker had a very relaxed admissions standard, which made playing football there very inviting for "student-athletes" who perhaps had spent more time in the weight room than in the classroom.

Well, not long into the game we learned something else about the Becker College Hawks; they were fast. And we learned that the hard way, by watching their tailback rip off an 87 yard touchdown run on their first offensive possession. We were quickly down 7-0. We also learned that they could talk some trash.

"Hey number two? Number two?" screamed their Safety as he walked up to the line of scrimmage and lined up across from Fletch. "I'm gonna getcha. Uh, huh. That's right, I'm gonna getcha. You're mine!" And at the snap of the ball that guy would "get him" all right, jacking Fletch up and holding him at the line of scrimmage nearly every time. Sometimes he'd get into him pretty good, and sometimes just enough to knock him off his route. Either way, he always seemed to get his hands on Fletch, making it difficult for our receiver to get downfield.

Dima Rossoshansky ran the ball off tackle for a gain of five or six yards before being tackled to the ground by three or four Becker defenders. Hopping up off the pile, one linebacker stood over Dima and barked down at him.

"Bring it again! Come on, bring it again!"

Dima would, of course, do just that, un-intimidated by the particularly aggressive nature of the defensive players. And each time that he ran the football, he would once again encounter that same guy, who would let Dima know that he was there, too.

"That's what I'm talking about! That's what I'm talking about!" the linebacker shouted.

Dima, not knowing what the linebacker was actually yelling at him, would just look at the Becker player like the guy was crazy or something, smile at him, and then trot back to his position in the backfield with JC. Afterward, when he came off of the field, Dima would look at me, shake his head, and laugh.

And then there was my favorite Becker player, number eighteen, the Right Cornerback who lined up opposite our number eighteen, Kevin Alley. He was a tall, thin, black kid with long dreadlocks that fell out from under his helmet and down below his shoulder pads. With the shaded visor across his facemask, he reminded me of the New Orleans Saints' wide receiver, Donte Stallworth, mostly because of his dreadlocks and visor, not because of the way he played. Anyway, this kid just ran his mouth incessantly.

"Hey, come on eighteen! You're mine! You're mine!" he yelled at Kevin.

He yelled at Kevin loud enough that everyone on our sideline, who could hear, took notice. Now you're getting the picture. Our sideline couldn't hear a thing these guys were saying. I mean, I'm sure that our boys could see the lips of the Becker players moving and such, but they couldn't hear the trash talking. Only about three or four of us coaches could hear it, and maybe a few of the boys who were hard of hearing, Jon, and the referee.

"Watch your mouth, number eighteen," warned the side judge.

But number eighteen just wouldn't stop and after a few more plays, drew a personal foul for taunting. Unfortunately for us, it would be one of our best gains of the day, fifteen yards.

"Eighteen?" the referee called out to the player after the play as he walked away. "You know they can't hear you? You know that, right?"

"Oh they hear me, all right! And they gonna keep hearing me!"

"They're deaf, son. They can't hear you," continued the referee, "It's a deaf school!"

"I don't care if they dead or not," he said, putting his mouthpiece back into his mouth. "It makes no difference to me."

He walked toward one of his teammates and motioned back toward the referee.

"Man says them boys is dead," he said to a teammate and pointed across to our offensive players who were lining up for the next play.

"Ain't that some shit?" the other player remarked.

Well, after a prolonged time of having to listen to such language and disrespect, I found myself sinking to his level, and perhaps one of the more embarrassing, and unprofessional moments, in my coaching career. I looked over at Brian and saw him sign in a slant pass to Kevin Alley, who was lining up on our forty yard line, just in front of me. Becker's number eighteen strolled out to where Kevin had lined up and positioned himself directly in front of Kevin, about a yard away. I moved just a little to my left, so that I'd be just a few yards from the defender, but on the sideline, of course.

"Hey, Eighteen?" I called out to him, trying not to move my lips. All the while I was staring into our backfield at the quarterback. "You suck!"

Number eighteen snapped his head toward our sideline and then quickly back at Kevin.

"You heard, me, Eighteen," I said again, moving my lips as minimally as I could so no one could see that I was talking to the player. Crossing my arms, I continued to look intently at JC as he barked signals from his position in the shotgun formation. "You suck, shit head!"

The boy's head again snapped toward our sideline and in my direction. At the same time, Justin delivered the ball between his legs to JC. Kevin Alley leapt off the line of scrimmage and cut inside of number eighteen, who was obviously distracted and failed to get his hands on our speedy wide receiver. Kevin hauled in the pass from JC and ran twenty four yards before being tackled by the safety near the Becker thirty-five yard line. I felt pretty childish about the incident and worried that Ed might have heard me, but it turns out that he was too far away. I didn't know, though, if anyone else had heard me. If they did, they never said anything. As childish as it might have been, it was fun. We ended up scoring on the drive.

But that would be about the only fun that I'd have that day, or anybody else on the team, or the coaching staff, for that matter. We self-imploded with six turnovers, three of which occurred in the red zone to kill potential scoring opportunities. One, in particular, was an interception that put JC and I at odds afterward. He made a good read of the cover two safeties and threw the ball to a receiver running a post route between them. But, instead of putting the ball directly onto the receiver's hands, he floated the pass down the middle, effectively leading the receiver up field. By doing so, JC gave the defensive backs time to converge and easily intercept the pass in the end zone. I quickly strode over to meet JC at the bench.

"Quarterback 101," I signed to JC as he grabbed a cup of Gatorade from the trainer's table. "Never float a pass across the middle of the field. We talked about that the first week of practice!"

When I signed this to him, I did so with some forcefulness, much more than I usually did, and JC interpreted that as me being angry about the play. I don't know if he was insulted or embarrassed, but he blew me off, picked up his helmet, and casually walked away from me. I wasn't so much angry as I was frustrated. But, when I looked down the sideline, I caught a glimpse of Ed looking our way and I could see that he was angry. Oh, was he angry.

I couldn't blame him, though. Self-inflicted errors were something that no head coach would tolerate. They were signs of poor discipline, poor preparation, and in some cases, poor coaching. Our three fumbles were mistakes just as careless as that interception. Of the three, none were forced fumbles, or in other words, caused by a defensive player. They were just the result of poor ball security skills. On one fumble in particular, the football just popped out of our player's possession and right into the hands of a Becker defender.

JC threw two more interceptions during the game, and we committed a season high six turnovers in all. It was agonizing, especially since Becker was not a better football team than we were. Yes, they had a lot of speed, and they used it to rack up 310 rushing yards, but we'd killed ourselves with the turnovers, and were the cause of our own demise. The final score felt more like an indictment than a loss:

BECKER 30 GALLAUDET 6

Our encouraging 2-0 record had sunk to 2-4, and it was a

very bitter disappointment for Ed. After the game, he summoned the entire coaching staff into Ryan's office where, once again, we had front row seats to another vein popping, visor hurling, conniption. It was the Greensboro post-game tantrum on steroids. In no uncertain, or pleasant, terms, Ed expressed his frustration with our offense, calling it a joke and an embarrassment before finally storming out of the room.

No one in the office said a word after Ed left, not a single thing, from any of the eight assistant coaches. Brian put his earpiece back into his ear. Harold grinned, and Chris just looked down between his legs and shook his head. Ryan remained seated in the chair behind his desk, staring at some scattered papers left strewn about the floor in the wake of Ed's departure. I'd always been told by my parents as a child, and maybe several other adults as well, that if you can't say something positive then don't say anything at all. I hadn't really ever heeded that advice, but now seemed to be a pretty good time to practice it. And so with nothing to add on a positive note, I left.

On my way home I received a text message from JC on my cell phone. He apologized for his behavior on the sideline during the game. I didn't need or expect an apology, but I pulled into a KFC parking lot along New York Avenue and thanked him for it just same.

JC said that he wasn't having fun and took responsibility for much of our offensive woes. In doing so he texted, "I don't think my shoulders are broad enough to carry the load." While I've said many times that I thought JC to be a very insightful guy, I perceived his forlorn text to be a display of self-pity. And I'd never much cared for the "woe is me" approach to dealing with adversity, not even with my own children. And I wasn't going to tolerate it from JC, either. So, I told him that if he wanted to quit, then he should just do so; he should just quit and walk away from the game and the challenges that it presented; just leave it and his teammates behind. But not to blame it on anything other than the fact that he no longer had a desire to compete. JC still had some fire in his belly, at least I hoped he did, and I was trying to stoke those embers a bit. Otherwise, I couldn't imagine what Ed would have done if JC had walked in and said, "Coach O told me to quit, so I quit."

The following week was a bye week for us, and I encouraged JC to take advantage of his time off to gather his thoughts and try to rekindle his competitive passion. He repeatedly assured me that he'd consider all that I'd said and that he appreciated my approach and guidance. A few days later he texted me again, this time to ask if I could get him two tickets to a Ravens game. I hoped that that meant he wasn't quite ready to walk away from football, just yet.

With a bye on the schedule the following weekend, Ed didn't plan for any football related activity on Sunday or Monday. Our next opponent was a non-conference, club team that Ed simply referred to as Williamson Trade, and they apparently weren't very good. Gallaudet had played several games against Williamson Trade over the years and had come away with lopsided victories each time, so there was little belief among any of the players or coaches that we needed the extra practice time. Instead, I think Ed knew that the boys needed a little down time, a little room to breathe, and he took advantage of the opportunity offered by the schedule to give them a respite.

The bye week had indeed arrived in a timely manner. Not only did the boys on the team need some time off, so, too, did the coaches. Brian needed some time to cool off. Kerry would need the time off to be with his wife, who gave birth to their second child, a boy, just hours after the Becker game. Ryan, I guess, could use the break to work on his marriage. And me, I needed to help my wife with our oldest son's birthday party the next day. Otherwise, had I gone to a football practice and left her with a dozen ten and eleven year old boys with noise makers and party favors, my marriage would have required some work as well.

16

He Works in Mysterious Ways

Undoubtedly, you've heard the phrase, "God works in myste-rious ways." To me, that usually means that one doesn't see God's work while in progress, but rather in hindsight. Some-times we receive the blessing of actually seeing Him work in real time. In church on Sunday, I sat with my family and listened to the sermon being preached by our pastor, Dr. Robert Parsley. Pastor Bob, as we called him, was a good old boy from Arkansas, trans-planted by God into a chic, suburban neighborhood.

Being from the "back woods," as he called it, Pastor Bob had a way of delivering his sermons in the simplest of terms, easy to un-derstand. The message that morning was preached just that way, "simple-like," as Bob would say, and it was received right on time: How was God using you to do His will and carry His message? Ob-viously, He had used many people throughout the Old Testament to accomplish this, but that would be using hindsight. How about the here and now? How was He using me? And I thought about how easily the door to coaching football at Gallaudet had been opened for me. And I thought about Ryan, and Brian, and Rusty, and so on. And with that I realized that He had blessed me with the ability to see Him working through me in the here and now.

Planning to perhaps one day write about my coaching experience at Gallaudet, I'd generally considered the obvious: my writing would focus on the deaf community and how its culture contrasted with my own. But I came to the realization that, although God was indeed working through me as a coach, I hadn't given much thought about His plans for me as a writer. Obviously, He had me working two jobs, if you will, and He was using me both as a coach *and* as a writer.

Considering such, I sat in the pew and began to think about how I'd change the theme of my literary project from one that focused on deaf culture to a faith-based work. But after some prayer, and the events that transpired during the week to follow, I knew that I was to somehow blend the two together, weave a story of how God works in everyone's life, in every community, and in every culture. But, in order to do so, God had to bless me with that vision then and now, so that my eyes would be open to all that He would reveal to me. In hindsight, I think my vision was just about 20/20.

Courtesy of the bye week in our schedule, Sunday and Monday were planned days off for both the players and the coaching staff. And again, the bye week came at just the right time. On Sunday afternoon, my wife and I teamed up to throw a birthday party for our son, Mark. There were about a dozen boys in attendance and coordinating such a posse was no small task. We hosted the event at a local family fun center that featured miniature golf, a driving range, batting cages, a video game room, and multiple basketball hoops of varying heights. I did everything from feeding tokens into the pitching machines, to holding the boys up to the basketball rim so they could dunk a ball, to keeping score for their miniature golf tournament.

"Dad, you get everyone's score for that hole?" asked Mark.

"Yeah, I think so, buddy."

"Ok, because from my group Joe got a six, David got a five, and Robbie got a six!"

"How about you, what was your score?" I asked.

"Oh, I got a hole-in-one!" He smiled and ran toward the next tee.

After we were done with all of the games, I loaded the gang into one of our Coach & Courier 15 passenger vans and took them to Friendly's for ice cream sundaes and the customary birthday cake ceremonies. Everyone had a great time and I was happy to have been able to be there to help make it happen for a change. Although my wife, as usual, had done the lion's share of the planning, I was there to do the heavy lifting, which she appreciated immensely.

On Monday morning while dropping the boys off at their bus stop, which was behind that same Friendly's Restaurant, our younger son, Tyler, asked me if I was able to come to his flag football practice.

"Hey, Dad, since you don't have to go to Gallaudet today, do you think you might be able to take me to practice tonight?" he said as he hopped out of the car and closed the back door.

"I think so, Ty," I told him. "Yeah, I'll take you to practice."

He smiled as he pulled his backpack onto his shoulders and began walking toward the open doors of the awaiting, yellow school bus from the Annapolis Area Christian School. Once on the steps of the bus, he stopped to look back toward me, and waved. "How could I not go to his practice?" I thought to myself? And so later that evening, I took him to his football practice and remained on the sidelines throughout. Each time that his coach gave the team a water break, I was right there to hand him his water bottle and give him a few words of encouragement.

As I watched his team of six-year old gridiron masters dart about the practice field, I spoke occasionally with a few of the other parents. Standing next to me on the sideline was the father of one of Tyler's friends, who was also playing flag football. Don Wiley was the Dean of Students at Annapolis Area Christian School, where our sons were classmates. I'd met Don several times in the past since his daughter was in the same grade as Mark. So we were not even close to being strangers. And knowing that I was coaching at Gallaudet, he asked me how things were going and how I was adapting to the culture there.

"You know," he said, "it's interesting that you're learning sign language."

"Learning sign language?" I responded with a slight grimace. "Okay, we'll call it that."

"Because at the high school," he turned and looked at me, "the Board of Directors is considering the addition of American Sign Language to the curriculum as a foreign language."

"Is that right?"

"Yeah, they are," he went on. "The deaf community is a target rich missionary field."

Imagine that.

*

Tuesday, October 9 brought a little something that we hadn't seen for quite some time, rain, and a hard, cold rain at that. Although we were able to get in some stretching and light drill work, the intensity of the rainfall soaked the fields pretty quickly and Ed, not wanting to risk injury to any of the players, looked as if he were about to call practice to an end.

"What do you think?" he asked me and Chris Burke as one of the players slid across the turf and mud and into a few of his teammates. "Should I call it?"

Chris was looking up at the clouds moving rapidly across the skies above the campus. Of course, he didn't hear Ed. I thought it was probably a good idea to call it, considering the sloppy field conditions. Suddenly, there was a deafening clap of thunder and everyone, including Chris, either heard it or felt it, and the players immediately looked toward us. Ed motioned to them to get off the field and into the field house.

"I think that's a good idea," I said to Ed.

"I bet you do," he grinned.

The service entrance to the field house quickly became a mess of water, mud, and abandoned pieces of athletic tape. On their way to the locker room, the players deposited their wet practice gear into a rolling bin adjacent to Kris's equipment room. He would need to get to work on the laundry in short order. I stood alongside the bin and kept a hand on it to prevent it from rolling away from the boys as they cast their heavy, wet garments into it. After it seemed that everyone had made their way through the process, I began to roll the bin into the equipment room. It was much heavier than usual now that it was full of dirty, wet jerseys, t-shirts, and socks, so I decided to push, rather than pull, the bin.

Inside the equipment room, Kris had started the washing machines and was waiting to receive the bin from me. He saw me coming and smiled, then nodded for me to look behind me. When I turned, I saw Rusty in his gym shorts carrying his wet practice gear in his arms. I stepped aside and let him deposit the garments into the bin.

"Thank you," he signed. As he began to walk away, he hesitated and then turned back to me and began signing slowly. I watched and mouthed the words to myself as best I could.

"Do you know?" I repeated aloud, but softly, while watching Rusty's hands. He repeated whatever it was that he was trying to sign several times, but I didn't understand anything beyond, "do you know?"

"Sorry, Rusty," I signed. "I'm not following you."

"Jon, Coach," said Kris from behind. "He's saying, 'Do you know that Jon is a believer?'"

"Jon," I asked out loud, "our trainer?"

"Yes," Rusty signed with a smile. "He is a faithful believer."

"Hey, that's great," I signed back to Rusty as he left for the locker room. I turned and pushed the bin gently toward Kris.

"Thanks for the help there, Kris."

"No," Kris said as he reached for the bin of clothes, "thank you, Coach."

I went to the coach's locker room where I washed up a bit

and put on some dry clothes for the ride home. As I made my way toward the stairwell exit, I saw Jon walk from the hallway into his training room. I thought that maybe, if he wasn't busy, I might ask him about what Rusty had said. And so I changed course and began walking toward the training room. Jon looked up from his desk as I walked into the room.

"Hey, Coach," he said.

"Hello, Jon."

"What brings you by?" He pushed a roll of tape across the surface of his desk and sat back into his chair.

"Oh, I just thought I'd say, hey," I said as I leaned against a training table and faced him. "And mention that Rusty spoke of you this afternoon."

"Nawrocki?" he said.

"Yep," I nodded.

"And what did Rusty have to say about me?"

"Well, for whatever reason, he felt compelled to tell me that you were a believer," I said. "And he looked pretty happy to share that news, too."

Jon had been wrapping athletic tape around some sort of device when he stopped for a moment to look up at me. He smiled, picked up the roll of tape, and continued taping.

"Rusty is a great kid," Jon said.

"Actually, he said that you were a 'faithful believer.'"

"Oh, yeah?" He smiled and nodded. "Well, I guess maybe I've made an impression upon him after all, eh?"

"It would appear to me that you have," I agreed.

"Rusty leads our Athletes in Action group. Did he tell you about that?"

"No, he didn't," I said, "but I've seen the posters around the field house. What, uh…."

"Christian athletes," Jon said. "It's a fellowship group for Christian athletes. You're welcome to attend any time you'd like. We meet on Monday evenings."

"I'd like that. I'll see if I can make it one week after practice."

"That would mean a lot, Coach. You've already had a positive influence on these boys, yourself, you know?"

A little flattery now and then feels good. It felt especially good in this case since it appeared to be a clear message from above that I was doing a good job, and that He was pleased with my work thus far.

Jon Vaughn was an interesting young guy, newly married and recently hired as the Athletic Trainer by Gallaudet. He'd graduated from James Madison University just a few years earlier. A rather quiet and subdued fellow, he was extremely confident about his skills. He certainly wasn't shy when it came to presenting his opinions regarding our player's treatment regiments, but he always did so with respect for Ed and other members of the coaching staff. Ed generally deferred all of our player's health issues to Jon and followed his recommendations.

My conversation with Jon only lasted about twenty minutes or so, but I remember it well to this very day. Jon told me that he had specifically chosen to come to Gallaudet because it was a "target rich mission area," the second time in twenty-four hours that I'd heard that phrase. I guess God wanted to make sure that I clearly understood His reason for planting me there at the school. I got the message. Anyway, Jon went on to tell me that he'd recently prayed throughout the spring that God would send him help. He was overwhelmed with God's immediate response. Within a few months' time, Gallaudet had four new faces in the field house, all Christians: Ryan (though Jon expressed concern for Ryan's walk with The Lord), a new basketball coach, a new volleyball coach, and I all arrived on the scene before summer.

"I asked God for help and before I knew it, He sent me reinforcements," Jon said. "He answered my prayers." And with that response to prayer, Jon, was sure that he, too, was doing as The Lord had planned for him.

The schedule for the week called for very light practices with only one day requiring the players to practice in shells, meaning their helmets and shoulder pads. Both Ed and Ryan were noticeably relaxed. I thought perhaps the bye week might be the primary reason for their ease in intensity, but as it turned out, Ed was a bit worried about his heart. In fact, he disclosed that he was wearing a heart monitor so that doctors could evaluate his cardiovascular condition. Ed's father had passed away prematurely, and he wasn't taking any chances with his own health. He lived on the edge, emotionally, and in doing so feared that he might be at risk of stroke or heart attack. Regardless, he had suddenly toned down his ferocity to that of a big cat at rest, like a tiger on a tree limb.

Ryan appeared to have settled down a bit as well, even asking me for my input on some modifications to our offense strategy. Originally dismissive of my suggestions in the past, he now planned on installing some of them, which surprised both Brian and me. But his change of heart was a pleasant surprise; the assistant coaches all welcomed it as they would a breath of fresh air. Ironically, the fresh air outside had turned brisk and chilly as the fall season finally broke the warmth of the extended summer. We had a cool, windy week of practice, which gave me the opportunity to break out my navy blue, Gallaudet Football jacket.

Since some of the receivers had experienced difficulty catching passes of late, Ed decided to introduce an interesting gadget for the receivers to practice with on Wednesday afternoon. The training gadget featured a football shaped "waffle ball." The ball was attached by a thin bungee cord to a nylon belt that was to be worn around the waist of the player. The idea behind the gadget was for the receiver to throw the ball up and away from his body, and then quickly prepare to receive it upon its return. JC, Jimmy, Fletch, and I all watched in amusement from several yards away as we worked on footwork drills.

Ed handed the gadget to Shawn Shannon. Shawn strapped the belt around his waist, grabbed the ball from Ed, and hurled it downfield. The ball travelled about ten or fifteen feet before quickly snapping back to strike Shawn directly in the face. He reached for his nose, laughing aloud as the ball fell to the ground below him.

"You're supposed to catch the ball when it comes back, you idiot!" Ed laughed. Of course, the quarterbacks and I laughed as well, and they were unable to proceed with their own work after witnessing the folly of their teammate. Shawn tried it once again, this time reaching out for the ball, but missing it once again. Only this time, the ball struck him flush between the legs, and Shawn collapsed in agony. All of the players in the vicinity broke into tears of laughter and ridicule. Shawn was done with the gadget.

Ed then handed it to junior wide receiver, Derrick Williams, who was frightened by the exercise and reluctant to give it a try. With Ed's encouragement, Derrick put the belt around his waist and accepted the ball from Ed. Derrick had it in his head that he was going to throw the ball as hard and far as he could, giving him more time to react and catch it upon its return. That way, he might avoid the same embarrassing disaster that had befallen Shawn.

And so Derrick heaved the ball up and away and immediately positioned his hands out in front of his face to catch it before it could return and hit him, as it had Shawn. Only when he threw the ball, he threw it so hard that it separated from the bungee cord. The ball continued on its flight path, but the bungee cord snapped back and stung Derrick in the shoulder. All the while, there stood Derrick, hands out in front of his face, awaiting a ball that was bouncing harmlessly on the ground about thirty yards away. Ed looked downfield at the ball, and then back at Derrick with his hands out in front of him, still waiting for the ball to return. He motioned for Derrick to take the belt off and hand it to him, which he did, and we never saw the gadget again.

The practices remained light for the rest of the week, only lasting about an hour and a half each day. And we were off for the weekend, which gave me an opportunity to take my youngest son, Tyler, to M&T Stadium to experience his first ever NFL game; a game featuring the Baltimore Ravens and the St. Louis Rams. Everything was just right. The weather was perfect: sunny and mild. And for Tyler, the chicken fingers from the concession stand were downright delicious with honey mustard and fries.

"Dad, you want to try a French fry?" he asked me. "They're great!"

"No, thanks," I said, standing in front of my seat and applauding a big play by the Ravens. I looked down at him, seated in the chair next to me with the basket of fries and chicken on his lap. The crowd began to cheer wildly as the Ravens scored a touchdown in the end zone directly in front of us. The fans in the seats around us reached out to me to give me a "high five" in celebration of the score. I reached out to Tyler to give him a "high five" as well. Still seated, he dropped a French fry back into the basket and slapped the palm of my hand with his own.

"Did you see that touchdown, Ty?" I asked him.

"Nope," he said, but not upset about it, "people were standing up in front of me."

"Yeah, they tend to do that at football games," I told him.

"You want a chicken finger?" he asked.

Well, the Ravens went on to win the ball game, crushing the Rams 22-3. And a Ravens photographer snapped a photo of Tyler and me in our seats during the game, which we were able to purchase on-line a week later. We had a really good time together and that framed photograph is on his wall today to prove it.

*

With Homecoming on the horizon and an easy game against Philadelphia's Williamson Trade, the players were very loose, as were Ed and Ryan. So Monday's practice, while a rare occurrence, was still pretty relaxed for a practice leading up to a game. But the team followed its normal pre-practice regimen, and once on the field, a normal practice plan. However, when we broke from our Flex formation and Fletch went to work with the special teams, JC was absent. That left me with just Jimmy to work with during our Indy segment of practice. I asked Jimmy where JC was, but he shrugged his shoulders and indicated that he didn't know, and began his footwork drills in the ladder by himself.

"Hey, where's JC," I called out to Ryan as he chatted with Kerry several yards away.

"He's with Jon," Ryan said. "His shoulder is bothering him."

Well, that certainly came out of nowhere, I thought, since JC hadn't indicated to me at any time that he was experiencing any pain or discomfort. And so Jimmy had my undivided attention during "Indy" that day. Although Ed and Ryan had never given Jimmy any serious consideration as a football player, and certainly not as a quarterback, I really liked what I saw in him. The only thing about Jimmy that I wasn't crazy about was that he was a lefty, which meant that I had to see everything backwards while evaluating all of his mechanics and techniques. But he had a strong arm, was pretty tough, and genuinely eager to learn how to succeed at playing quarterback. I didn't know if Jimmy was going to get any playing time that weekend, but it was obvious that he was going to finally get some practice reps with the offensive unit. And he did.

About half way through the team segment of practice, I saw JC walk onto the field and make his way toward me, Jimmy, and Fletch. He was walking very casually with his left hand in the pocket of his sweat pants.

"Hey," he signed and nodded with a slight smile.

"What's the problem?" I asked as I stepped toward him. Fletch was watching JC intently from over my shoulder, knowing that an injury to JC would result in his having to fill the void under center.

"It hurts when I throw the ball, so I went to see Jon," JC signed.

I'd always watched the hands of the person signing to me so that I knew what they were saying, of course. But, since I'd improved a bit at reading the language, and also had a sense of what was being said, I was able to glance quickly between JC's hands and his face. And I was a bit surprised at how casual he seemed. He didn't seem very concerned, but I didn't know if that was because it wasn't a serious problem or he just didn't care. Fletch quickly signed something to JC as Jimmy looked on.

"I have to go work with Jon every day until the pain eases," JC said.

"No playing?" Fletch asked.

JC shook his head, no. My guess was that JC had tendonitis, which would require several weeks of rest in order to fully recover. A player could still play, though, if he managed the pain with ice and ibuprofen, which most players did at this point in the season. But maybe Jon feared a greater injury, without having the benefit of an MRI or X-ray, and my guess was that that was why he was shutting him down for a while. Fletched turned his stern gaze toward me.

"You're the man," I signed to him.

Fletch quickly flashed a "thumbs up."

Like most high school and college football coaches during the practice week leading up to Homecoming, Ed repeatedly warned the boys about maintaining their focus, staying out of trouble during Homecoming events, and making good decisions off the field. When you think about the sheer number of student-athletes involved in a football program, the fact that only a few usually get themselves into trouble is really astounding, considering the naturally aggressive nature of the boys who play the game. Gallaudet was no exception. To my knowledge, though, we didn't lose anyone that week to mischief or misfortune.

We did, however, have an unusual incident on Tuesday amongst the players themselves. Apparently, some of the Jewish players were not getting along with a few of the black players, and vice versa. And several racial and religious slurs were used. Obviously, this didn't sit very well with Ed. But it especially bothered Justin Lathus, our long, curly-haired offensive center with a bad hip. Ed decided to let the team captains have first crack at resolving the issue, and so Justin called a team meeting after practice to address the matter.

Justin, like many of the boys, was a very emotional guy, and after assembling the team in the wrestling room, the room where they met as a team before each home game, he conveyed his disappointment with their behavior very passionately. A few of us coaches monitored the player meeting from the rear of the room to ensure that no hostilities broke out, but things were well in hand and orderly. The players on the team paid close attention to Justin, although most of them couldn't hear him finish just about everything that he signed by mouthing the phrase, "Fugg you, fugg you!" But, that's what he did, at the conclusion of nearly everything that he said, "Fugg you, fugg you!" It was short and squeaky, but obviously Justin's preferred exclamation point.

Daniel Alexander, a black, sophomore wide receiver from Phoenix, Arizona got up from among the group of players seated on the floor and stood alongside Justin. He agreed with Justin and reiterated the same message to the team, albeit without Justin's exclamation points. The two put their arms across one another's shoulders as a sign of unity. The sentiment was well received by the rest of the players as they, too, made amends with one another. With the matter apparently resolved, the team had begun to leave when Ed stepped forward and demanded their attention.

"Gentlemen, every Saturday we go out onto that football field and play the physical game of football, not just to win the contest, but to earn the respect of our opponent, the league, and the football community as a whole," Ed spoke while he signed. "How can you expect to earn that respect if you can't respect yourselves, your teammates, each other?"

And with that a lot of the players nodded their approval of Ed's message, and all seemed well as the team departed the room for the evening, except with Rusty. Rusty left the room with his head down, tormented by disappointment in his teammate's behavior, despite reassurances by them that everything was okay. As Ron Luczak and I watched Rusty walk dejectedly down the hallway toward the locker room, Ed approached us with an open palm raised before him.

"He's okay, he's a big boy," said Ed. "Rusty's a super Christian and easily bothered by these things. He'll get over it."

When Justin filed by me, I stopped him to ask what he'd said to the guys, apologizing for my not being able to keep up with his signing. He took a few moments, but then explained that the main points of his address where about teamwork, being brothers, and having respect for one another. He signed to me slowly, watching my eyes as I followed along, and in such a way that I could easily interpret. And then, before leaving, he patted me on my shoulder.

"Thanks for asking, Coach," Justin signed.

"Thank you," I said.

Ed looked on at Justin and me as he stood with his arms crossed and his back against the door. He straightened out his back and began to walk away.

"Thank God I have several weeks of leave after the season is done!" he said. "I think I'll request to add a little maternity leave as well."

Like Kerry, Ed's expectant wife was due to deliver any day.

*

JC had a physician's visit on Wednesday to have his shoulder looked at. On Thursday, he gave us the news that he was done for the year with a worn out rotator cuff. That was shockingly bad news, indeed, but JC didn't seem too upset about the prognosis. In fact, I got the sense that maybe JC was actually relieved to have a good reason to finally step down as the quarterback of the team. The transition from club ball to Division III had been frustrating for him. He wasn't exactly a spring chicken, either, at twenty-five years of age. And living with his fiancé, both of whom were hoping to get a job following their upcoming graduation, maybe his priorities were no longer set upon gridiron achievements. I think that it might have been a combination of each, but only JC knows that for sure.

The news upset Ed quite a bit, though, at first. Initially, he assigned some of the blame to me, referring to my use of the weighted football for a few of our quarterback drills. Jon quickly rejected the notion that the ball had caused the injury. He told Ed that using the ball had probably extended JC's playing time a little, since it likely had helped to strengthen the muscles around the joint. The injury had been incurred over a long period of time, according to the physician's report.

Not ready to give up on his favorite athlete, Ed asked Jon if the injury precluded JC from playing another position on the field, like wide receiver. After all, JC was a superb athlete and would be a tremendous asset as a receiver opposite Kevin Alley. Jon agreed and assured Ed that the joint would suffer no further damage if he played wide receiver. And so JC became a wide receiver, which seemed to suddenly make JC very happy once again. Brian later told us that JC had wanted to play wide receiver since 2002, but being the best athlete on the team, the coaches had always stuck him at quarterback. After just one look at JC jogging back to the locker room to put on his practice gear, I could see that we'd a rejuvenated Jason Coleman on the team. And that would be good.

So as you might expect, Fletch and Jimmy split the reps at quarterback from that day on, although it wasn't clear if, or when, Jimmy would actually get any playing time in a game. It was understood that Fletch was now the team's quarterback, and neither player assumed an arrogant or defensive posture about it. Instead, they were very supportive of one another. In fact, most of the boys on the team went out of their way to ensure that Fletch and Jimmy knew that they each had their support as well. Fletch was relieved of his special teams duties, and was now able to spend that portion of practice with Jimmy and me working on his footwork, defensive reads, responsibilities, and the proper mechanics of passing the football.

Throughout the week, we had a lot more visitors than usual at practice, probably because of Homecoming. There were a half dozen people or so in the stands, or along the track, watching practice on any given day. In addition, there were one or two older boys on the sideline who had declared their intentions to enroll at Gallaudet and play football for the Bison the following year. Ed made provisions for them to hang around the team to get a feel for the environment. I met one kid who was an offensive lineman from California, and another who was a running back from Wisconsin. They were pretty big boys, too, and appeared to be very athletic. And like most of the freshmen currently on the team, both were already nineteen years old, even though they were still high school seniors.

Williamson Trade, formally known as The Williamson Free School of Mechanical Trades, was nearly as old as Gallaudet. Founded in the mid 1800's by philanthropist I.V. Williamson, it had served as a school for financially disadvantaged young men. Williamson was from a Quaker family, and thus, the school operated based on Judeo-Christian principles. At the school, teen-aged boys could learn a trade by which they were able to secure jobs and provide for their families. It wasn't until the 1960's that the school became a post-secondary institution, an alternative to public and private colleges and universities. To this day, Williamson Trade provides a free, quality trade and technical education to qualified young men of all backgrounds.

Although Williamson Trade wasn't a football powerhouse, I was impressed that the school not only had the financial resources to support a team, but the administrative desire to do so. They obviously took pride in their team, too, since it appeared that it travelled well, meaning that there were a good number of supporters along their sideline, cheering on their team in the baby blue, black, and white uniforms.

On the opposite side of the stadium, there was a lot of pride as well, as Gallaudet fans crowded the streets outside of the small stadium. The smell of grilled hamburgers and sausages wafted through the air and the large crowd was full of smiles, laughter, and celebration. It was the scene of a typical pre-game tailgating party, only this week was Homecoming Week.

There were no marching bands, no speakers blasting music, and obviously no pep rally chants or cheers. Gallaudet graduates from the classes of 1957 and 1967 marched around the track as part of the organized festivities, with each group carrying a class banner across the front of their ranks. Several much older graduates rode ahead of them in golf carts. The game and the festivities were such a popular event that the school had provided for the contest to be broadcast on the Internet for the viewing pleasure of Gallaudet graduates across the country. It was easily the biggest turnout of the year to watch a Gallaudet home game, despite the fact that we were playing a less than formidable foe.

Our players may not have been able to hear the excitement of the crowd, but they saw it and they felt it. After warm-ups, they returned to the field house and assembled behind the closed double doors of the team meeting room. The coaching staff remained in the hallway outside of the room to allow the boys to "do their thing." Excited to play their Homecoming game, they hooted and hollered like I hadn't heard them do all season long. And the building was filled with what sounded like the inaudible wailing of ghosts and the howling of unleashed beasts. But then suddenly, the raucousness inside stopped, and the building went silent again as one of the two double doors began to open slowly. Andrew Zernovoj, a reserve wide receiver from Woodside, California, referred to by his teammates simply as "Z", popped his head out, and smiled calmly at us.

"You can come in now," he said in a very soft voice.

How things had gone from the loudness of a rock concert to the hush of a library in the blink of any eye was beyond us, and quite surreal. The coaches all looked at one another as if to ask, "Did that really just happen?" It was oddly humorous when we stopped to think about it for a moment. And we had to refrain from chuckling as we joined the boys inside, where we were greeted by a room of seriously determined game faces.

Once the game finally got underway, the looseness of the team rapidly dissipated. It quickly became apparent to the players, and the coaching staff, that someone had forgotten to tell Williamson Trade that they were a less than formidable opponent. Despite their lackluster performances in years past, it appeared that this time they'd come to Washington ready to play some football. In fact, they jumped out to an early 7-0 lead with a long, gritty drive to begin the game, followed by a short touchdown run. Our defense struggled early and often, despite stellar play by the Doudt brothers, Joshua and Calvin. Josh scored our first touchdown of the game by intercepting a pass and rambling forty yards for the score. He also recorded eleven and a half tackles on the day, which represented an individual game high for the season. Calvin had a great game as well, recording several tackles and an interception. But, like I mentioned, the defense struggled to get off the field in the first half, allowing Williamson Trade to move the football up and down the field and use up the clock.

Fletch notched the first start of his career at quarterback, and was played very well in the first half of the game. He was cool and collected and exhibited a good deal of confidence. After returning to the sideline between each offensive series, he sought me out, eager for evaluation and advice. Jimmy, meanwhile, stood at my side and "listened in" as I discussed strategy and play execution with Fletch. They were both bright young men and each welcomed the position coaching that I provided. JC, now playing wide receiver, quickly became a favorite target for Fletch, and scored on a pass that gave us a 13-12 lead with just a minute to go before the half.

But the lead was very short-lived. Williamson Trade returned a poor kick-off to mid-field. And a few short plays later, with only 14 seconds remaining before the intermission, our defensive back allowed his receiver to beat him down the far sideline for a twenty-six yard touchdown pass, giving Williamson Trade a surprising 19-13 lead.

We made it interesting, though. With one shot to score on the final play of the first half, Fletch passed the ball to Kevin Alley on a twenty yard curl route. Kevin caught the pass and immediately tossed the ball to Cole Johnson, who was sprinting across the field directly in front of Kevin. Cole took the football from Kevin and dashed to the outside of the hash marks and down the field toward the end zone for an additional thirty yards. For a moment, we thought that Cole might score when he dodged a Williamson defender by spinning inside of him at about the twenty yard line. Instead, Cole bounced off of our offensive lineman, Phil Endicott, who was downfield trying to block. As a result of the collision, Cole lost his balance and fell to the turf at the ten yard line. Time expired. Phil felt badly about the unfortunate contact, but who could blame an offensive lineman making that kind of effort fifty yards down field? Not me. Not Cole. Not Ed. At halftime, we were quite surprised to be trailing on the scoreboard.

The locker room was surprising calm during the break. There was no dissention, finger pointing, or fireworks from anyone upset with how the game was progressing. And there were no theatrics from Ed either. Instead, everyone seemed to be quite resolute and eager to get back onto the field. Their emotional balance would pay dividends in the second half.

On our first offensive series of the third quarter, Ryan engineered a long drive from the "coach's box" above the home crowd. And Fletch executed it on the field masterfully. After a series of running plays and play-action passes, Fletch capped the drive with a one yard scamper for a score, one of his two rushing touchdowns for the game, and giving us a quick 20-19 lead.

The offense continued to execute just as efficiently the next time we gained possession of the ball as well. Eventually moving to within the Williamson thirty yard line, it appeared that we might be on our way to another score. But when Fletch pitched the ball to running back, Daniel Alexander, on a read option play, Daniel took his eyes off the ball, allowing it to bounce off his hip and onto the ground. The ball was recovered by a Williamson player. End of the drive.

But that would be the only snafu for us for the remainder of the game. In his first start as a quarterback, Fletch was "in the zone" and ended up passing for 240 yards and two touchdowns, in addition to his two rushing touchdowns. And although it continued to struggle, the defense seemed to bend, but not break, against the determined Mechanics of Williamson Trade. We did not allow our Homecoming opponent to post any additional scores.

With less than five minutes to go in the game, and comfortably ahead by a score of 40-19, I managed to convince Ed that Jimmy needed to get a few reps under his belt. He was now the team's primary backup and gaining some actual game experience would be greatly beneficial should we have to turn to him in an emergency. After all, Fletch, while having a good game, was more of an athlete than a natural quarterback, and as such played the game in a way that placed him more at risk of injury. He agreed.

"He better not screw up, Coach," said Ed, looking over his shoulder at me while placing his hand around the microphone attached to his headset.

"He'll be fine," I smiled. "We're just going to hand the ball off anyway."

"Just make sure he knows that," Ed scowled.

I jogged over to Jimmy and told him to warm up because he was going in for the final series. I told him that we'd be running the ball and that he should be prepared to just take the snap and hand the ball off to the running back. He didn't care about that, though, he was just happy to get into the game. Jimmy smiled, grabbed a football, handed it to Justin Lathus, our center, and began taking practice snaps.

A couple of minutes later, Williamson Trade scored a touchdown to make the score 40-26 with 2:26 remaining in the contest. We recovered their on-side kick off attempt and began our final offensive series around mid-field. I patted Jimmy on the top of his shoulder pads as he began his jog onto the field. But just as he stepped onto the playing surface, Ed reached out and tugged on Jimmy's jersey from behind, pulling him back to the sideline. I thought Ed was going to give him a few words of encouragement before sending him out, and I watched as he signed instructions to Jimmy. But I could see disappointment on Jimmy's face, and I knew what had happened. Ed had changed his mind and decided to keep Fletch in the game. As Jimmy returned to my side, Ed looked over at me.

"Not taking any chances," he said as he returned his gaze to the field. I guess he was comfortable with a three touchdown lead, but not two. If it was up to me, I'd have put Jimmy into the game.

Jimmy was frustrated, of course, and probably angry. I know I'd have been. I tried to encourage him, and assure him that he was indeed a competent quarterback, and that his time would come. He just nodded, thanked me, and walked away toward the bench. Out on the field, the offense ran out the clock against Williamson Trade to secure the Homecoming victory.

GALLAUDET 40 WILLIAMSON TRADE 26

Ed approached me on our way into the field house and congratulated me on Fletch's success during the game. He was pleased with how well we'd prepared Fletch to play in JC's absence. And although I didn't see Ryan following the game, he called me later that night to tell me the same. He said that he appreciated my work with the quarterbacks and was impressed with the results he'd seen with Fletch. I responded by thanking him for the kind words, but insisted on giving the credit to Fletch. For the first time all season I'd been able to work with him during our practices, instead of watching him participate with the special teams units. Fletch had simply responded very well to my coaching instruction, and benefitted from the extra game preparation. I was very happy to be appreciated, though, and able to feel that I'd had a positive impact upon the team. But I wasn't about to take any credit away from Fletch.

Fletch got to keep the game ball.

17

Land of the Giants

During our Sunday afternoon film review of Saturday's game, Ed saw something of interest in the film and asked Ryan to re-run a particular series of plays several times without explanation.

"Again," he said from his seat in the darkened classroom. "Run that series again."

"What?" asked Ryan, "You see Justin slip and miss the Mike linebacker? I wondered what had happened on that play, how he got into the backfield so quickly."

"No, go back two plays," chuckled Ed as Ryan reversed the play film. "Go back one more play. Go back."

"What?" Ryan said, sounding worried.

"Look at that!" exclaimed Ed as he broke out in bold laughter. "What the hell is that?"

But none of the coaches could figure out what Ed was referring to, much less what it was that had prompted him to laugh aloud.

"Look! On our sideline, at the top of the screen," laughed Ed. "What the hell is Overmier doing?"

The film showed me standing on our sideline, hastily snapping my hands back and forth above my head, trying to get the attention of the players on the field. Had I jumped up and down a few times, I'd have resembled a spastic chimpanzee. I suddenly remembered that particular series. We'd gone to a hurry up, no huddle offense, and I was trying to get Fletch to speed up the pre-snap process. I'd seen Brian doing the same thing while mouthing the words, "Hurry up! Hurry up!" And so I thought I'd do the same, even though my signing wasn't necessarily as intelligible as Brian's. Obviously, I hadn't gotten it right.

"Oh, my God," Ryan laughed, joining Ed in the light-hearted moment.

"That's too funny," chuckled Brian.

All I could do was shake my head in embarrassment, because I really did look funny out there, especially with Ryan playing it over and over again. Although everyone knew what I was trying to do, it just looked pretty silly on film. I made a note to myself to never let that happen again. Maybe something else that was silly would happen, something else I'd sign wrong, but never like that, for all to see. It didn't bother me too much, though. But, thinking that the players might have thought the same way during the actual game was a little humiliating, I must admit.

Before leaving for the day, Ed laid out our practice plan for the week leading up to our game against Mount Ida on Saturday. He wasn't going to be around on Monday; doctors were going to induce his wife's labor and delivery and he wanted to make sure that we kept things simple at practice. I think that was code for, "Don't screw things up because I won't be there to fix them." That's just the way Ed was, which was okay by me. He also informed us that he'd made arrangements for the team to get in a pre-game, walk-through practice while en route to Newton, Massachusetts. We were going to practice at Giants Stadium in East Rutherford, New Jersey. How cool was that? My guess was that it was awful hard for The Meadowlands to reject such a request from the world's only deaf college football team. In the past, Ed had obtained similar courtesies from The New England Patriots and Ohio State University as well. And so the prospect of a ten hour bus ride was a bit less unpleasant for the players and coaches that week.

The game in Newton, Massachusetts would put me in the vicinity of my twenty-one year old daughter, Valerie, who'd moved to Rhode Island a few years earlier to attend college. I hadn't been crazy about her decision to leave the family, but her boyfriend had been headed in that direction and, well, you know the rest of the story. While the relationship with her boyfriend fizzled out within a few months, she'd come to enjoy living in Jamestown. And being the self-sufficient, independent, young woman that she is, she chose to make Rhode Island her new home. So, I called her and told her that we had a game not too far away that weekend and that it would be nice to see her if she had the time. Unfortunately, Valerie had to work on Saturday, but she said she could drive up to Newton to meet me for dinner after we arrived on Friday night. So I, too, had a little extra something to look forward to on the trip.

The weather that week was mostly cool and dreary with a light drizzle. Fletch and Jimmy challenged each other during their footwork drills and decision-making exercises on Tuesday. We spent Wednesday's Indy segment of practice working on ball handling skills and play-action execution. They were really improving immensely with their practice time together and the two-to-one coaching attention, which was a luxury for any small football program. While surveying the practice field, I'd occasionally catch a glimpse of JC, now playing both wide receiver and defensive back. He appeared to be much more content to be just one of the guys now, relaxed and friendlier than he'd been during the first several weeks of the season. I was seeing a very different Jason Coleman than the one that I'd first seen in that original ESPN documentary.

With a new baby in the house, Ed was getting little to no sleep. He was an early morning person and preferred to go to bed early in the evening. But the baby wasn't exactly cooperating with that game plan just yet, and Ed was struggling mightily with the little guy's schedule. It was one of those little daily blessings that you have to be thankful for, though. You see, Ed began to leave for home right after practice each night, which gave the rest of the coaching staff an opportunity to breathe a little easier at the end of the day.

Following practice on Wednesday, Ryan mentioned that Ed was taking a good look at several other coaching opportunities. We had all thought that Ryan might leave to follow Ed should that transition take place, but we thought wrong. If Ed left to coach elsewhere, Ryan said that he would probably return to Ohio instead, and that he definitely was not going to apply for the head job at Gallaudet. Well, it turned out that Ryan wasn't as tight with Ed as the rest of the coaching staff had thought. The two just shared a little history together and now, being the only two full-time coaches, they'd developed a closer working relationship with one another than with any of us.

Without the chief around, the rest of the coaching staff spent a little more time after each practice sitting in Ryan's office chatting. We talked about normal stuff for a change, like our families and our kids, the high cost of living in the Washington area, and other non-football related subjects that we wouldn't normally have the opportunity to discuss with Ed around. He always had our noses to the grindstone each day. Well maybe not mine so much. Brian, though, just had to talk football. He was much younger than most of us and being a big fan of the New York Giants, he was terribly excited about getting to practice in Giants Stadium on Friday. In retrospect, these chats became a bonding experience for our coaching staff, an opportunity to get to know one another a little more personally. It was good. The tension between Ryan and I began to dissipate, and our relationship, which had become adversarial, became much friendlier.

With the practice plan for the week simple and routine, very little happened that was out of the ordinary. Following practice on Thursday, Ryan gathered the coaching staff in his office and discussed with us the schedule for Friday morning's departure. As usual, my primary job in the next morning was to make sure that we had enough footballs for the trip; several for practice and several more for the game. And so while we met, I scrubbed down three new footballs that I intended on taking with us. Following the meeting, I gathered the three balls and placed them into a black, mesh bag. I then put three used game balls in a blue, mesh bag. And finally, I put four practice balls in a red, mesh bag. One might assume that my next question would be, "Now how many balls did I have altogether?" I'll admit that it might sound a little odd, my system of ball maintenance, but it really was simpler than trying to keep track of every ball all of the time. Regardless of whether we were at our pre-game walk-through in Giants Stadium, warming up before the game at Mount Ida College, or actually playing the game itself, I didn't have to tote all of the balls everywhere we went, only the color-coded bag of footballs that we needed.

*

After just four hours of sleep, I awoke on Friday morning at 5:15 a.m. I kissed my wife goodbye, covered our boys as they lay in their beds, and packed a cooler of food and drinks for the long day's journey ahead. I was out the door at 5:45 a.m. and on the campus of Gallaudet in plenty of time for our scheduled 7:00 a.m. departure. But, of course, Ed and Ryan had long since arrived, the early birds that they were. They stood on the walkway outside of the field house and directed foot traffic while players, trainers, and student managers loaded the buses parked along the curb. With the cloudy weather, it didn't seem much like a new day, but rather the remnants of the night before, especially on the faces of the players. They looked like zombies. Mostly a team of night owls, it probably seemed like the middle of the night for many of them.

I grabbed the footballs, along with some other equipment that Kris asked me to help him with, and stowed it all in the storage compartment under the offensive team bus. All, but the black, mesh bag, that is. The game balls stayed on board with me, always.

I didn't want there to be any chance that they would somehow go missing by the time we arrived in Massachusetts or become damaged along the way. And so they travelled in the overhead bin above my second row seat. I boarded the bus, sitting across the aisle from Brian again, and took a personal inventory of myself and my belongings. I nodded over toward him that I was ready to go. Brian smiled and nodded back. The players were onboard and ready to go, as well. The equipment managers, with all of the teams gear, were onboard and ready to go, as were the trainers and all of their equipment. It was seven o'clock and time to depart.

But, Ed and Ryan remained on the sidewalk outside, talking to one another between the chattering diesel engines of the buses. Ed was clearly agitated and after a few more minutes, he beckoned for Chris Burke and Brian to join them. Adam Brimmer, one of our few remaining offensive linemen, was missing. The senior lineman from Indianapolis wasn't in his room when Ed and Ryan had gone door to door to get the players up; he still hadn't arrived.

Justin Lathus, his long, curly hair still a tangled mess from his morning shower, stepped off of the bus to talk with Ed. Justin explained to them that Adam had gone out drinking that night in College Park, near the University of Maryland. When he'd returned to campus, he went to the dorm room of his quasi-girlfriend and found her with another guy. To make matters worse, that guy was a player from the football team. I never learned who that player was, but from what I understood, it was someone sitting on the defensive bus. Adam was angry, of course, and he left the building without returning. No one had seen him since.

With that, Mount Edward blew. He quickly dispatched Ryan, Chris, and Brian to find Adam. Now, I'm sure that Harold would have been useful in the search as well, but he, too, was AWOL. Chris grabbed the keys to the Gator and sped off toward the dormitories with Ryan and Brian in tow. Meanwhile, Ed paced back and forth alongside our bus, getting angrier and angrier with each passing minute. Watching Ed, I wasn't quite sure that finding

Adam was going to be a good idea for any of the parties involved. When they returned without the big kid there was no big blow up, no spectacle, and no fisticuffs. There was only the look of angry resignation from Ed as he nodded for the other coaches to board their buses. We left the campus of Gallaudet at 8:00 a.m. without Adam Brimmer, and without Big Harold.

The setback in our departure time put us in the middle of Washington's rush hour traffic, which is one of the worst in the country. Falling further and further behind schedule, we finally cleared the District and headed north on Interstate 295, through the suburbs of Maryland toward Baltimore. Once in Baltimore, we would pick up Interstate 95 for most of the remainder of the trip. Unfortunately, we didn't quite make it to Baltimore before the second bus, the one in which Ed was riding, blew an oil seal and was unable to continue the journey. Again with maintenance issues, both buses pulled over along the median strip between the dual lanes of The Baltimore-Washington Parkway. After several minutes of deliberation, the decision was made, between Ed and the bus company manager, to continue on the trip with just the one bus, and have another bus dispatched to meet us at Giants Stadium later that afternoon.

The next dilemma to be faced was the transfer of players and equipment from one bus to another. The bus was able to accommodate all of our players and coaches, but not all of the gear and equipment. And so Jon and Kris decided that it would be best if they and their assistants remained with the disabled bus. Once the replacement bus arrived, they could transfer all of their equipment and be on their way toward New York. Did we have the footballs? Yes, we did. Did we have the bass drum? Yes, we did. And so we were finally good to go. As we pulled away and merged into traffic, Ed's cell phone rang.

"Coach Hottle," he answered. "What? Yep, yep, go ahead. All right, thanks, Jon."

Ed looked over at Ryan, who was seated in front of me, and

told him that Allison, Jon's assistant trainer back at the school, had called Jon. She said there was a football player in her office looking for the football team. The player was Adam Brimmer. Jon called to ask Ed if he wanted Allison to drive Adam to the disabled bus. Adam could then rejoin the team in New York. Ed signed off on the plan, although I'm sure he did so with reluctance. It was another example of Ed having a bit more bark than bite. But it made sense. Ed needed Adam to play more than he needed the opportunity to make an example of him.

"Dumb ass," was Ed's only comment as he reclined into his front row seat.

Although crowded, our bus ride was pretty quiet from that point forward as most of the guys either caught up on some reading or napped. I partook in a little of both. About three and a half hours later, though, the bus began to come to life as a few of the guys caught a glimpse of Giants Stadium in the distance up ahead. Of course, their excitement intensified with every mile that we drew nearer to The Meadowlands Sports Complex in East Rutherford, New Jersey. I must admit, I was a little excited myself. I'd visited several professional stadiums in the past, but walking on the game field at Giants Stadium would be checking a new box for me, too.

We arrived at the stadium shortly after one o'clock, and stadium personnel marshaled us to a parking location just outside of the facility's main service entrance. As our bus maneuvered into position, we could see through the over-sized portal and onto the playing surface inside the stadium. The bright, yellow goal posts contrasted sharply with the green grass and canyon-like walls of dark blue seats that rose high above the playing surface. Just the weekend before, the New York Giants had begun their unlikely run into the playoffs by defeating the San Francisco 49er's on that same field. The Giants went on to win The Super Bowl later that winter.

Although the end zones that day were still painted Giant blue, the stadium was also home to a second NFL team, the New York

Jets. There were large, green and white NY JETS murals on the walls throughout the stadium's service area below, the largest of which was on a high, concrete wall leading from the service area to the field. This was where one would normally see the players gather as they prepared to enter the arena upon pre-game introductions. On game day, these service areas and walkways would be crowded with media personnel, sports announcers and television broadcast equipment, players, trainers, coaches, and cheerleaders, as well as concession suppliers and security crews. It was normally a very busy place, but not during our visit. It was just us and a few dozen maintenance type folks, amused by the silent disposition of our own football team.

Besides the green and white murals, there were also several NY GIANTS logos around the stadium, but it largely seemed like there were more JETS logos than GIANTS. Maybe that was because the Giants got to have their name on the front of the stadium, I don't know. Plus, all of the stadium seating was Giant blue. Maybe it was because the Jets were in the midst of a pretty miserable season and would win just four games all year long. In fact, that weekend the Jets would lose to the Buffalo Bills and score a measly three points. Whatever the reason, it was hard to not consider the contrast between the two teams and their destinies. Would the path before us resemble that of the Giants, or that of the Jets? That remained to be seen, although while on the field that afternoon, we all felt like giants.

Most of the players quickly donned their cleats and eagerly took to the field for the short practice session. A few remained behind to assist Chris and Brian with getting the bass drum to the sidelines before joining their teammates. Ed wasn't in a hurry to get practice rolling, though, and gave the boys plenty of time to satisfy their curiosity and take pictures of one another with their cell phone cameras. It was an exciting moment for them, though some just stood in awe as they stared up and around the stadium.

Giants Stadium was pretty antiquated by today's standards,

but it was still a professional arena. It's steep, sharply inclined decks and rows of seating gave one a sense of what it must have been like for the gladiators in the Roman Coliseum. It might also be difficult for someone struggling with claustrophobia as well, since those towering walls of seats and promotional signage were within just a few dozen yards of you, no matter where you stood on the field.

After a short while had passed, Ed sent Brian to midfield to begin pounding on the bass drum, a signal to the team that it was time for them to assemble for Flex and prepare for practice. And as they did, Brian, on the field of his beloved Giants, began to beat on that drum like I don't remember seeing anybody beat on it all year long. He was a pretty big guy, too, so he put that drum skin to the test. And boy did the drum bellow out that day. The empty seating and concrete walls magnified the drum beat by what seemed like seven fold. And if you couldn't hear the drum, you could definitely feel its percussion.

Deaf or not, the sound of the drum captured the attention of everyone in the stadium, and within a few short minutes had attracted dozens of curious stadium employees. They gathered in small groups in portals, walkways, club levels, and end zones to catch a glimpse of us as we practiced. I guess they were all curious to see a deaf football team and to witness the pounding of the famed Gallaudet bass drum. Practicing in an NFL stadium was the closest that any of our players would ever get to being part of "The Big Show." I don't know how many of them actually appreciated him for it, but Ed had given those boys a wonderful experience.

We practiced for about an hour or so and then returned to our bus. By that time, the second bus had arrived, and with it Adam Brimmer. A caterer had assembled several large tables a few dozen yards from the buses and brought submarine sandwiches, chips, cookies, and drinks for the team. And while we partook of the meal, Ed met with Adam on the other side of the two buses. Knowing Adam, he'd either already eaten or had stashed away some of the prepared food for the continuation of the trip. He wasn't one to miss a meal.

We departed Giants Stadium at three o'clock, still well behind schedule, and were immediately engulfed by rush hour traffic again, this time outside of New York City. The team was a lot more comfortable, though, now that we had the second bus. But the DVD player on our bus was inoperable, which meant more reading and more napping. I called my office a few times to check on how operations were going there, praying that our Coach & Courier vehicles were faring better than our team's buses. I also continued to work on my signing by engaging in conversations with some of the guys about their homes, families, and aspirations. And every half hour or so, I'd text my daughter, Valerie, to keep her informed of our progress. Her plan was to arrive at our hotel at approximately the same time as we did, perhaps a little before in order to find a restaurant for us.

Unfortunately, upon reaching the state line between Connecticut and Massachusetts, the turbine on the replacement bus failed.

"Good grief," I said to Ryan. "How did this bus company manage to stay in business?"

As a result, the bus could only maintain speeds of forty miles per hour for the remainder of the trip. Unable to nap or read any longer, I sat and watched our bus driver rock back and forth in his seat as we crawled along the highway, regardless of whether or not the Friday night traffic dictated such. All the while, he spoke silently to himself, his lips moving rapidly as he did. He was probably praying, worried that the other bus might not hold on too much longer. Either way, it had been a long day for the old fellow. The nine hour journey had become one of nearly fourteen hours. We finally arrived at our hotel in Natick, Massachusetts at 9:45 p.m., just a little more than fifteen hours before game time.

The hotel was very accommodating and had set up a buffet dinner for our team, even though they normally would have already closed their dining room for the night. Rather than send the boys to their respective rooms right away, Ed and Ryan held onto all of the room keys until after dinner. This way we were sure to have one hundred percent attendance for the meal and subsequent team meeting. We piled up our gear in the foyer across from the concierge before heading to the dining room.

Valerie met me inside the hotel lobby and had brought her girlfriend, Devin, along with her for the ride. That was fine by me since that meant she'd have someone to share the drive home with late at night. I thought that she might have brought her new boyfriend with her, but that didn't happen. Perhaps she was worried that I might be a little intimidating to him. At six foot four inches tall and about two hundred forty pounds, I guess I could be a little intimidating to a boyfriend, even though I was just a big old teddy bear. Okay, maybe I wasn't the teddy bear type, but I wasn't exactly a grizzly bear either. Honestly, I was more like a Yogi Bear, to tell you the truth.

Instead of going out to find a restaurant at such a late hour, Valerie and Devin joined the team for dinner at the hotel, sitting with me and Ed at our table. Of course, flanked by two very attractive young ladies, I was a very popular coach among the players that evening. And Ed, to my surprise, was extremely cordial, considerate, and downright hospitable. I was impressed by Ed's alter ego, to say the least.

My daughter and I'd grown somewhat estranged over the last few years as the result of a conflict between her and my wife, Mary-Ellen. Valerie's mother and I divorced when she was just three years old and, determined not to be an absentee father, I made a conscious effort to be very involved in her life. Mary-Ellen and I usually planned our weekends and vacations around Valerie's visits, and we'd even travel an hour to see her school concerts and sporting events. She and Valerie seemed to have a fairly healthy relationship. But, once Valerie became a teenager and moved in with us full-time, the relationship between her and her stepmother quickly became adversarial. Still unable to come to terms with my second wife, even several years later, Valerie was now satisfied with just an occasional call or text to her father and her two half-brothers. She wouldn't even "friend me" on Facebook. But our visit that night, was mostly warm and friendly, which made me feel like her dad again.

"So, is everything going well?" I asked her as we ate. "You look great."

"Thanks, yeah, everything is fine," she assured me.

"Planning on coming back home any time soon, maybe at Christmas?"

"Probably, but I'll be staying with Mom, though. And I won't be staying long, so I doubt that I'll be able to get over to your house."

"Does that mean you won't be coming over to the house for Christmas Eve?" I ventured to ask. You see, my daughter had a tendency to get angry with me quite easily and I didn't want to 'stir the pot' any more than necessary. But I knew that my wife and our boys would later ask me if she was coming to dinner or not, so I just had to put it out there. Otherwise, I'd get into trouble back home *for not* asking such things.

"Dad, I don't enjoy coming to your house, you know that," she huffed.

And so I backed off and instead asked the two girls if they wanted dessert or something more to drink. After dinner we retreated to the sitting area outside of the hotel lounge and spoke about her job, her horses, and her apartment. The subject of her boyfriend never arose and so I again, I ventured forward to bring about another sensitive issue. But, you know, isn't that kind of what a father is supposed to?

"How's your boyfriend doing?" I asked, watching as her friend, Devin, smiled nervously and rolled her eyes. She sunk further into the wing backed chair next to our couch.

"I'd rather not talk about it, Dad," she said, "I'm sure you already know everything."

"How would I know everything, Val?" I shrugged my shoulders and smiled nervously.

"Grammy?" She said, smugly, referring to my wife's mother. My mother-in-law, who lived on Long Island, had oddly enough become my daughter's confidant.

"Uh," I hesitated. "Yeah, we talk. She talks more with Mary-Ellen than she does with me, of course. But I don't think she's said much about him."

"Oh, yeah, I'm sure," she said sarcastically.

"Really, Val," I shook my head, "she hasn't. Those are the types of things you find out on someone's Facebook page."

Valerie shook her and sat back into the couch next to me. I didn't press the issue any further, instead redirecting the conversation into generalities that would incorporate Devin, to diffuse the tension. She asked her friend to take photograph of the two of us, and it turned out to be a really photograph. Although not very photogenic, I looked pretty good in the picture, even after the long day of travel. And, of course, she looked spectacular. Valerie was a very pretty, young woman.

The two of them hung around until midnight and by then it was time for her to hit the road back to Rhode Island. I'd hoped that she would be able to attend the game against Mount Ida the next day. So, too, did about fifty-three football players. But, she insisted that she had to work the following afternoon, and the ride home was a bit long. And so after a hug I gave her a kiss on the cheek.

"Hey, remember that I love you," I told her.

"I will. I love you, too, Dad," she smiled.

And with that they were on their way back to Rhode Island.

After talking with several of my players, who were naturally interested in knowing more about my daughter, I learned that quite a few of them had experienced similar relationships with their parents. Some of the boys, as small children, had been enrolled by their parents at schools like MSSD, the Model Secondary School for the Deaf co-located on the campus with Gallaudet University. And since those schools were often boarding schools, the child may see his or her parents only a few times per year, making it very difficult to establish a normal parent-child relationship.

I also found out that a lot of the boys on the team had a parent who was deaf and a parent who wasn't. That, too, could really make things particularly difficult on a domestic relationship. You see, among those types of families, the divorce rate in the United States is nearly 90%! And almost nearly as high is the divorce rate among hearing couples who have a deaf child in the household. That rate exceeds 80%. This was in sharp contrast to the national average of just over 50%, which is also the divorce rate among marriages where both spouses are deaf. And so it made sense that they would understand how my relationship with Valerie had become distant. Several of the players, including both Fletch and Jimmy, encouraged me to "keep trying" with Valerie. I knew that my two quarterbacks were sincere, but the other guys, well, I think that they were just hoping to get some contact information out of me.

*

Newton, Massachusetts was a historic town of old homes and cobbled streets dating back to more than one hundred years before the Revolutionary War. The colorful fall foliage helped to portray the town as one from a Norman Rockwell print. About a twenty minute drive to the west of Boston, Newton was exactly what one might imagine a New England town to be, except for one small detail. I don't know why, but I guess no one had ever told me that turkeys ran wild in Massachusetts. At first I thought I was seeing things, and I was amused at the sight of a turkey running through someone's yard. But then, as we drove through the town toward the campus of Mount Ida, I realized that there wasn't just one turkey running through someone's yard, but dozens, maybe hundreds of turkeys running about the town and through the yards, parks, and other open areas. They weren't as plentiful as pigeons, like on the streets of downtown New York City, but there were lots of turkeys, wild turkeys.

Mount Ida College was yet another small, but scenic campus. The private school wasn't nearly as old as the town, but it dated back to the year 1899. Enrollment at Mount Ida was comparable to that of Gallaudet, about 1,500 students, but the campus sprawled out across almost one hundred acres of rolling hills and clusters of large trees. Of those 1,500 students, about 900 lived on campus. And of those 900 students, about one out of every nine was a Mustang football player. And so obviously, the campus was somewhat consumed by football.

Currently, the football field at Mount Ida College has a state-of-the-art sports turf surface, lighting, and ample sections of stadium seating for spectators and fans of the boys wearing forest green uniforms. But, back in 2007, they played their games on an old, grass field surrounded by trees, shrubbery, and a few long sections of wooden bleachers behind the home team bench. On the opposite side of the field, and behind the visiting team's bench, was a much smaller section of bleachers. About a hundred yards behind the visiting team's bleachers, and beyond a patch of tall trees, was an old gymnasium, which would serve as our locker room that day.

We arrived at Mount Ida at ten o'clock the next morning and, after disembarking the two buses, Ed let the team mill about for about thirty minutes. Following the break, we assembled all of the players, training equipment, and gear inside the old, open air gymnasium. There were no lockers or benches in the relic of a building, so the boys just found a spot on the floor of the basketball court, mostly along the walls, and dropped their bags. Some of the guys sat on the floor and dressed, while others stood.

After Jon and a few of us assistant coaches finished taping the ankles and wrists of the players who needed to be taped, Ed brought the team together and delivered his standard pre-game speech about playing with intensity, heart, and desire. He stressed that he wanted them to be remembered for how they played the game on the field, and not necessarily the outcome on the scoreboard.

Afterward, he directed me to get the quarterbacks out onto the field to warm up. As we left the gym, though, the heavily overcast skies began to pour forth a steady rain. And when it didn't let up, we decided to warm up Fletch and Jimmy right there in the gym, on the floor of the basketball court. It worked out okay for us, though. By the time that we'd completed our warm-up drills, the rain storm passed, and the team began its walk to the playing field. By then, the skies had returned to just a gloomy, but not quite as dark, cloudiness.

The game got underway right on time at one o'clock. Despite the weather, there were several hundred Mustang fans lined up along the end zones and throughout the bleachers across the field from us. There was no actual stadium structure, so the football field was just that, a grass field with white lines and a set of goal posts at each end. Not far beyond the end zones was a parking lot on one end and tennis courts at the other. Behind us sat sixty or seventy Gallaudet fans and supporters in the one small section of bleachers. Included among those folks were three young women from Boston who had come to see some of our players play. The three former co-eds had attended Gallaudet University a few semesters ago as part of the school's translator training program. While at the campus they had come to know many of the boys on the football team and continued to stay in touch with them.

Out on the field of play, our boys were faring pretty well and giving the Mustangs a real run for their money. Although the team from Mount Ida was impressive at first glance, it was mostly because of their physical size. They were much bigger than we were, especially across their offensive line. But, I didn't think that they played with all that much skill or aggressiveness. Maybe they'd underestimated us, or maybe it was our own aggressive style that was playing out in our favor, but like I said, we were giving the "Ponies" a run for their money. I say that because Fletch was the only true mustang on the field, at least during the first half. He was on fire. Fletch was executing the read option to perfection, ripping off several long runs, including a sixty-nine yard run for a touchdown.

Our defense was giving Mount Ida all it could handle as well, especially our defensive end, Josh Ofiu. Despite their size advantage on the line, the offensive tackles from Mount Ida simply didn't have quick enough feet to counter Josh's speed and strength. He was a constant disruption in their backfield. But late in the second quarter, Josh made a big mistake. With the score still tied at seven points apiece, Mount Ida was punting on fourth and long from midfield. Josh, rushing from the right side of the line broke through protection and drove himself quickly toward the punter. He went all out. He left nothing to chance. It was either going to be a blocked punt and a destroyed punter, or he was going to miss the ball and just destroy the punter, which, of course, would result in a fifteen yard penalty against us. Unfortunately, Josh missed the ball and the result of the play was the latter. Mount Ida retained possession of the football and scored a touchdown later in the drive to take a seven point lead just before the half.

On the way in to our makeshift locker room for the half-time break, one of our volunteer team managers, Matt, nervously approached Brian. Matt wasn't a big guy, neither tall nor thick, with dark hair and pale complexion. I didn't know him all that well, since he'd only worked with the team recently, but he seemed like a nice kid. He'd been filming the game for us from atop the home team's bleacher section. Matt looked fearful, though, as he tapped Brian upon his shoulder. He held out in both of his hands something that resembled electronic parts.

"What the..?" exclaimed Brian, looking bemused.

It was the team camera, or what was left of it. Ryan walked by and stopped to examine the debris himself, taking the pieces from Matt to look more closely at them.

"What happened?" asked Brian.

Matt explained that he'd stumbled along a section of railing while filming the game and accidentally kicked the tripod. The tripod collapsed and over the edge went the camera, smashing as it landed on the concrete pavement below. He was scared to death that he was in big trouble, although it was actually Brian who would end up taking the fall.

"Oh, God," said Brian.

Brian was somewhat in charge, if not by de facto, of the managers filming the game, the equipment, and the post-game editing of the film. Ryan then handed the pieces of camera back to Matt and reached into a cooler on the ground next to the entrance to the old gym. He pulled out a can of soda and looked innocently at Brian.

"Good luck telling Ed about that," he said as he popped open the can and walked inside.

As you might expect, it wasn't a pleasant scene when Brian showed the camera to Ed. He screamed at Brian for several minutes outside of the locker room, so loudly that everyone within a city block could hear him. Ed was so angry that he didn't say a single word to Brian for the remainder of the trip. The ride home that night was probably eight of the longest hours in Brian's young life, as he and Ed both rode in the same bus all the way back to Washington, D.C.

Matt used the team's portable camera to finish filming the game, although he missed a good portion of the third quarter. Of course, he was just terrified to be anywhere near Ed, and cowered at the sight of Brian. I assured him that things would work out, and that he had to put the incident behind him so that he could do a good job of filming the second half.

Because of the camera incident, Ed had little time to address the team before the end of the intermission. He managed, though, to reiterate the importance of putting forth a solid effort and making good decisions. And when the game resumed it appeared that the boys would do just that. After receiving the second half kick off from Mount Ida, our first drive began with promise as we moved the ball downfield pretty quickly. Unfortunately, the drive ended abruptly when Fletch decided *not to run* for a first down, but to pass the ball instead. Running to his right, he attempted to pass the ball by throwing it across his body, causing it to "float" in the air toward JC, who was about ten yards downfield. JC had broken away from his defender and was in the open, but without any zip on the ball, the inside linebacker was able to recover and intercept the pass. It was a great effort by Fletch, but not a good decision.

Mid-way through the third quarter, Mount Ida's advantage in size began to wear down our defensive players. Early in the game, with fresh legs, our defensive linemen and linebackers were able to get around their big boys, avoid their hands, and spin freely into the backfield. But that energy wasn't there after the first series of the second half, not with a depleted corps of linemen. The offensive linemen from Mount Ida were now able to get their big paws on our guys and control them. After that we were just no match for them, not even Josh.

And if even if they had been able to get past them, their quarterback was no little guy either. He was a big, strong, black kid who reminded me of the former quarterback of the Minnesota Vikings, Daunte Culpepper. He wasn't nearly as skilled as Culpepper, but with his size and athleticism he proved to be awfully tough for our guys to tackle, especially in the later part of the contest. Although he passed for 178 yards and two scores, it was his size and legs that proved to be the demise of our defense. We just couldn't seem to get that guy to the ground, even after flushing him from the pocket. He seemed to always break free of a tackle to gain positive yardage after what appeared to be a sack or a tackle for a loss.

Late in the quarter, Mount Ida marched down the field, still leading on the scoreboard by a seven point margin. Taking advantage of their strength inside, they began to pound the ball between the tackles, driving down to our thirty yard line. On a first down run play, Josh Ofiu, engaged with the Mount Ida offensive tackle, attempted to reach out and grab the ball carrier with one hand. Unable to make the tackle, and off-balance, Josh was driven into the ground by the offensive lineman. He sprang to his feet, but was grimacing in pain as his right arm dangled by his side. He managed to stagger to our sideline before falling into a heap just outside of the boundary, and at my feet. The referee blew the whistle to halt play due to the injury.

"Game over!" I could hear Josh saying in his high-pitched, squeaky voice. "Game over!"

I summoned Jon and he was quickly at Josh's side. At first, it appeared to me that Josh had suffered an arm or shoulder injury because of how he held himself, but that wasn't the case. Josh was a really tough kid and could withstand the pain long enough to focus on reading Jon's lips as he asked him questions regarding his injury. His ability to mouth his responses verbally was a big plus as well, since he clearly wasn't going to be able to sign effectively with just one hand and in a great deal of discomfort. This enabled Jon to quickly determine that the nature of the injury was actually neck related. Not wanting to take any chances with the complexity of a neck injury, Jon called for the paramedics and had Josh transported by ambulance to nearby Newton Wellesley Hospital. Jon accompanied him so that he could help translate between Josh and the medical staff at the hospital.

The injury turned out to be what's called "a stinger," basically a pinched nerve along the neck and shoulder area, and something that Josh had never experienced before. A stinger is a very painful injury that temporarily renders one almost paralyzed. Albeit it for only a short period of time, it can seem like an eternity to an injured player. If you've never experienced a stinger before, it can also be really scary. And it scared Josh a good deal. Like he said when he collapsed to the ground, it was 'game over' for him.

Following the delay, the Mount Ida offense continued to take advantage of its size and power, running the football effectively and using play action passes for solid gains. Several plays after Josh's injury, the Mustangs scored to extend their lead to 21 -7, which was the score of the game at the conclusion of the third quarter. Did we have anything left in the tank or had all of our hopes just left the field with sirens ablaze? The final period of play would show us what our players were made of and Ed challenged them to not give up, but rather to play hard and fight through the physical challenges ahead. And play hard they did.

The fourth quarter was virtually a draw, a battle of field position where the two teams struggled for every inch of yardage gained. It was like watching two boxers exchange body blows in the late rounds of a prize fight. And when it was over, our boys had gone toe-to-toe with the mighty Mustangs of Mount Ida, having given it everything they had. Although the story on the scoreboard said one thing, the feeling in their hearts said another: they had played like giants!

MOUNT IDA 28 GALLAUDET 14

While the scoreboard favored Mount Ida, the stat sheet was virtually a tie. Mount Ida rushed for 261 yards and passed for 178. Gallaudet had rushed for 242 yards and passed for 174. The difference was in the turnover column, where we'd struggled with the growing pains of a new quarterback: three costly interceptions, each of which brought potential scoring drives to an end. The mistakes, though, were not the result of poor effort, but rather a few bad decisions that the Mount Ida defensive players simply took advantage of. Fletch had nothing to hang his head over, nor did the team.

NFL coaching great Vince Lombardi once said, "The measure of who we are is what we do with what we have." In his own way, that was the message that Ed had for the team in the locker room following the game. It was a positive talk, well received by the team. Unfortunately, sophomore wide receiver, Cole Johnson, couldn't enjoy the satisfaction of the team's physical effort on the field. Instead, he sat motionless with his back arched and his head against the wall. He was in obvious pain, physical pain, grabbing for his neck and unwilling to sign to Ed what was bothering him. Cole, like Josh, had suffered some type of head or neck injury, and so we again called 911 for the paramedics. Ed contacted Jon by phone and told him that he was sending Cole to the same hospital Josh had been taken to. He asked Jon to meet Cole in the emergency room. Ryan and Ron Luczak rented a car and left the team to meet the trio at the hospital after the game. When the players were released from medical care a few hours later, they drove the entire crew back home to Washington.

Oddly enough, Cole Johnson's injury was also a stinger, just not as severe as the one sustained by Josh. Apparently, Cole's helmet had been struck by the knee of a defensive back while he was cut blocking late in the game. He was fortunate not to have suffered a concussion as well.

Meanwhile, during the game the bus drivers had called for roadside service to repair their bus in the gymnasium parking lot. The turbine was replaced in the disabled vehicle and we were good to go. And so after eating pizza that had been delivered to the old gym building, we left Mount Ida, just a few minutes past five o'clock. Even though the ride home wasn't nearly as long as the trip up, we still didn't arrive back at Gallaudet until just before 2:00 a.m. It had been yet another very long day.

18

You're Either in or You're Out

"I'd say maybe ten percent of the team will quit this week," Ed said to Ryan in the semi-darkness of room G40 on Sunday afternoon following the Mount Ida game. "No way, ten percent?" asked Ryan.

"Ten percent," Ed said with confidence.

"Not this year, Coach," said Brian. "I don't think so. Things are different."

"Ten percent," Ed said once more.

"Why?" asked Ryan.

"It's just the way these kids are. There's no brass ring to reach for anymore, no playoffs, and no winning record. The luster's worn off for them," Ed explained. "I don't know what to tell you, Hite. It's just their nature."

"That's crazy," Ryan said, shaking his head and sitting back into his seat. "How about playing for a little pride?" Ryan was a competitive a young man and he just couldn't imagine our players not relishing the opportunity to play two more college football games.

Most college athletes appreciate every game that they are able to play, knowing their playing days are numbered due to their limited eligibility to compete. And so when seniors get down to their last few games, they hope to play as well as they possibly can, and may even play if injured. That's because an athlete's last few games can define his or her career. And of course there's the difficulty of dealing with the finality of one's last game. That's always tough for an athlete to cope with or handle emotionally. I saw it at the high school level every year. On the night of a senior's last game, it finally hits him that he'll never play college football, and that after all of the years of little league ball and high school practices, the final game was just that, final. I can remember a good many boys breaking down in tears both before and after the last game of their senior season.

The football players at Gallaudet, though, had never really known such parameters. They had always played club ball and could pretty much do so for as long as they had the desire to play. There were no such eligibility requirements limiting the number of seasons they could participate. Chris Burke had played for more than a half-dozen years and JC was already in his mid-twenties and still playing. There had even been some players in their thirties. For them there had always been a "next year," and always another chance to play.

Things would change for them from this point forward, however, since the team was now a member of a NCAA Conference and having to comply with the regulations thereof. But for now, Ed was concerned that, for the boys, it was all about moving on to their next interest, and that maybe things would go better next year. Not all of them, of course, but for many of them. I hoped he was wrong, but Ed was a pretty savvy guy, and he was usually right.

As far as watching the game film, well, it was the same old story. We felt that we could have won the game. Notice that I didn't say that we should have won the game, but that we could have won the game. The most frustrating thing for us was that our team's level of physical talent and lack of size had little to do with us losing the game. Again, what did us in were the numerous missed opportunities. Watching the film, I recognized a similar pattern of mistakes made by our team in the Mount Ida game that I'd seen in several other game films. The mistakes being made were not made routinely, but mostly at critical moments in the game. During key plays, players would miss an assignment, line up incorrectly, or use particularly poor technique. I didn't want to attribute the deficits to their lack of experience or maturity, because I was sure that wasn't the issue. It appeared to me, though, that in certain situations, some players just abandoned most of what they'd been coached to do.

I'm sure that Ed had long ago discovered the pattern himself and identified the problem. But for me, it was as if a light switch had just flipped on. I didn't bring my observation up for discussion because, quite frankly, I was a little embarrassed that I hadn't picked up on it long before then. After all, my quarterback had been one of the main culprits. But, I'd focused more on our quarterbacks' physical approach to the game rather than their mental approach. After all, Ed had made it clear to me that I wasn't to mess around with JC's head because JC was a mature athlete. But that wasn't the case with Fletch and Jimmy; I was free to coach them however I pleased. In doing so, however, I hadn't made a habit of focusing on other player positions while watching game film; I'd mostly zeroed in on the quarterbacks and receivers.

So what was the problem and how could we fix it? I understood that these boys had faced varying degrees of learning adversity throughout their young lives, even well into their secondary education, but they weren't un-trainable. And it wasn't a matter of attitude or effort, either. And so I brought the matter to the attention of some of the players during conditioning that afternoon. After doing so, I came to the conclusion that what appeared to be a lack of discipline was actually a matter of trust. They didn't trust our coaching. Not that they didn't trust us as coaches, because they did. But they didn't fully trust what we were coaching them to do. It wasn't so much my quarterbacks either, because I think that Jimmy and Fletch had learned to trust my coaching from the very beginning, or so it seemed. There were some issues with Fletch, but for the most part I think Fletch accepted my coaching very well. But for many players on the team it was a different story.

The learning process can be different for a lot of people, but for most of us it is often with the guidance of a teacher or mentor; someone to talk us through a problem or procedure. These kids had experienced a similar process, but with quite a rougher go of it. Their deafness created a very difficult learning environment. For example, it was much more difficult for a deaf student to take notes in the classroom; they could not watch an instructor and write at the same time. Or when learning to do something with their hands, they could not work and listen to instruction at the same time; they had to physically look up at an instructor. As a result of that inconvenience, the learning process could quickly become one of trial and error in many cases, especially with an impatient student. If they could solve a problem or figure out a solution without having to look up then the process was much more rewarding.

And so as a result, the student who successfully learned by his own devices developed a strong sense of confidence and independence. They would also have a tendency to trust more in their own judgment and rationale than that of others. This was especially so in adverse conditions or critical moments, both of which present themselves throughout the course of a football game. Their incredible independence was a product of their learning experiences, but also a detriment to their development as football players. Players need to be coachable.

What I had been seeing in the game films were football players, faced with the physical challenge of an opponent during a critical moment, not doing what they'd been coached to do, technique-wise or strategically. Instead, they were resorting to their own devices and judgment as a means of overcoming such challenges. And they weren't having much success as a result. It was clearly a matter of not respecting, or trusting, a coach's experience and instruction, as it related to the accomplishment of that player's task or responsibilities. Coaching a deaf football player presented a unique set of challenges, but the most important challenge was developing a solid player/coach relationship. It didn't matter if the coach himself could hear or not.

At our staff meeting on Monday, we learned that Harold was struggling with the loss of a friend who had died of meningitis the week before. Like Harold, the young woman was a teacher at MSSD and they were apparently pretty close friends. That explained why he hadn't made the trip to Massachusetts, but I imagined that Ed would have at least liked the courtesy of a text from Harold. Regardless, Ed didn't seem too upset that Harold had missed the trip and wasn't at practice on Monday, either. Personally, I liked Harold, but I was beginning to see that Ed valued Harold's physical presence as a coach much more so than his coaching talent. My guess was that Harold had never established himself as someone that Ed felt he could count on. But, Harold was deaf, and it was important to Ed that he had at least a few deaf coaches on the staff, coaches to whom the players could relate.

Earlier in the day, Ed called Brian into his office and instructed him to go get Matt from his dormitory room. The two returned to Ed's office a short time later, expecting maybe at least forty lashes apiece over the incident with the camera. But instead, Ed assured them both that all was forgiven and that things like that just happened sometimes. He apologized for being so angry before and told them both not to worry about it anymore.

On Tuesday, practice began with an "I told you so" from Ed as he spoke to Ryan outside of the football office in the field house. He told him that Ben Taylor and Justin Grigsby had quit the team, probably dissatisfied with their minimal playing time. Ben, a sophomore, was an undersized, defensive lineman from Indianapolis and Justin, a junior, was a defensive back from Phoenix. Neither had garnered much playing time to this point in the season, if any at all, and I guess they didn't figure on getting playing time against either SUNY Maritime or Juniata. As Ed had said, maybe they had better things to do with their time.

Losing those two players would probably have little effect on the competiveness of the team's defense, but losing our center, Justin Lathus, would definitely have a negative impact on the offense. And for a little while at practice that day, I thought that just might happen.

During the team segment of practice, Justin was having difficulty with his shot gun snaps. He was off target with some of his snaps, and on a few others he actually rolled the ball back to Fletch. At one point, Justin stood up and tossed the ball to Ryan, asking him for a new football.

"That ball is bad," signed a frustrated Justin.

"No," Ryan signed and spoke loudly as he tossed the football back to Justin at the line of scrimmage. Justin caught the ball at his waist, but didn't return to his stance. Instead, he flipped the ball back to Ryan.

"Give me a new ball," signed Justin. "That one is bad. I can't grip it."

"No," repeated Ryan, "the quarterbacks aren't having any problems with it. I want you to use this ball."

"I want a new ball," Justin forcefully signed again. "Give me a new ball."

"No. You're not getting a new ball. Use this one or I'll find a new center," Ryan signed, getting angrier by the moment. He tossed the ball back at Justin, but Justin just let it bounce off of his thigh and onto the ground.

"Fugg you," Justin mouthed aloud in his soft, but high pitched voice as he walked off the field. "Fugg you!"

"Bauman!" called out Ryan as he turned and signed toward where the sideline. "Bauman, let's go. Get under center," he signed. And out jogged little Richard Bauman, a 5'6" freshman from Hollywood, Florida. Good luck, kid, I thought to myself.

Did this make three students quitting in one day? I thought.

That would be six percent.

I watched from the sideline with my arms crossed as Justin went to the trainer's table. He grabbed a cup of Gatorade and then joined several other players, who were lined up to my right, watching the practice. They looked over at him but Justin didn't acknowledge them. He simply stared out onto the field, sipping Gatorade from the cup. Jimmy and I'd been watching the practice, reviewing the quarterback's responsibility on each play. I asked Jimmy to give me a moment and after doing so, I leaned forward to look down the line of players to my right. Justin was standing about a dozen players away with his helmet off, staring angrily out onto the field. He glanced over at me and I nodded for him to come over to where I stood. He did.

"What's up?" I signed.

"I needed a new ball and Hite--" he started to sign, but I stopped him, raising both of my palms toward him.

"I know what happened out there," I signed. "I saw it. But, what's wrong?"

I looked him in the eye. He grimaced and tilted his head. I glanced back out onto the field as the shot gun snap from Bauman sailed over Fletch's head. Jimmy, standing on my left, shook his head. I turned toward Justin and tapped on his shoulder pads.

"Does that look good to you out there?" I asked. Remember, I had a limited vocabulary when it came to signing. Justin looked out onto the field. The next snap from Baumann rolled to the right of Fletch. "Isn't that your offense?"

"What?" signed Justin.

"Isn't that your offense out there?" I asked again. "You're the captain of the offense aren't you?"

Justin looked back out onto the field, and as he did another snap went over Fletch's head.

"I'm just having a bad day," he signed, adjusting his grip on the facemask of his helmet.

"We all have bad days, Justin," I said. "We still have a job to do."

My signing might not have been the greatest, but it was good enough. Justin apparently got the point. He tossed the Gatorade cup to the ground, slid his helmet back onto his head, and with his bad hip limped his way back out onto the field. Ryan acknowledged him as he returned to the formation, and then sent Bauman back in our direction.

"Tell Baumann to work with Jimmy on his snaps," yelled Ryan.

I looked over at Jimmy and he was already smiling, nodding his head up and down, and giving me the thumbs up. He had read Ryan's lips. As he grabbed a football and headed over to work with Baumann, I thought to myself, 'I sure hope he gets a shot to play soon. The kid really deserves it.' When I looked back to the field, Justin's snaps had returned to normal, and Fletch was clapping his hands with approval. And Ryan hadn't changed the ball.

It was a difficult week of practice for us, not because of any adverse weather conditions or unusual physical duress, but mostly because the boys were just plain worn down emotionally. Football teams generally only play about ten games during the course of a season, but it's a long, grueling season. It's especially tough when one considers that in addition to the physical rigors of football, the players are also carrying twelve to fifteen credit hours of college studies. So it doesn't usually come as a surprise, to most experienced coaches, when their team's attitude begins to suffer a general malaise in late fall. Ed was an experienced coach and he'd known this was coming. He was right. Without the prospect of earning a play-off berth, or winning a title, there was little left for these guys to accomplish that season, other than in the stat book. But on the whole, that alone wasn't much of a motivating factor for most of them. This seemed to have been a little more expected at Gallaudet than most colleges. But I think that's because Gallaudet had been a club team for so long, and not that most of its players were deaf.

*

Our opponent that week was SUNY Maritime from just outside of New York City. They ran the offense that Ed swore was garbage, the triple option. That was largely because their head coach was a former player at the U.S. Naval Academy, where they employed the triple option offense very effectively and with a great deal of success. The triple option offense can be a very difficult offense to defend against since most teams had little time to prepare for it, usually just the week or so and against their scout offense. A scout offense is usually a team's own offense trying to run plays that they expected their opponent to run in the game. But the triple option requires a lot of timing and practice, a luxury that offensive scout teams just don't have. So they are not usually very good at running the triple option against their own defense in practice. Thus, their defense doesn't "get a good look" to learn from, making it difficult to defend against in the actual game.

Well, it wasn't any different for our offensive scout team either, especially Fletch. He just couldn't get a handle on the quarterback's triple option responsibilities. And Pierre Price, one of our talented, freshman running backs, couldn't maintain proper spacing from Fletch. The young, light skinned, black kid instinctively rushed toward the quarterback instead of running parallel to him about five yards away. At times, he was so close to the quarterback that the pitch key, the defensive end, was easily able to defend both the quarterback and the running back at the same time. That obviously wasn't how it was supposed to work and not what we'd see from SUNY. And so our team practice segment on Tuesday, designed to prepare our defense for the SUNY offense, was mostly a waste of valuable practice time.

The execution of the scout offense didn't improve a bit on Wednesday and patience began to wear thin for both Ed and Ryan. In fact, Ryan got so frustrated with Fletch and Pierre, in particular, that he yanked both of them off the field at the same time, complaining about their lack of focus. He took Fletch's helmet from him, put it on his own head, and attempted to run the offense himself, from the quarterback position. It wasn't pretty, but I have to say that he was much more efficient at running the offense than

Fletch had been. And so the defense finally got a chance to see how difficult defending the triple option offense really could be.

Fletch, meanwhile, was standing a few feet from me, smiling and laughing at the idea of Ryan playing quarterback with the scout offense. Every couple of seconds, he'd point out to the field for me to watch Ryan. Then he would mock Ryan's performance as quarterback, giggling loudly as he did. As much as he was a man physically, Fletch was still just a kid at heart. Pierre, though, a really good athlete from Illinois, wasn't so amused. He left the field and headed for the locker room, throwing his hands up in disgust and embarrassment. It was a good thing that Justin Lathus decided to hang around after his incident with Ryan, because if Pierre had just quit the team, then we'd have been down 8.3 percent of our players, really close to Ed's prediction of 10.

During a break in practice on Wednesday, there was a sudden commotion among a group of players as the team gathered on the sideline. Several of the players dashed away from the scene hysterically, as if frightened by something. Well, that something was Bill Jacobs, one of our offensive linemen. He'd donned a red and black face mask and put his helmet back on over it. It was one of those rubber costume masks that resembled a professional wrestler who called himself, "The Undertaker." At first glance, he was a pretty scary sight, especially for those guys who had been caught off guard by it. It was Halloween and Bill had scored himself a pretty good trick.

Just like many people refer to Wednesdays as "hump day," Halloween had always been a sort of "hump day" for me as a high school football coach. The day after Halloween is obviously the first day of November. And once November showed up on my football calendar, I knew that the end of our season was just around the corner. Halloween was a harbinger of that. Regardless of how well the year was going, our last game would be quickly upon us. Sometimes that meant that we had to ratchet up the intensity in order to maintain the team's focus as we prepared them for the playoffs. In other years, we had to lighten up a bit, let the kids relax and enjoy their final week or two of football. When Ed left Wednesday's practice early, to take his children out for trick or treating, I knew that our last week and a half was going to be the latter.

So did the boys. And on Thursday, that became very obvious.

"Coach," Jimmy signed to me, "are you coming back next season?"

Scott Lehman, our other freshman running back, stood beside Jimmy and watched attentively for my response. Jimmy's face was sincere, almost forlorn.

"Well, probably," I signed back to him. "I'd like to."

"Good." Jimmy smiled and signed, "If you're coming back then so am I."

Jimmy looked quickly at Scott and then back to me, nodding his approval. Scott smiled as well, and gave me a "thumbs up." That's when I realized that not only was the end of our season upon us, but that Jimmy had all but thrown in the towel in hopes of actually getting to play. Both players were apparently already looking toward next year, the kind of attitude that hits football players on the day after Halloween. And for the first time, I seriously started thinking about whether or not I really would be back the following season.

I spent a lot more practice time than usual working with Fletch and Jimmy on Thursday afternoon. Ed and Ryan had expanded the defensive segment of practice to further prepare the defensive players for SUNY Maritime's triple option offense. That gave me more time to work with the quarterbacks than I normally enjoyed. And, we also had the luxury of Kevin Alley and Cole Johnson working with us the entire time. The two quality receivers had become quite adept at running their routes, so we were able to work a lot on the timing of our short passing game. Richard Baumann, the back-up center was with us as well. He needed the practice, too, but was throwing our timing off with erratic snaps.

"Do you have a ball with better grip?" Bauman signed to me.

"Seriously," I asked, "are we really going to go there?"

Baumann looked at me nervously, although I wasn't angry, nor did I sign my response with any kind of emphasis. Jimmy, though, walked over to our bag of quarterback practice balls, reached in and grabbed a relatively new football, and then tossed it to Baumann. That's when I knew that Jimmy had really become quite comfortable with me as a coach. I gave Jimmy an amused look.

"It's okay, Coach," Jimmy signed as he nodded and held the old ball up for me to see, "this ball is a little worn, harder to grip."

"Okay," I signed. I looked at Fletch and Fletch just smiled at me.

It didn't matter to me which ball they used, although I really didn't see that much of a difference between the two footballs. Like Ryan, I thought that complaining about the ball was mostly just an excuse for the bad snaps, but I wasn't going to make a big deal about it. As long as the new ball resulted in better snaps I was okay with whatever excuse they needed. It's still amusing to me, though, that the boys on the Gallaudet football team were a lot pickier about the texture and feel of a football than any kid that I'd ever coached up until then, and since.

Ed stayed home on Friday to help his wife with their newborn child. And so he wasn't at practice the day before the game, if you can imagine that. But Pierre Price was once again at practice, and so was Justin Grigsby. Pierre had just needed some time to cool off following his little spat with Ryan on Wednesday. And Justin had contracted pink eye, so the doctor had told him to not to go to class for a few days and to definitely stay away from the football team while he was contagious. So not only did Ed miss practice, he missed his target of ten per cent. Brian was right for a change; maybe things really were different now. Ed, though, wasn't around to appreciate Brian's gloating.

Clayton Kendrick-Holmes was the head football coach at SUNY Maritime in Throgs Neck, New York. He'd arrived there a few seasons earlier after coaching the football team at the Naval

Academy Prep School in nearby Newport, Rhode Island. We'd actually met right about that time, while he was on a recruiting trip to nearby Annapolis. He'd been interested in a couple of boys from our Severna Park team. And so we were familiar enough with one another that he recognized me in the hallway of the field house on game day, just outside of his team's locker room.

We greeted one another and spoke briefly about how things were going for one another, coaching quarterbacks, and how the season had progressed. While he was very happy with his team's development over the past two years, he was very disappointed with how the current season had unfolded. His Privateers were not playing very well. After giving him a synopsis of my experience of Gallaudet, we shook hands, wished each other 'good luck,' and went about the business of preparing our players for the game at hand. I enjoyed speaking with him again, but my gig was up for that weekend; I wasn't going to be able to casually overhear any of our opponent's strategic plans this time.

A 1992 graduate of the U.S. Naval Academy, Kendrick-Holmes had played defensive end for the midshipmen. Hence, he was a believer in the triple option offense, because after practicing against it on a daily basis, he knew first-hand just how difficult it could be to defend. For us, it was going to be especially difficult as we were missing not one, but both of our starting defensive ends. Josh Ofiu had not yet been medically cleared to resume playing after suffering the neck injury against Mount Ida the weekend before. Michael Daze, not pleased with his own academic standing, backed away from football to focus on his studies, and wasn't playing either. I remembered Ed saying that he hated the triple option, calling it a garbage offense. But I knew better, especially after getting to know Ed. He didn't hate it because it was a garbage offense; he hated it because it was tough to defend. It was going to be especially tough to defend without both of his starting defensive ends.

The game got underway with SUNY Maritime receiving the opening kick-off. Running the triple option offense to perfection, they made little haste in marching seventy yards down the field to score and early touchdown and assume a quick, seven point lead. Well, so much for the end of season, relaxed attitude from Ed. The gloves came off right then and there as Ed went ballistic following the Privateer's touchdown drive. In fact, one might say that he became "inter-continentally" ballistic, screaming like a madman at his defensive players as they returned to our sideline. And it was just the first series of the game!

Watching from our sideline, Josh Ofiu was disgusted by what he'd just seen on the field, and pleaded with our team doctor for permission to play in the game. He harassed the doctor into to re-assessing his neck injury. Apparently Josh did enough to convince the doctor that he was okay to play, because the doctor gave him the green light to do so. Josh then ran back to the field house, put on his uniform and gear, and returned to the field of play just a few minutes later.

I don't know why Ed became enraged so quickly. Maybe he thought it would motivate his players or quickly get them focused. But I thought that he had acted a little prematurely in doing so. On our first offensive play of the game, Fletch kept the ball himself, on our own option play. He ducked inside the defensive end, and then evaded the outside linebacker as he ran with the ball. He scampered untouched for sixty-two yards and a touchdown to tie the score, just like that.

The defense got a huge boost from the returning presence of Josh Ofiu. They did not allow SUNY Maritime to gain ten yards and a first down on the following series, and the Privateers were forced to punt the ball away. But, for whatever his reason, Ed wasn't easing up. He continued to yell profanities at both our players and the referees. He received a warning from the umpire, after which he calmed down a notch. But from that point forward, it was obvious that the referees were making an intentional effort to ignore everything Ed barked in their direction. In fact, later in the half, Ed actually had a good point regarding what I thought was clearly a missed call by the referees. But like I said, the referees had turned a deaf ear to him.

"Bob!" Ed called out to the referee following a play in which the SUNY quarterback had thrown the football into the ground to avoid being sacked for a loss, "Bob, he can't do that! That boy can't do that! That's intentional grounding!"

But Bob didn't answer.

"That's bullshit and you guys know it!" Ed screamed louder. "That's grounding!"

The referees were suddenly deaf themselves. And that just infuriated Ed even more, but to no avail. The referees placed the ball on the ground at the original line of scrimmage and blew their whistles to signal the start of the next play. And that's the way it was for the remainder of the game.

After returning the SUNY punt to about our thirty five yard line, the offense went back to work with Ryan calling the plays from above and Brian signaling them to the team. On the second play of the series, Fletch rolled out to his left, looking to pass the football. He saw his receiver open about ten yards away on a crossing route and he turned to pass the ball to him. But he didn't get his shoulders square to the line of scrimmage before doing so. As a result, his feet became tangled up beneath him and Fletch fell awkwardly to the ground, immediately grabbing for his right ankle. Jon and his assistant ran onto the field to tend to him. After a few moments, they stood him up and, with the assistance of a couple of sideline players, helped him off the field and to the training table behind the bench.

Ed immediately pointed to JC and summoned for him with his right index finger. I watched as JC grabbed his helmet and ran over to his beckoning head coach. Walking toward the two, I overheard Ed's instructions to JC. Ed still had a tendency to mouth his words as he signed, like me. He told JC that he had to go into the game until Fletch was able to return.

"But I can't throw," JC replied, holding out his palms and

shaking his head.

"I don't give a damn," Ed said. "We're going to run the fucking ball!"

JC resigned himself to once again taking charge of the offense, at least for a series or two. Thinking that Fletch might not be able to get off of the training table, I walked over to Jimmy and instructed him to begin warming up, which he eagerly did. He was a little nervous, but I convinced him to relax and, if Ed called him into the game, to just run the plays as he'd practiced them during the week. He didn't need to go in and win the game, but just do his job the best that he could. The team would do the rest.

"Overmier!" called out Ed. "Get over here!"

I approached Ed with caution.

"Don't worry about Jimmy, because that ain't happening," he said. "Go help get Fletch ready to go."

At the training table, Fletch was in obvious pain. Jon and the doctor were working on his lower leg. It wasn't looking good. I handed him a cup of Gatorade as they gingerly maneuvered his leg about. Fletch looked up at me and shook his head from side to side, indicating that he didn't think he was going to be able to continue playing. I patted him on his shoulder pads. Jon stood up and told me that Fletch was done for the game with what he thought might be a high ankle sprain.

"You want to tell Ed or do you want me to?" Jon asked me.

"I'll tell him," I said. "The mere fact that you asked tells me that you don't want to be the bearer of bad news. Not today anyway."

Jon smiled and walked toward the Gator.

Meanwhile, JC and the offense were having success running the football as Ryan avoided calling any pass plays. SUNY Maritime, though, didn't know that JC had an injured should or that he wasn't able to throw the football. They'd seen him throw the ball in game film, I'm sure. So they had to respect the threat of a pass, even though it didn't exist. That made it possible for JC and the offense to run the ball more effectively, especially in situations when conventional wisdom would have dictated a pass. And so on that first drive following Fletch's ankle injury, the offense actually moved the ball down the field for a touchdown without passing the ball a single time. At the end of the first quarter, we'd lost our quarterback, but gained a seven point lead.

As the offense returned to the sideline following that drive, I approached Ed to give him the news about Fletch.

"Coach, it doesn't look like Fletch is going to be able to finish the game," I said.

"What? Don't give me that shit!" he complained loudly. "Tell him to tough it out. I want him back in the game on the next series."

"It's a high ankle sprain, Ed. He can't go."

Ed knew that a high ankle sprain was a serious injury that would prevent a player from continuing to play, but he didn't want to hear it from me. He needed to hear it from Jon or the team doctor. And so off he went in their direction where he was given the news directly from the horse's mouth. Even then it didn't sit very well with him, and his mood soured even further.

His defense continued to play remarkably well, though. Perhaps Ed's early theatrics had worked. Perhaps Josh Ofiu had inspired them. I wasn't really sure that it mattered; what mattered was that they were playing much better than they had on the game's first series of plays. About mid-way through the second quarter, the SUNY quarterback and running back collided in their own backfield, causing a fumble. Our defense recovered the ball, giving us great field position just inside the fifty yard line.

Once again, JC took the field and directed another scoring drive consisting of nothing other than running plays. Even the plays that resembled play action passes were actually one hundred percent quarterback keepers with JC running with the ball. Kerry Phalen, our line coach, was having a blast. He was excited about the fact that there hadn't been any breakdowns in our pass protection to that point. He was being sarcastic, of course, since there hadn't really been any passing plays. But he was still excited.

One guy who wasn't too excited was Jimmy Gardner, who by this time had stopped warming up. He wasn't pouting, or in any way demonstrating a bad attitude. I could just tell that he was deeply frustrated, and I'd have been, too. We'd both thought that he was now our back-up quarterback, not JC.

The defense continued to stymie the SUNY offense and forced another punt with just two and a half minutes to play in the second quarter. This would have been the perfect situation to insert Jimmy and let him finish out the half, I thought. I figured it was a great opportunity to get him comfortable in the offense in case we needed him in the second half. What if we had to start passing? What if JC got hurt? We might even need him for our final game the following week, depending on the severity of Fletch's injury. In either case, the time seemed right to me. We were winning 21–7, the defense was playing great, and the offense was just running the ball anyway. Maybe we'd get in three or four plays before halftime. To me, it was a win-win situation, and so just before the punt, I walked over to offer Ed my suggestion.

"Coach, do you want to let Jimmy run these last few plays of the half?" I asked. "If we need him in the second half he'd at least have a few plays under his belt." And so there it was. I'd stuck my neck out for my back-up quarterback.

"I'll tell you what I want," Ed said without so much as looking at me standing next to him. "I want you to shut up."

"Alrighty, then," I said under my breath as I just stood on the sideline and stared out onto the field. I could see Ed in my peripheral vision as he walked away from me. I was a bit stunned by the manner in which he responded to my question and needed a moment to compose myself. "I shouldn't be surprised, though," I thought. I'd been around him for several months and I should've known that that's just the way he was, maybe even expected it. It's not the way I was. It's not the way every head coach was, although many are. But that's the way Ed was. Should I have asked the question of him? Well, obviously not. But I didn't regret it since I felt that I was doing what I thought was right, and in the best interest of the team. When I finally turned around after a minute or so, I saw Jimmy looking in my direction from his seat on the bench. He held out his hands and shrugged his shoulders.

"Sorry, Jimmy," I signed to him. "I tried."

He put his fist forward and motioned as if knocking on a door, meaning that he understood. At that point, though, he finally appeared to become angry. Fletch wasn't the only one in pain at the end of the first half.

In the locker room at halftime, many of the boys expressed concern that SUNY knew of our intention to simply run the ball with JC playing quarterback. They feared that the SUNY defense would stack the line of scrimmage against us in the second half, in other words bring all of their defenders right up to the line to stop us from running the ball. But Ed convinced them that SUNY had known in the first half that we were just going to run the ball, and yet they still couldn't stop us. He told them that the game was in the hands of the offensive line, and that they'd have to carry us if we wanted to win the contest.

As the team left the locker room, though, Ed instructed Ryan to use JC just like he was any other quarterback, despite the doctor's recommendation that JC not throw the football. The way Ed saw it, JC's rotator cuff wasn't going to get any worse than it already was, so he wanted to see if JC could work through the pain. I felt all along that Ed probably doubted whether or not JC was really injured. We would soon see if the injury was for real.

"Better continue sticking to play-action, Ryan," I suggested as we left the locker room. "Maybe a few dump-offs to the backs, nothing where he has to get that elbow too high."

"Yeah," he said. "I hear you."

On our first series of the second half, SUNY did indeed stack their players on the line of scrimmage to defend against the run.

We didn't know if they were aware of JC's injury and had made a halftime adjustment, or if they were simply calling a run blitz. Regardless, they stuffed the run on the opening play of the second half. On second down, JC faked a handoff to Dima and rolled to his right. Kevin Alley was wide open down the sideline in front of him, having streaked past his defender. JC attempted to throw the ball to Kevin, but the ball barely traveled twenty yards before falling harmlessly to the ground. JC grabbed for his shoulder. Now, SUNY knew for sure that JC was hurt. And they had a lot of time to take advantage of his limited capabilities.

The SUNY offense just couldn't muster any momentum, though, and I could see why Kendrick-Holmes had been frustrated about his team's development. By now, they should have been much more adept at running the option offense. While they moved the ball pretty well, they continued to make costly mistakes, putting themselves in tough down and distance situations and turning the ball over. They were not a very good passing team either, managing just eighty yards through the air for the entire game.

Undoubtedly, however, their main frustration had to be that they knew we couldn't pass the ball, and yet they still couldn't stop us from running. It was a reversal of roles, if you will. A team that runs the triple option offense usually frustrates the other team in a similar manner.

Near the end of the third quarter with the score still in our favor, 21–7, we faced a third down with just one yard to gain. With both teams almost running the football exclusively, the game had become one of field position, and the ball was deep in our own territory. As long as that remained the case, SUNY still had a chance to win the game. We really needed to 'flip the field' or risk yielding a score that would tighten the game.

Brian signed in the play call from Ryan to the team on the field. When Ed saw JC toss the ball to the running back, who was tackled right at the yard to gain marker, he flipped out. He turned and screamed up to the top of the stadium to where Ryan was calling plays via headset down to Brian. Ed was upset that we hadn't run right at the defense, between the tackles, in a situation that required just a single yard. I think we all understood that part. It was the whole yelling up to Ryan thing that was pretty embarrassing. I could only imagine what the SUNY sideline was thinking.

"Coach," Ron Luczak said to Ed, trying unsuccessfully to get his attention, "Coach!" But Ed continued pacing back and forth along the sideline, openly berating Ryan's play calling. "Coach," Ron repeated, still trying calm Ed down. Ed snatched his headset off his head and glared right at Ron. "We got the first down, Coach," Ron said.

The offense ran several more plays and Ryan mixed in some play-action passes just to try to keep the SUNY defense honest. For the most part, that plan worked, but JC really struggled to get the ball to his receivers. He finished the game having completed just six passes for forty-seven yards, most of which were yards gained by the receiver after the catch. But, we continued to run the ball incredibly well. I don't know if the SUNY defense just wasn't very good, or if they never figured out that JC was limited. But we ran for 350 yards that game, including three touchdowns.

Even though we were playing well, things got a little 'squirrely' for us about halfway through the final quarter. If Shakespeare was calling the game on the radio broadcast, he may have declared that perhaps, "the worm had turned." Again facing a third down with one yard to gain and deep in our own territory, our offense approached the line of scrimmage. A first down would give us a fresh set of plays and pretty much ice the game for us. Instead of calling a toss or counter, Ryan this time had called a simple dive. The running back took the hand-off from JC, dropped his shoulder, and dove hard into the line. But a SUNY linebacker was already there in the hole, and the two players collided violently. The ball was jarred loose and wound up on the ground, where a SUNY defender recovered it, giving SUNY great field position. Just a few plays later, their offense scored on a short touchdown run. Their kicker pushed the extra point attempt wide of the goal post, though, leaving them eight points behind with just over six minutes remaining to be played. Still, they were within a touchdown and a two-point conversion of tying the game.

Along our sideline, Ed was calling for our "Hands Team" to field the kick-off return. A "Hands Team" was a group of players who were usually very good at handling the football, like running backs and receivers. When a team anticipates that their opponent might try an onside kick to quickly regain possession of the football, they usually employ their "Hands Team" to minimize the risk of that happening. The "Hands Team" would be put on the field for the kick-off return instead of their usual return team. Players on a "Hands Team" generally stood a much better chance of recovering a ball kicked across the ground than players used to just blocking during a normal kick-off return. It was a Special Teams unit and Ed was in charge of Special Teams.

But with all of the excitement and commotion on the sideline, Ed was having difficulty conveying to the players that he wanted the "Hands Team" on the field. Players and coaches alike were moving all about the bench area, frantically using sign language to corral those designated players. With the SUNY kick-off team already in place and ready to go, the referee called for our players to take the field. Seeing that we were not ready yet, Brian panicked, ran over to the referee, and called for a time-out. Although well intentioned, it wasn't something Brian should have done. We didn't have a time out remaining, nor did Ed want to call one.

Ed sent his "Hands Team" out onto the field, at least most of them anyway, plus a few players who had some idea of what to do. He then turned to the referee and yelled out that only the head coach could call for a time-out, and that being the head coach, he hadn't called for one. The referee stared at Ed for a moment and then turned back to the field of play. After seeing how we'd lined up, Kendrick-Holmes called for a time-out, and waved his team over to their sideline.

Ed, meanwhile, made a bee-line down our own sideline toward Brian. Brian saw the storm approaching and stood expressionless with the innocence of a five year old who didn't know what he'd done wrong, but knew that he was about to find out. Ed went chest to chest with Brian and pushed his own nose right up against Brian's, telling him in no uncertain terms that he wasn't very happy with Brian calling a timeout. It was pretty ugly.

By now, the actual "Hands Team" had assembled and awaited instructions from Ed. Ed spoke to them briefly and then dispatched them onto the field for the on-side kick attempt from SUNY. Most of our players were right in front of us, on the left side of the field, in anticipation of the on-side kick from SUNY's right footed kicker. But SUNY had changed their minds and instead of attempting the on-side kick, they "pooch" kicked the ball much deeper, and away, from where most of our players had positioned themselves.

Our kick returner, Pierre Price, raced over toward the SUNY sideline to field the ball, and picked it up at about the twenty yard line. If a SUNY player had beaten Pierre to the ball, they would have gained possession of the ball themselves. At first, Pierre attempted to run the ball right up along their sideline to get as many yards as he could. But then he quickly realized that most, if not all, of his blockers were on the opposite side of the field. That or he probably saw about nine, unblocked SUNY defenders, who had him dead in their sights. I think a lot of us on our side of the field cringed in anticipation of the physical engagement that Pierre was about to suffer if he didn't get out of bounds. Had it had been me, I'd have chosen to gain a few yards and then just skip out of bounds, happy to have possession of both the football and all of my limbs.

Pierre had other plans, though, choosing instead to change direction and attempt to outrun the SUNY defenders back across the field toward our sideline. There wasn't a whole lot of football IQ factored into that decision. Just about the only chance that SUNY had of winning the ball game at that point was via a turnover, in other words a Pierre Price fumble. But being a freshman, Pierre wasn't thinking about such things, he was just being an athlete. Fortunately, so, too, were his teammates as one by one the SUNY defenders were knocked off their feet by Gallaudet players crossing the field from the opposite direction. Pierre managed to get all the way to our sideline where again he decided not to just run out of bounds, happy with possession and good field position. Instead, he chose to run all the way to the end zone for a touchdown. Although in the books it was an eighty yard kick-off return, Pierre had actually run about one hundred and seventy yards on the play. And that was the proverbial frosting on the cake. A few minutes late, the game was over.

GALLAUDET 28 SUNY MARITIME 13

It was the first official Division III victory in school history and merited a Gatorade bath for Ed at the final whistle. Usually after a victory, players would try to sneak up from behind their head coach and dump a cooler of Gatorade over his head. The Gallaudet players were no different, except that they weren't very good at sneaking up on anyone. They didn't know that they were being so noisy, and that Ed had heard them grunting and laughing from about twenty yards away as they approached him with the cooler. He tried to scurry away, but a few of the players standing nearby grabbed hold of him and held him in place as their teammates dumped the entire contents of the cooler over Ed's head and shoulders.

In the locker room afterward, the mood was mostly upbeat in the wake of the victory. But there was some pause for concern, too, like for Fletch and his ankle injury, and JC's shoulder, which Jon had wrapped in ice. There was also a lot of disappointment on behalf of many of the players that Jimmy hadn't played in the game. While he'd participated in the team's victory celebration, Jimmy clearly felt dejected, and was the first to leave the field house afterward. A lot of people, including myself, of course, felt that he should have been given the opportunity to play. That was his job; to be the back-up quarterback should the starter suffer an injury.

We felt Ed could at least have given the kid a chance to earn some respect from his teammates, and feel like he'd made a contribution to the team effort. Unfortunately for Jimmy, Ed, still soaked in orange colored Gatorade, felt otherwise.

Sitting in my car and looking out across the football field, I thought about the differences between Ed and I related to Jimmy. Maybe it was the high school coach in me, but I still thought that it was a coach's responsibility to help shape his players into men, both physically and emotionally. If Ed's lack of compassion and respect was what a college coach was supposed to be like, well, then I probably wasn't meant for the job. And although Ed had a much stronger coaching background than I did, I couldn't help but wonder if the team would have preformed differently under my style of leadership than it had under his, especially Jimmy.

19

Jimmy Cracks Corn, but Ed Don't Care

Sunday was a day off for both the team and the coaching staff. My family and I went to the eleven o'clock service at church and then home for lunch. In the afternoon, we all chipped in and got some yard work done. We lived in a community with more than its share of mature oak trees and the leaves were about knee deep by this time each year. It wasn't uncommon for us to have to spend several weekends raking leaves.

While we raked and bagged leaves, my son, Mark, told me about how well he'd played in his youth league game on the day before. He knew that I liked to hear every little detail of how things went, so he was quite explicit about exactly what he'd done on just about every play. Of course, doing so took away quite a bit of time from the yard work at hand, but that was fine. The leaves could wait another week, if need be. My other son, Tyler, he wasn't very good at raking leaves. Raking leaves is an awfully hard thing to do when you're racing up and down the street showing your parents how well you ride your bicycle.

My wife needed some time to talk about things as well. But, unlike with Mark, I hadn't always been so willing to listen to every detail of what she had to say. That was another deficit on my part as a husband. Since she was, in essence, holding the fort down so that I could coach college football, I made sure to listen to everything she wanted to tell me that afternoon.

"Your sister wants us to come over for Thanksgiving dinner on Saturday this year instead of Thursday," she said as she began filling a lawn bag with leaves. "She's going over to her in-laws for Thanksgiving this year, but still wants to have everyone over for dinner that weekend."

"Ok. Is that alright with you?" I asked.

"Well, no, not really," she stopped bagging for a moment to look at me, "it's our anniversary that weekend."

"Huh? I thought our anniversary was the week before Thanksgiving."

"Not this year. Thanksgiving is November 22!"

Our anniversary was November 23. She resumed bagging leaves as I raked more of them into the pile in front of her and Mark.

"So I thought that maybe your father and Teresa would watch the boys Friday night so that we could go out to dinner," she said. "Maybe keep them overnight and bring them to your sister's house on Saturday afternoon?"

"And we'd just meet them there?"

"Yeah," she said as she rubbed her nose with the back of her hand.

"Ok, sounds good to me," I said. "I'll call Dad this week and ask him."

I knew that she felt the satisfaction of some adult conversation with her husband. With her, it wasn't really the content of the discussion that was the most important thing, but rather that I was spending time talking to her. And she went on talking about things like both boys needing new khaki pants for school, our dog, Toto, having to go to the groomer, and getting someone to come out to repair our dishwasher. A lot happened around my house while I was on the football field. While she had been very supportive of me all fall, she was happy that the end of the football season was drawing near.

*

At Monday's team film review, wide receiver Derrick Williams showed up with his arm in a sling. Apparently, he'd fractured his collar bone at some point during the game on Saturday. And so Derrick's season was over just a little sooner than he'd expected. Fletch was on crutches, his ankle still badly swollen and discolored. At the least, he wouldn't be able to practice before Wednesday. And with JC's shoulder still ailing him that meant that Jimmy would get most of the snaps with the first offense that week. But, when the coaches gathered for our staff meeting following the film review with the team, Ed wasted little time putting to rest any ideas I might have had about starting Jimmy against Juniata College that weekend.

"I'll suit up before I play Jimmy, Coach Overmier," Ed said, starting the staff meeting.

Most of the coaches turned to glance in my direction, waiting for my response. They knew, and appreciated, my advocacy of Jimmy.

"Well, there goes the threat of the deep ball," I said, trying not to be lured into a futile argument on Jimmy's behalf. Ryan chuckled.

"I won't gamble my mortgage on Jimmy Gardner. So understand that," Ed said, intent on reeling me in.

"You could always refinance," I smiled. "I'm sure that Ron knows a few good lenders." Ron Luczak worked with Freddie Mac, one of the nation's largest mortgage insurers. Ron leaned forward in his seat and clasped his hands together in front of him.

"I do actually," he said.

"The boy broke his ankle last year when he showed up for school," Ed continued. "He got out of the car and dropped a television on his foot."

Like the rest of the coaches, even I chuckled at that one. After the meeting, we all walked out to our cars together. Ron's motorcycle was parked next to my car.

"Hey," Ron said, as he strapped on his helmet and mounted his bike. "At least you're standing up for your position player. That's good."

"Thanks, Ron." I smiled.

"See you tomorrow," he said. Then he started his engine, revved it up a couple of times, and took off through the gravel.

The next day dawned cold and windy. And to make things just a little bit colder, Ed had the team practice on the MSSD football field at the far end of the campus. The MSSD field was located on a much higher piece of ground than our stadium, and the swirling winds up there made it feel much colder than the thermometer indicated. The only player prepared for the rapid change in the weather was Josh Ofiu, the kid from Alaska. He loved the suddenly winter-like conditions. The rest of the team, though, scrambled to find long johns and sweatshirts to wear under their practice gear. Of course Ed didn't really move the practice to the MSSD field to make it a little colder. Ed moved it there because the MSSD field had lights and we could get more practice time in. The sun was setting around a quarter to five in early November.

The long jog from the field house to the MSSD field served as conditioning for the players. For the coaches it was about a three minute drive while crammed into a couple of SUV's. It was my first time actually visiting the Model Secondary School for the Deaf, even though it was just several blocks away. I was pretty impressed. Besides academic buildings, there were residence halls, a separate dining facility, and a gymnasium with an indoor pool. Plus the football field with lights.

During the first segment of Tuesday's practice, Ryan reviewed and ran the offensive unit through the running plays that he hoped to use against Juniata that weekend. JC took two reps and Jimmy ran every third. Despite his excitement, Jimmy handled the ball well, and had a good grasp of each play. His teammates were very supportive of him.

"All right, time for "Little Jimmy O" to get some reps," Ed called, drawing snickers from the other coaches. Ryan began coordinating the team passing segment of the practice.

"Little Jimmy O," Ed repeated. "This ought to be good."

Ed put his defensive backs and linebackers onto the field rather than allow the offensive receivers to practice on air. He grinned broadly as he slowly made his way from the defensive side of the ball to where we stood behind the offense. JC took the first set of snaps, but threw with great difficulty and discomfort. As one might expect, he only completed one pass and missed badly on several other attempts, grabbing for his shoulder after each throw. Even Ed knew that wasn't going to cut it against Juniata. They were too good of a football team for us to try to get by with a one dimensional offensive game plan. If Fletch couldn't play, Ed would have to rely on Jimmy. And Fletch was no sure bet to recover in time for the game on Saturday.

"It's show time!" Ed smiled as he peered out over his glasses at Ryan. "Let's see what Little Jimmy O can do."

The coaches all grinned at Ed's suddenly playful attitude. Fortunately, Jimmy couldn't hear any of the disparaging rhetoric as he called the huddle together and signed to them the first play from Ryan. He was all business. To my right, Fletch was grinning as well, eager to see how Jimmy would fare.

The first play was a perfectly executed bubble screen to Jimmy's left. The next pass was a curl, and the third was a crossing route. He completed all three passes with spot on accuracy. His teammates offered him high fives and pats on the back. Ed stood and watched with his arms crossed against his chest. Jimmy completed a slant pass, and then another crossing pattern, both with excellent velocity. He looked good in the pocket, too, poised and relaxed. After completing seven passes in a row, Ryan called for Jimmy to throw a fade in the direction of Kevin Ally. Kevin attacked the cornerback and then took off down the sideline on a fade route. Jimmy received the snap, took his drop step, and lofted the football over the defensive player's head and into Kevin's waiting hands for a touchdown. His offensive teammates were giddy over Jimmy's successful performance.

"Hite, let me see a deep curl," Ed tugged on the brim of his visor and called over to Ryan.

Ryan called for the curl route.

Cole Johnson took off on what appeared to be a go route, straight down the field and just outside of the hash marks. After he'd run about twenty yards, he turned back inside, in front of the dropping cornerback. The safety, recognizing the curl pattern, broke hard in Cole's direction, but was too late to break up the play. Jimmy had delivered the ball to Cole with laser accuracy and perfect timing. He completed nine passes in a row. Suddenly, the coaches were not laughing at Jimmy any more.

"This is scary," commented Kerry with a look of bewilderment on his face. "I'm starting to believe in the kid."

"You and me both," Ryan said after spitting a glob of tobacco juice out onto the ground. "That was unbelievable."

Fletch was laughing so hard he almost fell off his crutches. Standing alongside of Fletch, Dima and AJ Williams were amazed at just how well Jimmy had passed the football, especially considering the cold weather. Cold weather can cause the leather football to be rather slick. It also numbs one's hands. Justin Lathus returned to the huddle and smiled at Jimmy, swatting him on his backside as he did. Shortly thereafter, the other linemen enjoyed repeating the same. But even though we hadn't seen a quarterback complete all of his passes like that all season, Ed was still not a believer.

"Let's see what he does when I put a pass rush on his ass," Ed smirked as he looked over at us. "You'll see the real Jimmy then."

"Uh oh, Coach," Ron Luczak said to me as he walked by me on his way to assemble a defensive line. "Looks like it's sink or swim time for your boy."

"I guess so," I said. "But at least he didn't fall out of the boat on his own, if you know what I mean." I was referring to Ed's story of Jimmy hurting himself while getting out his own car.

"I got you," Ron smiled.

But the rush of the defensive linemen didn't seem to faze Jimmy at all on that clear and crisp evening. He continued to complete passes with an incredible rate of proficiency. He carried out excellent ball fakes on play action passes, and got plenty of depth on his drops to make good reads downfield. He even hit his receivers in stride on a few sprint out passing plays where Ryan put Jimmy on the move to get him away from pressure at the line of scrimmage. And after he'd badly fooled the defensive end on a bootleg, even Ed began to laud the youngster's performance.

"Damn," Ed said. "Jimmy even fooled me that time."

When the practice was over, Jimmy was overwhelmed with accolades from teammates and coaches alike. And Ed recognized him for his preparation and performance in the team huddle before releasing the squad for the evening. Jimmy had brought about a renewed sense of excitement among the boys and it was refreshing to see and experience. Afterward, Jimmy made his way to where I'd been standing behind the huddle, listening and watching Ed as he addressed the players.

"Well," Jimmy signed, "How do you think I did?"

"You were great," I signed back to him. I put my index finger to my temple and then pointed directly at him as I continued signing, "I knew you could do it."

Jimmy smiled as he turned away and jogged across the field to join his teammates, who were already en route back to the Gallaudet campus. As I watched him descend down the hill toward the stadium, the brightly lit dome of the U.S. Capitol Building appeared to rise above and beyond him. To the right of the Capitol dome, the illuminated Washington Monument majestically pierced the darkened sky. I paused for a moment to take in the gorgeous and surrealistic, panoramic view of Washington's skyline at night, which for that brief moment in time, included Jimmy Gardner.

We practiced at MSSD for the remainder of the week. With the days becoming so short there was little else that we could do other than practice inside the field house. Practicing in the gym was seldom an effective use of practice time, though. Football teams generally got very little accomplished on the wooden floor of a basketball court. That's why colleges built indoor practice facilities similar to the one that Penn State would allow us to use that Friday.

Penn State University was a relatively short distance from Huntingdon, Pennsylvania where Juniata College was located. As he'd done for all of our away games that season, Ed had worked his magic to get permission from Penn State University to use their turf lined, indoor practice facility. It was the same building that the famous Nittany Lions of Penn State used for practices during inclement weather. That was going to be pretty cool, too, I thought.

It was another kind of cool on the MSSD field for our final two practices, though. High school coaches usually had to wrap up practice a little early at this time of the year because very few high schools have the luxury of a lighted practice field. And most athletic directors didn't want the football team damaging the playing surface of the stadium, so teams just got a lot less practice time once Daylight Savings Time hit. Not us, though, we were practicing through dusk and into the night. And the dew moistened air made it a little extra cold.

Fletch was at practice on Wednesday, x-rays on his ankle had returned negative. He was without crutches and moving around pretty well. But since he still hadn't been medically cleared to resume participation, he remained undressed for practice. While the team worked on special teams and defensive strategies, Fletch challenged my developing ASL comprehension skills by signing to me about his own experience while a student on the MSSD campus. He was a high school freshman when his parents applied and received acceptance for him to attend the school. Enrolling Fletch as a full-time resident student was a very difficult decision for his parents, because they lived so far away in Austin, Texas. But they felt it was in their son's best interest and they took advantage of the opportunity.

Fletch had resided at the secondary school for three years before graduating and moving across campus to Gallaudet. All in all, he'd been on the school campus in Washington for the last six years. On occasion, his parents would come to visit him, and at other times they'd send him a plane ticket so he could visit the entire family back in Texas. Unless I was mistaken, and that could easily happen the way I interpreted the rapid ASL of a twenty one year old, Fletch had a younger sister now at MSSD. That made things a whole lot easier on him, his sister, and their family.

With Fletch not practicing, Jimmy once again assumed most of the quarterbacking reps with the scout offense, and shared snaps with JC once we went to team offense and worked on running plays. JC, though, did launch a beauty of a fade down the right sideline, and appeared to do so effortlessly. Ed wasn't paying attention, though. But Kerry and I were.

"How the hell did he do that?" Kerry asked me.

"Beats me," I said. I wondered again if perhaps Ed was right about JC and his shoulder injury. When I looked over at JC after watching him throw the pass, he just smiled and shrugged his shoulders. Looking back at things, I think JC might have been the one dealing the cards all along; maybe he suffered a little tendonitis, but probably not a rotator cuff injury.

Meanwhile, Jimmy continued to perform well in practice, this time handling several full series of offensive plays. Harold, now back with the team following his prolonged absence, saw Jimmy throwing for the first time. His eyes seemed to pop to twice their normal size as he grabbed my shoulders to turn me in the direction of Jimmy and the offense. Then he smiled, tapped his fingers hard upon his chest, approving of what he saw of Jimmy's play. The smile was unmistakably Harold.

"So who do I go with, a quarterback with bad wheels or a

rookie?" asked Ed as he walked up behind us.

"Me, I'd go with the rookie, especially since the strength of Fletch's game is his mobility and speed," I suggested with an analytical tone. "And we don't really know how well that ankle is going to hold up for him." I wondered if Ed was signaling that he might actually consider using Jimmy on Saturday if Fletch wasn't one hundred per cent healthy. "Plus, Jimmy has really looked sharp all week. He's ready."

"I figured you'd say that," Ed mumbled as he drew his right hand to his chin.

It's a funny thing about football players and the cold weather; they tend to have very little patience and sometimes fights break out as a result. You might think that that happens a lot when the weather is hot, and it can. But under hot and humid conditions guys usually brush off an infraction, too tired and worn out to counteract an overly aggressive foe. But guys don't want to be messed with in the cold, especially during practice. And so it was that Wednesday evening.

Calvin Doubt was cold, and therefore not particularly aggressive, that night at practice. And so he was often just standing around at the end of a play, trying to stay warm. Well, at the end of one play, offensive tackle Adam Brimmer knocked Calvin off of his feet as the linebacker casually approached a pile of players on the ground. That caused a bit of a ruckus, an offensive player roughing up a defensive player. And then a defensive player mixed things up a bit when defensive back Marty Blomquist gave receiver Chester Kuschmider an extra shot to the facemask with his hand. Those two went around and around.

But those two incidents were just bouts on the undercard. The main event occurred when little Richard Baumann, our backup center, retaliated from a little extra-curricular activity on the behalf of linebacker Joe Scroggins. Joe was the kid from Little Rock, Arkansas who wanted to play quarterback at the beginning of the season. I guess he was still playing with a chip on his shoulder, which I could appreciate, but Baumann didn't. It took us a little while to get those two separated from one another.

Come Thursday, though, we were back to being just one big, happy family once again, probably because it was our final practice of the year. As such, there was a positive degree of team synergy unlike any since week one, making the transition from one practice segment to another smooth and seamless. And even though it was just as cold as the two nights before, and they still had to run as a group all the way up to the lighted field of MSSD, the boys each seemed to have a little extra bounce in their step that night, except for Fletch, of course.

Fletch did manage to practice, though, his injured ankle heavily taped. But he shared the practice time with JC and Jimmy. Oddly enough, it was the last practice of the year, but the first time all season that each of the team's three quarterbacks took practice reps with the first unit offense.

*

Huntingdon, Pennsylvania was only a three hour drive from Washington, D.C., almost due north, and nestled quietly among the heavily forested hills of South Central, Pennsylvania. I don't know about today, but in 2007 it was quite the sleepy little town. There was the Huntingdon County Library, the Huntingdon County Jail, a few motor lodges, and an Amtrak station. There wasn't much else, except for Juniata College. So Ed wasn't in all that much of hurry to get there. In fact, our buses actually bypassed the town of Huntingdon by about 30 miles to the west en route to State College, Pennsylvania, the home of Penn State University. It was almost an hour north of Huntingdon.

If you've ever traveled Pennsylvania State Highway 220, or any of the roads that traverse the higher elevations throughout that region, you know that the weather can change quite rapidly. Once in Pennsylvania, we encountered a little light rain, then a mix of snow and rain, and then snow, and then a mix of snow and rain, and then again a light rain. We even experienced a few white out conditions along the way. But by the time we pulled onto the campus of Penn State University, the precipitation had pretty much ceased and the skies were just slightly overcast. The boys on the bus were in awe of the famed Beaver Stadium as we passed beside it. That's where the legendary football coach, Joe Paterno, had patrolled the sidelines for as long as I can remember.

Shortly after arriving in front of Holuba Hall, the Nitanny Lion's indoor practice facility, several representatives of the university's athletic administration greeted our team and escorted us inside. Holuba Hall was an integral part of Penn State's athletic facilities, which are second to none in the nation. Inside its walls were two full-sized, turf football fields, complete with hash marks and large yard line numerals every ten yards. The fields extended the width of the building, from left to right, with one field behind the other. The Penn State football team wasn't practicing during our visit, of course, but I could see the immense benefit of having the two fields. They could run two simultaneous practices, both offensive and defensive, and fully maximize every practice session, regardless of the weather conditions outside. That was big time college football. And so for about an hour and a half, while we practiced inside on the turf, we felt like a big time college football team.

Before leaving the campus after practice, we were given a tour of the spectacular Lasch Football Building next door to Holuba Hall. We were shown meeting rooms where the football team would meet and review game film. Some rooms were like auditoriums, large enough to seat the entire team. Others were much smaller and used for a position coach and a few of his players. All of the meeting rooms had big screen televisions and video projection systems. We saw the team's locker room, their weight training center, and the athletic trainer's facilities. And we saw the player's lounge, complete with pool tables, foosball games, televisions, and refreshment centers. It was easy to see why so many great high school football players had chosen to play their collegiate football at Penn State. And the school had recognized many of those players for their collegiate gridiron achievements by lining the hallways of the building with bronzed busts, action photographs, and memorabilia. It was an inspirational visit for the boys and a nostalgic one for me.

Ed had had sandwiches and chips delivered to the buses outside, and when we returned from our tour, lunch was served. Shortly thereafter, we departed the campus of Penn State University and headed back south. Rather than a motor lodge in Huntingdon, Ryan had booked us into the Ramada Inn in Altoona, about forty minutes to the west of Huntingdon. Perhaps that had been the only place that could accommodate us. The two buses arrived at the hotel around four o'clock. By four-thirty, the hotel's indoor pool was filled with deaf college football players.

A few hours later, we once again boarded the buses for a short ride to yet another local buffet style restaurant for our team dinner. Afterward, when we returned to the hotel, most of the players were pretty eager to get back to their rooms to watch a little television and settle in for the night. Some of the coaches, on the other hand, well, let's just say that they were a little curious to explore the Altoona night life. After all, not only was it our final road trip of the year, but it was the night before our final game. So, Harold and Brian went to the front desk to arrange for a taxi cab ride. Ron Cheek and I agreed that we'd better go along to keep an eye on the young lads. Ed and Ryan, though, relaxing in the comfort of Ed's suite, were out of the loop regarding our little foray into town. They had a big screen television, a twelve pack of beverages, and a couple of reclining chairs. They were two happy clams.

Once crammed into the taxi, we were at the mercy of our driver, Chuck, to take us somewhere where we could enjoy a few beverages ourselves. Declining the familiar environs of restaurant chains and sports bars, we ended up in a seedy little joint about ten or fifteen minutes from the hotel. I handed Chuck a twenty dollar bill and asked him to return for us at 1:00 a.m. He tipped the bill of his cap and assured me that he would do just that.

The club, from the outside, looked like an ordinary neighborhood bar. There were a few neon lights that hung from the building's white stucco walls and, although I didn't notice it at first, there weren't any windows. Had I detected this sooner, it probably would have been my first clue that things might be a little freakish inside. And they were.

It was a very familiar setting, for a B Class movie that is, the type of bar that television detectives would search out when looking for suspects or informants. We grabbed a few chairs and sat down at a small round table just a few feet from the bar. A cloud of cigarette smoke hung across the room, reflecting the bright flashing of multi-colored strobe lights. I looked over my shoulder in search of a waitress, but instead saw a couple of guys who reminded me of the television detectives, Starsky & Hutch. That was a quick reminder that I wasn't a clubber, that's for sure.

But Harold and Brian, they loved the sights and sounds of the Altoona underground that night. I didn't want to spoil things for them by suggesting that we find another place. And I couldn't use the excuse that it was too loud to talk, because we were all signing to one another anyway. Harold couldn't hear the loud music that blared from large, overhead speakers, nor could Brian without his hearing aids. But they obviously felt the rhythmic pounding of the base guitar as they smiled at me and Ron, and then fist bumped one another.

A waitress eventually came by and we ordered four draft beers. When she returned with the drinks, we quickly realized that one's hard earned money went a lot further in Altoona that it did in Washington, D.C. She set four very large glasses of draft beer on the table, maybe sixteen ounces or so, at just $3.50 per glass. At such a reasonable price, we wouldn't have to nurse our drinks for hours on end just to remain at the club.

I took a sip of beer from my glass and looked over at Harold, rocking back and forth in his chair and smoking a cigarette. I'd no idea that Harold smoked cigarettes, but there he was with one dangling loosely from his lips. He and Brian were busy checking out the club's clientele, drinks in hand, grinning like a cat at a canary buffet. Ron had somehow attracted the attention of two lesbians, who tried to pull a chair up next to him at our table. Fortunately, some popular song began to play and they scurried off to the dance floor with one another. I don't know if he was disappointed, but he smiled and raised his glass to toast their acquaintance as they did.

I really hadn't spent much time at nightclubs in the past, say, twenty-five years since college. And I wasn't that much of a partier then, either. But it turned out to be a fairly entertaining evening as Ron and I watched all of the characters and charades in the club that night. We chuckled at the sight of Harold and Brian, who had blended surprisingly well into the club's decor, "working the room" as they milled about. Being deaf wasn't a problem for either of them that night, they were having fun regardless. But while they seemed to draw energy from the noise and excitement of the atmosphere inside the club, for me it was just the opposite. And when the hour finally came that we should leave, I was more than ready to go.

When we left the club and walked outside into the brisk, night air, Chuck's taxi cab was waiting for us in the parking lot, just as he had promised. Again, all four of us squeezed inside the sedan and began the trek back to the hotel. Just a few miles down the road, though, Brian caught sight of a Denny's Restaurant and wanted to stop to have breakfast. Harold and Ron, having developed a late night appetite themselves, agreed. But again, I was tired. Sitting in the front seat, I instructed Chuck to drop the guys off at Denny's, take me back to the Ramada Hotel, and then return to get them at 3:00 a.m., which he agreed to do. When Ron returned to our hotel room, whenever that was, I was already fast asleep. And so unlike our previous road trips, there wasn't any late night chatting about our common interests in music or old television shows. Not from me anyway.

20

The Season Finale

I n week one of the season, we'd played St. Vincent College in Latrobe. Their football stadium was named after the longtime head
coach of the nearby Pittsburgh Steelers, Chuck Knoll. Now, here
we were some ten weeks later at another Pennsylvania college stadium that was also named after a former NFL head coach named
Chuck. This time, the football stadium at Juniata College was
named after an alumni named Chuck Knox. Knox, who coached in
the NFL for more than thirty years, had played his collegiate ball at
Juniata in the early 1950's. In fact, he'd captained the school's first
undefeated football team in 1953.

In 2005, Coach Knox donated one million dollars to his alma
mater for the purpose of improving the athletic facilities. If being
an esteemed alumnus of the college, as well as one of the most successful coaches in the history of the NFL, wasn't reason enough to
name the stadium after the guy, I guess the donation was, although
I think the stadium had been named in his honor many years beforehand.

About an hour and a half prior to kickoff, the three quarterbacks and I left the locker room and walked down the street to the
stadium, a block or two away. It was a chilly 38 degrees outside with

a light breeze that seemed to draw wisps of moistened air down from the heavily overcast skies and across the grass playing surface of Knox Stadium. It was the kind of weather that makes some people say, "It smells like snow." It was also the kind of weather that made me glad that I'd brought my insulated gloves.

About ten minutes into our warm-up, JC nodded for me to turn around. Without saying a word, I turned and saw a coach from Juniata walking toward us. He smiled kindly and waved as he approached. I could tell that the man wasn't quite sure about whether to speak or not. I just smiled and waved back.

"How are you, Coach," he asked with a slight degree of apprehension.

"I'm a little cold," I replied, "how about you?"

"Yep, it's getting to be about that time of year, all right." I sensed a slight easing in his nervous posture. "It's a little cold, but that's football weather, you know?"

"It sure is."

"If there's anything that you guys need just let me know. I'm Coach Launtz, quarterback coach here at Juniata."

I introduced myself, and then each of our three quarterbacks as they continued to proceed through their drills. For the next several minutes, the two of us talked shop about coaching and how our teams were playing. He told me that he was fascinated by the challenges that we faced coaching deaf football players, especially the quarterbacks, of course. He was also amazed by how well we'd managed to overcome our communication deficits. Coach Launtz was also quite impressed by the athleticism of Fletch and JC, and equally so by just how skilled the three quarterbacks appeared to be, especially Jimmy. He really liked what he saw in Jimmy's footwork and quick release. Like many coaches with whom I'd spoken throughout the year, he thought that they might be somewhat behind the learning curve without the experience of playing high school football at the most competitive levels. After he commented on Jimmy's delivery, I told him that Jimmy hadn't played a single snap all season long. He just shook his head in disbelief. And with Fletch's amazing recovery from his ankle injury, it was doubtful that things would change for Jimmy that day.

Juniata was finishing up a terrible season of football, one in which they had yet to win a single game. Their offense had managed to score just a little over fifteen points per game during the first nine weeks of the season, and you don't win many college football games that way. Their quarterback was doing well, though, and their passing game had been fairly productive. But they couldn't run the ball a lick. And when you can't run the football, it's awfully hard to win football games at any level. Coach Launtz didn't say as much during our little chat, but I could tell that it would not come as a surprise to him if his team walked out of the stadium that day winless. And that would be a far cry from the 1953 team of Chuck Knox.

As the special teams units from both schools jogged onto the field for the game's opening kickoff, the twelve hundred or so fans on hand to cheer on their local college football team began to chant, "JC! JC! JC!" The chant sounded pretty cool, I thought, but they couldn't be cheering on our marquis player, Jason Coleman, could they? If so, JC wouldn't know it because he obviously couldn't hear them. When I told him that the crowd was chanting, "JC", he smiled and turned to tell some of his teammates about the chant. A few of the boys could hear the chant, like linebacker Calvin Doubt, who confirmed with JC that the crowd was indeed chanting "his name." We quickly realized that the "JC" chant meant Juniata College, obviously.

Juniata won the coin toss and elected to receive the ball to begin the game. Our kickoff team covered the return pretty well, and the Juniata offense began their first offensive series at their own twenty-four yard line. Ed was chomping at the bit to get his defense onto the field and the opportunity to take advantage of Juniata's anemic offense. He called for several blitzes during that first set of downs. But Juniata began the game by running the football, and on several plays ran in the opposite direction of Ed's blitzes. With an unnerving ease, Juniata marched the football right down the field and scored a touchdown on a short run. They missed the extra point, though, when it ricocheted off the left upright of the goal post.

Their six point lead was short-lived, though, to say the least. On our first offensive play from scrimmage, after a nice kick return to our own forty-five yard line, Fletch kept the ball on what appeared to be a read-option sprint out to his left. Instead of taking the football and running with it, though, he instead flipped it to JC who was running from the left side of the formation to the right, the opposite of Fletch. It appeared to be a reverse and the play drew all of the Juniata defenders toward the line of scrimmage. Suddenly, JC stopped and lofted the ball down the field to his pal, receiver Shawn Shannon. Shawn was uncovered along the right hash marks. The safety covering him had abandoned his defensive pass responsibilities when he dashed toward the line of scrimmage to stop the reverse run. Shawn caught the ball, pulled it into his body, and sprinted thirty five yards to the end zone to complete a fifty-eight yard touchdown pass play.

For a while it appeared that it was going to be a real shootout as neither team's defense showed much of an ability to stop the other team's offense. The Juniata running game was full speed ahead as they ran through Ed's defense like a hot knife through butter, scoring again on another short touchdown run. But, we were able to pass the ball at will and scored again ourselves when Fletch threw a short slant pass to Kevin Alley, who hauled it in and scored from about ten yards out. At the end of the first quarter we were out in front by a score of 14-13.

The Juniata fans cheered their team on and continued to chant, "JC! JC! JC!" Their starting running back was having a career day running the football and their quarterback was doing pretty well, too, passing the ball effectively. Juniata certainly wasn't playing like a winless team without any offensive firepower. No, their offense was playing like a team possessed. And when their defense caught a few breaks in the second quarter, we were in big trouble.

Fletch fumbled a snap and Juniata recovered the ball. They scored on a twenty-nine yard field goal. Then Daniel Alexander fumbled at the end of a run and Juniata again recovered the ball. They scored on a touchdown run. And then Shawn Shannon muffed a punt return and you got it, Juniata recovered the ball. And again, they scored a touchdown, this time via a fade pass in the corner of the end zone.

Everything had suddenly gone south for our team at that point, on both sides of the ball. But when Shawn fumbled the punt return, I think Ed's frustration with our ineptness reached the level of maximum overload. In his despair, and with just a few minutes remaining in the first half, he called out for his backup quarterback, Jimmy Gardner.

"Coach Overmier, get Jimmy ready!" Ed shouted. "He's going in on the next series."

I sprinted over to where Jimmy stood near the far bench. I told him to get his helmet on and begin to warm up in a hurry, because he was going in following the kickoff return. The excitement on Jimmy's face was like that of a small boy thinking that Santa Claus had landed on the roof on Christmas Eve. He quickly donned his helmet and grabbed Cole Johnson to help him warm up. As he began to throw the football to Cole, I tried to convey to Jimmy that I wanted him to calm down and play like he'd practiced all week, with poise and confidence. I told him to make sure that he took the time to look across at his defensive reads, that he was a very good study--we weren't going to run any plays that he hadn't already practiced-- and that I was confident he would do well.

That was a lot to tell a young quarterback in such a situation, even by word, much less via sign language. It didn't really matter though. Despite how poorly I'm sure that I actually signed those instructions, Jimmy really couldn't see my signing anyway. While he threw the ball back and forth to Cole, he had to focus more on the football than my hands. And that was one of the communication deficiencies of working with deaf players.

Following their touchdown pass, Juniata's kicker didn't hit the ball very well, and he wound up with a very short kickoff. We were able to run the ball all the way out to midfield and into really good field position. And with that, I don't know what went through Ed's mind, other than a flash thought that perhaps we could turn our offensive misfortunes around with a good kick return.

"Fletch stays in!" he yelled aloud and into the microphone of his headset.

He didn't look at anyone in particular, but instead stared down at the ground, his head moving slightly back and forth. I was disappointed for Jimmy once again, but quickly turned to find Fletch, who to my surprise was standing right behind me.

"Fletch, you're in," I signed to him.

"What?" he signed back inquisitively. "Jimmy is going in!"

"Not anymore," I continued to sign. "Coach wants you back in. Let's go!"

Fletch fretted for a moment, but then snapped his chin strap back on to his helmet and ran out onto the field. Jimmy, obviously dismayed, remained at my side looking for the play call from Brian. Since he was naturally so much better at reading Brian's signing than I was, I counted on Jimmy to relay the play call to me before each play so that I knew what to expect on the field. Helping me that way usually kept Jimmy's head in the game, too.

I don't know if Fletch had anything up his sleeve on that day or not, and I still don't. But the combination of his suddenly poor execution and his reaction when I told him that Ed wanted him back into the game gave me reason to pause. Fletch was still a kid at heart, and a genuinely compassionate kid at that. But would he intentionally mess up so that Jimmy could get playing time? How well Fletch and Jimmy knew each other was unknown to me, and with one being from Texas and the other from Florida, I doubted they had much history together. But the players on the team had a unique, common bond; their deafness and their support of one another had always been demonstrably strong. So I simply couldn't dismiss the possibility that Fletch might actually be doing something to get his teammate playing time during the season finale, with or without Jimmy knowing about it.

But out on the field, it sure looked like I might be onto his plan. Again, I never asked him about it, and he never volunteered to tell me, but his next two plays lead me to believe that I might have been right. On the first play of the drive, he dropped back to pass and had a receiver open in the middle of the cover two defense, right behind the middle linebacker. He had to see him because he was looking right at him. But instead of throwing the ball, he feebly tried to roll out to his left and was sacked for a loss. On the second play, Fletch should have handed the ball off to the running back, Daniel Alexander, but instead kept it and ran laterally down the line of scrimmage, almost as if he wanted a defender to tackle him. It was third down and thirteen yards to go with only about a minute left in the half.

"Put Jimmy in," barked Ed as he stared out onto the field with his arms folded across his chest, "now!"

I turned to Jimmy and patted the top of his shoulder pads with my open hand.

"Go!" I signed to him and pointed out to the field. "Go!"

Jimmy couldn't hear the intensity in my voice, but he must have seen it in my eyes. He began to sprint out onto the field, but hesitated for a moment to ask what play had been called. I pointed to my eyes, using both my index and middle fingers, and then to Brian, indicating that I wanted Jimmy to look at Brian for the play call. Jimmy gave me the thumbs up signal.

"Coach," I asked Ed, "do you want to call a timeout, get him settled?"

"No, I don't," Ed said. "Just run the play and hurry it up, the clock's running." He walked to within a few steps of me, scowling out from under the brim of his visor and onto the field. "You wanted your boy to get a chance to play, well, here it is. But if he throws an interception he's done. He'll never play another down again, I swear it."

You talk about a tough situation. Fortunately for Jimmy, he couldn't hear Ed, and in his excitement he didn't seem to feel the pressure that Ed had just cast upon him. Jimmy received the play call, composed himself about four yards behind the line of scrimmage in shotgun formation, and waited for the snap from Justin. I watched with great anticipation, as you might expect. It was a good snap. Jimmy took the ball to his shoulder and stepped back onto his left foot, looking down the left side of the field. He saw the outside linebacker sprint out into the flats, leaving the inside receiver, Jason, open in the seam, and underneath the safety. Zip! Jimmy stepped forward and delivered a guided missile right into Jason's chest for a fifteen yard completion and a first down.

Yes! I said to myself as I clenched my right hand into a fist. The players on our sideline raised their helmets above their heads and cheered Jimmy on in every way that they could.

As in high school football, when a college football team gains a first down, the referees blow their whistle to momentarily stop the clock. This allows the chain crew to move and reset the down and distance markers without any valuable time elapsing from the play clock. Once the markers are reset, the referee will again blow his whistle to start the clock and resume play. Among the benefits of our no-huddle offense was that during the short period of time that the clock was stopped, our players could rush to the line of scrimmage and look to Brian for the next play call. When the referee again blew the whistle to start the clock, the offense could immediately run their play, wasting no time.

"Why is he wearing a glove?" Ed screamed as turned toward me. "Why is he wearing a damned glove?"

I looked and saw that Jimmy was indeed wearing a receiver's glove on his right hand. I didn't know why and, to tell the truth, I hadn't noticed the glove before. And I don't know when the kid had the time to slip the glove on, either. Maybe his hand was cold. Maybe he felt that it provided a better grip and improved ball security. Or maybe he just thought that it looked cool. I didn't know.

"Coach," I said to Ed, "it's not his throwing hand."

"I don't give a shit! Get it off of him, now!" Ed yelled. "Who does he think he is, Jim McMahon?"

I was thinking it was more like Kurt Warner, but that didn't matter. I stepped a few yards out onto the field toward where Brian was standing, waving my arms in front of me to get Jimmy's attention. When he looked over at me, I signed for him to take the glove off.

"Why?" Jimmy signed back.

I signed again for him to take the glove off, but he hesitated to do so. Then he looked to my left where he saw Ed screaming and gesturing his disapproval of Jimmy's wardrobe accessory. Jimmy then understood why, removed the glove, and swiftly flung it in my direction. I picked the glove up from the grass and returned to the sideline. By now Ed was seething.

As I jogged off the field, I looked over to see the play call that Brian was signaling in to the offense. It was Trips Right, Irish, one of our five-step passing plays. I then looked out at the defense and got that sick feeling in my stomach. The kind of feeling you get when you suspect something is about to go horribly wrong? I loved the play, just not the call, not out of that formation, or against the defensive alignment that Juniata was showing to defend it.

Essentially, Jimmy was going to be lured into making a bad decision, especially if he read the movement of the defenders and not the coverage. Even if he read the coverage it would be a really tough pass to complete because the defenders had positioned between the quarterback and his receivers. The only realistic chance Jimmy had was to put the ball down the sideline and let his receiver try to win a "jump ball" situation. Even then, throwing it out of bounds wouldn't have been the worst thing that he could have done. Given that we hadn't practiced this play against a cover two zone, I could only hope that Jimmy had somehow run the play on Madden '07 and knew that it was okay to throw the ball out of bounds. But, did I dare challenge the call and ask Ed for a timeout? Looking at the redness on Ed's face, I thought not.

Once the ball was snapped, all I could do was watch as the play unfolded, and grimace. The outside receiver ran a nine yard slant while the middle receiver ran a wheel route behind him; in other words he ran toward the sideline and then up the field. The inside-most receiver ran a bubble route out into the flats behind the line of scrimmage, sort of a shallower wheel route. None of the routes were hard passes to make for the quarterback, but to whom and when could be a difficult decision, depending on how the defense reacted.

Jimmy looked over his right shoulder, scanning the movement of the players downfield. He saw the linebacker who was over the inside receiver drop straight back about eight yards, which took away the slant route across the middle. Jimmy saw the safety over the top turn and run with the wheel route. Nothing easy there, either. It all happened so quickly for him, too quickly. That's just the way it is for an inexperienced player at first--fast. And so Jimmy threw the football in the direction of the receiver that he figured had to be open, the receiver running the bubble route. And it was a nice, crisp, well delivered pass, too, right on target. Unfortunately for Jimmy, he didn't take into account the cornerback who hadn't moved, but instead remained at the line of scrimmage in his cover two area of responsibility. The defender put his hands up over his helmet and caught the ball with ease, intercepting Jimmy's pass.

After catching the ball, the cornerback raced down the sideline with it, passing directly in front of Ed en route to the end zone. Jimmy was in hot pursuit, and gaining ground, as the two players neared the goal line following a sixty yard dash. I saw Jimmy dive and grab for the feet of the cornerback, causing the Juniata player to fall to the ground with the ball. But it was too late. The referee raised both of his hands to signal that the player had crossed the goal line with the ball for a touchdown, an interception return of sixty-eight yards.

And like the first half of the game, Jimmy was done.

We trailed at the break by a score of 36-14. Although Ed ripped the team pretty good in the locker room at half-time, he didn't single out Jimmy, or even mention him for that matter. I did what I could to console Jimmy, but sometimes there's not a whole lot to say to a player that he doesn't already know or feel. This was one of those times. And though I'd have come to his defense, it wasn't necessary, as neither the players nor any coaches placed blame on Jimmy. Stuff like that happens.

Fletch returned to quarterback the offense for the remainder of the game. He managed to settle down and played marvelously in the second half. He completed fourteen passes for a little over two hundred yards, including five touchdown passes, a season high. JC and Kevin each hauled in a pair of those touchdown passes. The offense would go on to put thirty-eight points on the board against Juniata that day, the highest game total of the season against a collegiate foe.

The defense, on the other hand, Ed's defense, struggled mightily. They surrendered over three hundred yards of rushing to a team that hadn't put a running game together all year long. The starting running back for Juniata ran for one hundred eighty-seven yards on his own. And Coach Launtz's quarterback turned in a very good performance too, throwing for two-hundred eighty-two yards and three scores. All in all, Juniata's "anemic offense" amassed just under six hundred yards of offense for the game! Juniata had come up with a solution to their ball control issues, and put on a ball control clinic. Their offense converted thirty-three first downs and ran an incredibly high eighty-seven plays. It wasn't a pleasant way to end the season for our defense, which yielded a season high fifty-six points for the game. And it could have been worse.

With a little more than two minutes remaining in the game, both the home team crowd and the players on the Juniata sideline were celebrating what would be their first and only victory of the season. Their offense was on one final march to the end zone and had pushed the ball all the way down to our twenty yard line. Usually, at that point of the game, good sportsmanship would dictate that Juniata simply have its quarterback take a knee and run out the clock. Doing so wasn't only a gesture of good sportsmanship, but it was the practical thing to do since it would minimize the unnecessary risk of injury to players. And I'm sure Juniata's intent was to do just that.

But there was a little bit too much time remaining. Taking a knee on four consecutive downs would have left some time on the clock for us to run several pass plays ourselves, though I'm pretty sure that we wouldn't have. So the Juniata coach decided to run one more play, an off tackle running play. And at the conclusion of that one last play, the coach did indeed signal to his quarterback that he wanted him to take a knee. Out on the field, though, a player remained lying on the turf, face down and motionless. It was a Gallaudet player, defensive end, Javier Goodwin. And suddenly, the cheering crowd went eerily silent.

Javier was a sophomore defensive end from the U.S. Virgin Islands. He didn't have much experience playing football and thus was a reserve player behind the likes of Josh, Rusty and Michael Daze. He was a quiet kid and often kept to himself. I didn't really know much more than that about Javier. Plus, since he played defense, we'd never had much of an opportunity to get to know one another. Still, the sight of him lying face down on the ground and not moving was of deep concern to me, regardless of how well I knew him.

The Juniata offensive players on the field jogged off toward their sideline and took a knee, followed in suit by the remainder of their team. Our boys, for the most part, remained standing since Ed preferred it that way. In his opinion, taking a knee was little league stuff. Ed walked out onto the field, joining Jon and the Juniata trainers at Javier's side. As time passed, though, and the severity of Javier's injury became more and more a concern, the Gallaudet players eventually went to a knee too, one by one. They continued to sign amongst themselves, though, and their muddled grunts and throaty voices carried throughout the stadium in the brisk, late afternoon air.

At first, I thought they were being disrespectful of their teammate who lay injured on the field, and that perhaps they should have been focusing a little more on him. But, after looking across at the Juniata bench, I realized that our guys were just engaged in the same idle chatter that the Juniata players were. It was the same type of small talk that even I remembered taking part in as a player myself at such moments. The Juniata players kept their chatter to a whisper, though. The Gallaudet players didn't know what that meant.

Javier remained motionless, face down. He'd suffered an apparent neck injury, an injury that trainers and paramedics treat with the utmost concern and precaution. One such precaution is to not move the injured player until the exact nature of the injury can be determined. And so Jon and the Juniata trainers made sure that Javier remained in the prone position until the ambulance had made its way onto the field. Obviously, the most effective way to determine the exact nature of an injury is to have the injured party tell you what the problem is, as well as when and where there is pain. So of course, the first thing that the paramedics did was to begin asking Javier such questions. Jon had to deliver the sobering news that Javier couldn't hear them. And so they all began to brainstorm for a solution to the problem---in no rush to board him up.

So, what do you do if you're a paramedic trying to assist someone with an apparent neck injury and unable to respond to your questions because he is deaf? Hopefully, someone like Jon, a trained medical professional, is nearby to sign and interpret, right? But Javier *lay face down* with his hands by his sides, unable to see Jon's signing. Nor could Javier sign himself. Time seemed to pass so slowly as the team of medical people sought ways to assess Javier.

Finally, Jon called over to Brian, who lumbered out onto the field in front of us.

"Is he all right?" Brian asked Jon.

"We don't know for sure," said Jon. "But, we think it's his neck."

"How can I help?"

"Well, I have an idea," Jon said. "Can you put Javier's hand into your hand and try to sign with him that way?"

"I think so," said Brian.

Jimmy watched with me from the sideline and explained to me that what they were doing with Javier is how they taught blind people to sign. He'd attended The Florida School for the Deaf and Blind and was familiar with the technique. His mother was a teacher at the school and so he knew just how difficult the process was, and the extraordinary degree of patience that it required. For a moment, I thought of the old fellow back at Gallaudet, who was deaf and blind, the guy who jogged the track every day. That must have been how he learned to sign.

Brian looked tense, but determined, as he kneeled on the ground next to Javier. Ed kneeled as well, beside Brian, and put his hand on Brian's shoulder to offer emotional support.

"Let's give it a try," Brian said quietly as he gently lifted Javier's hand and pressed his own fingers into Javier's palm.

"Go easy now," said Jon. "Try not to rotate his arm or shoulder too much."

"Got it," said Brian.

With painstaking slowness, Brian communicated with Javier by forming the letter signs of the ASL alphabet within Javier's hand. Javier was able to reply to Brian in the same manner. And eventually, through Brian, Javier was able to provide the information that the paramedics needed to stabilize his neck, get him strapped to a board, and safely onto a stretcher. As Javier was placed into the ambulance for transport, the fans and the Juniata players stood and applauded him, though he couldn't hear them. Brian walked back toward our sideline, and as he did, he noticed that our own players were not applauding, but just collecting themselves instead---putting their helmets back on, adjusting their shoulder pads, and stretching out their legs after the long delay. There was a look of disgust on Brian's face. He wasn't happy.

"What? The other team claps for Javier and his own teammates don't?" he cried out. "That's embarrassing!" But, again, most of the boys didn't hear his appeal.

I'm not sure why they responded, or didn't respond, the way that they did. I don't think that it had anything to do with the deaf culture, but it could have. I mean, why applaud if you know that the person for whom you're applauding is unable to hear or acknowledge your applause? He certainly couldn't feel or sense the adulation in such a wide open venue. And although I rejected the notion that it was a matter of the guys not caring about their teammate, it was the opinion of some of the guys on the team, that many of their teammates were only concerned about themselves. Whatever the reason for the way they responded, it did feel a little embarrassing, like Brian said.

By the time that the ambulance finally left the field and exited the stadium, there had been a delay of about forty minutes. That's an eternity in the world of athletics. The referee gave the two teams a few minutes to prepare themselves before blowing his whistle to resume play, but it wasn't necessary. We knew that the game was over and that Juniata's quarterback was going to kneel a few times to run the remaining time off of the clock. It was an anti-climactic ending to an otherwise very entertaining college football game. The final score was indicative of such.

JUNIATA 56 GALLAUDET 38

The bus ride home was the quietest ride of the year. It had been a long, cold day and perhaps the weather had taken a little more out of the boys than usual. I didn't know. Maybe for some of them, it had sunk in that their season was over and that all of the team's hopes and expectations of playing NCAA football had come to pass. They had proven themselves to be worthy opponents on the collegiate gridiron, deserving of the respect and admiration of those throughout the college football world. Whatever the reason, there seemed to be a collective sigh of relief on the faces of the players as they grabbed their submarine sandwiches and chips before boarding the bus.

For me, well, I knew that I was ready for the season to be over. Not because I didn't like coaching the team or playing away games, but because I realized that it had been quite some time since I'd been the central figure in my own family, a role much more important than that of a football coach. And so as the buses left the campus of Juniata College, I looked back at the stadium and wondered if I had just coached my last collegiate football game.

With the engine of the bus humming along down the highway, I called home and spoke with my wife. She told me how well Mark had played in his team's playoff game earlier that evening. He'd injured his knee early in the second half while making a tackle, but soldiered on to finish the game. And although he and his team were enormous underdogs, they had battled the defending county champions to a 13-13 tie at the end of regulation. They lost, though, on a controversial play at the end of the third overtime period. That must have been some game. And I'd missed it, again.

Mary-Ellen handed the telephone to Mark and I told him that I was very pleased to hear how well he'd played and how proud I was of his brave effort. And I apologized, again, for missing yet another game. I'd hoped to see his team play in the next round of the playoffs, but it wasn't meant to be, as the loss meant that his team's season was now over. He told me how crushed the boys on his team were after the loss, but that his coach was very impressed by how they'd come together as a team to accomplish so much. How ironic, I thought, that his youth league team had been able to achieve a goal that in the end, we had not quite attained--team unity.

After the phone call, I turned off the small reading light that shone from overhead, and sat back into my seat next to the window of the bus. Outside, the street lights and porch lamps of small towns and homes passed by quickly in the night and it reminded me that life at my own home was also passing by quickly. In just a few short years I'd be fifty years old, well past half-time in the game of life, I thought. I knew that I had a decision to make regarding whether or not to continue coaching college football the following season. And so I turned that little overhead light back on and began to jot down the pros and cons of me coaching college ball. When I was done I surveyed the list. Not to my surprise, the cons outweighed the pros. What grabbed my attention, though, was that most of the pros were related to me, and most of the cons were related to my family. I sighed deeply, knowing that I was asking too much of my wife and family.

When our buses finally returned to the campus of Gallaudet, it was a little past the hour of ten o'clock and by then Ed had received word from Jon regarding Javier. He'd been treated and released by the hospital back in Pennsylvania, suffering a damaged nerve in his neck. Thankfully, Javier was expected to fully recover within the next few weeks. Jon, who had escorted Javier in the ambulance, was driving the two of them home in a rental car. After getting off of the bus upon our return, I set my bags aside and helped Jon's assistants carry their athletic training equipment from the bus to their training room in the basement of the field house. I handed Kris the bag of footballs and went home to my family.

When I pulled into our driveway, the only light in the house was that of the table lamp in the hallway foyer. Everyone inside was fast asleep. My wife heard me though when I pushed open the door to our bedroom.

"Good, you're home," she said as she squinted; the side of her head was pushed deep into her pillow. "Now I can go to sleep for the night," she smiled and closed her eyes.

"Ok, see you in the morning," I said quietly.

"Oh, can you check on the boys and walk Toto one more time, please?" she asked.

"Sure."

The door to their bedroom was also ajar, and I pushed it open and walked inside. Unlike their mother, they didn't hear me enter. They usually slept with a loud fan running on the floor near the foot of their bunk beds. Well, really, I'm not sure if the fan was actually at the foot of their bunk beds or not. That's because Tyler slept on the bottom bunk with his head at one end, and Mark slept in the top bunk with his head at the other. Either way, I looked across at Mark as he slept with his blanket pulled tightly up to his chin. Tyler, though, his bed linens were a mess. They were all over the place. So I grabbed his fleece blanket, which was bunched up against the wall along the side of his bed, and covered him up, tucking it in across his shoulders. He awoke briefly.

"Oh, hey, Dad," he said. "You're home?"

"Yeah, I'm home, buddy, I'm home," I smiled, though he'd already closed his eyes again.

"Ok, good," he murmured as he rolled over and went back to sleep.

I leashed the dog and led her down the driveway toward the streetlamp, as I always did. It wouldn't be long, however, before she'd find the light on her own, as she would pass away of natural causes a few weeks later. When she did, I was there to help the boys lay her to rest in our backyard.

*

A few days after the Juniata game, on Monday afternoon, Ed held our final team meeting in Room G 40. By the time I arrived, which was about fifteen minutes prior to the meeting, the players had already cleaned out their lockers and returned their gear to Kris in the equipment room. Several of them had shown up clean shaven and dressed in business suits. Bill Jacobs, Chester Kuschmider, and the Doudt brothers were quite dapper. But, those guys hadn't spiffed themselves up for the meeting. They planned to attend a fraternity event afterward.

I made an effort to thank as many of the players as I could for their efforts throughout the season, and the patience and courtesy that they had afforded me as I learned to sign. I told the offensive players that it had been a privilege for me to coach them. They didn't know if I'd be back to coach the following year or not. Then again, many of them probably didn't even know if they, themselves, would be back the following year. I think that's just the way it had been for them, people coming and going all the time. And so there weren't any extended goodbyes and long, drawn out farewells.

When I shook hands with Jimmy, though, I think he knew that I wouldn't be back. He had that melancholy look upon his face.

"You," I pointed directly at him, "are a good quarterback!"

"Thanks, Coach," he signed quickly and dipped his chin before looking back up at me.

"Don't let anyone tell you otherwise," I signed, sort of, "Ok?"

"Ok!" he returned the sign.

Ed could probably give a dozen reasons why he didn't want to use Jimmy at quarterback that season. But the bottom line was that he just didn't trust him. Several chapters back, I wrote about the players not trusting their coaches, and making mistakes on the field of play as a result. Well, in Jimmy's case, I think it was the coach who had trust issues and had made the mistakes.

In the hallway outside of Room G 40, a television reporter interviewed several of the players before the meeting, including Phil Endicott, Marty Blomquist, and Daniel Alexander. A cameraman filmed both the player interviews and Ed making his final speech to the team inside the classroom. Earlier, he'd filmed some of the players as they turned their in their equipment to Kris. The reporter told me that their crew had also been on campus for our last home game, the victory over SUNY Maritime, filming then as well. They were from the local Fox affiliate; they'd been preparing a story about the Gallaudet team and the school's official return to collegiate football. They said that they didn't know for sure when the story would air and I don't know that it ever did. I kept an ear out for several weeks, waiting to hear something about when it might be broadcast. But, *alas, I never heard a thing.*

Epilogue

Whenever the subject of me coaching high school football comes up during a conversation, regardless of wherever it is that I'm coaching, the person with whom I'm speaking will generally ask one of two questions, "Oh? Did you play football?" or "Really? Do you know so-and-so?" Of course, there may be an occasional rogue question here and there, but those two questions are definitely the most commonly asked. However, when people learn that I coached football at Gallaudet University, the first and only question that I've ever been asked is, "Do you sign?"

It's only natural, I guess. Coaching football at a deaf university has always seemed to be of great interest to whomever it is I'm speaking. The 2007 season would be my first and last at Gallaudet. I'd return to the high school sidelines the following year. It wasn't because I didn't enjoy my time coaching the boys at Gallaudet, because I did, and I still very much value that experience. I grew to admire and respect all of those young men, as athletes and as people. And I sincerely appreciate the respect that they, in return, showed to me as both a coach and a person. Much of their respect for me was demonstrated by the patience they showed me as I struggled to learn their language.

I left coaching at Gallaudet because of the extraordinary commitment of time and energy required to coach college football, even on a part-time basis. At my age, time and energy was at a premium with another full-time job, a wife, and two small boys at home. The nearer we got to the end of our season the more frequently players began to ask if I'd be returning to coach the following year. I conveyed to them the dilemma that I faced back home and the possibility that I might not be returning to Gallaudet. Although seemingly disappointed with the possibility that I might not return, the players each said that they understood my concerns, having been raised with a strong sense of family values themselves. They understood that all of the time I spent on the football field with them was time away from my own family, and time that I could never recapture.

And with my wife trying to juggle the responsibilities of raising two young boys pretty much alone, as well as working a full-time job herself, well, it just didn't feel right that I should be off somewhere coaching football. Even though I was paid to coach, it really wasn't about the money, which was only a few thousand dollars anyway. It was more about my family back home who I'd been neglecting. Even if I'd chosen to continue coaching at Gallaudet, the option of me doing so would have been at Ed's discretion, anyway, which maybe he would've, and maybe he wouldn't have wanted. I never bothered to ask, though.

So the following year I returned to the friendly sidelines of Severna Park High School. Of course the boys at the high school were very curious to know what it was like to coach at the collegiate level. But more so, they wanted to know the specifics of what it was like to coach deaf football players. One of my players even wrote an article in the school's newspaper about my coaching experience at Gallaudet. But it wasn't until a few seasons later that my most unique opportunity presented itself to talk about coaching at Gallaudet.

It was during the afternoon session of our team's first day of practice in August of 2011. I walked over to a tree shaded hill at the far end of the practice field to greet a few parents. Parents of freshmen players often like to watch their boy's first few days of high school football practice. Doing so from that hill gave them a great vantage point, plus it was the only cool, shaded area around. As a coach, I'd typically go out of my way to make the trip over to welcome them to our program. My greeting was generally the same year in and year out.

"Which of those boys out there do you folks care to claim?" I'd ask.

This year there were about a dozen or so parents standing on the hill and they began to introduce themselves to me. Some went through the process of trying to point their son out from among the forty or fifty freshmen, all dressed in white football attire. If I heard the last name I usually knew who the player was; I was pretty good with names and faces. But I didn't hear the last name of the player whose dad seemed to be going to extra lengths to point out his son.

"I'm sorry, what is your son's name?" I said.

The man didn't reply, but just tried harder to direct my attention toward his boy out on the field. Eventually, he gave up and used his elbow to nudge the woman standing by his side, his wife. She excused herself from a conversation that she was engaged in with another mother.

"Yes," she said to the man. "What do you need, dear?"

The man began to sign to his wife. He was deaf.

"I'm sorry, Coach," she said. "My husband is deaf and he was just trying to tell you that our son is Max. Max Windham."

I smiled.

"Nice to meet you," I signed to Mr. Windham. "My name is Coach Overmier."

"Oh, how wonderful!" she said. "You sign?"

I signed to them that I'd coached football at Gallaudet several years earlier and that I had learned the basics of sign language.

Then I apologized for not being very adept at it, especially when it came to interpreting fluent signers like her and her husband.

"Don't worry about it, Coach," she said. "He's reading your lips anyway."

That worked for me, and apparently for Mr. Windham, as well. Later, his son, Max, would tell me on several occasions that his father was very happy to finally be able to carry on a conversation with one of his son's coaches. The thing about communicating with Mr. Windham was that it didn't matter whether he was walking by the practice field, sitting in the stands, or out in the parking lot, I didn't have to worry about hearing him to know what he was trying to say.

And so it has been with my command of sign language since my year of coaching at Gallaudet. I can still use it a little to this day. It tends to come back to me, though, when the person with whom I'm signing helps me along, especially by reading my lips. You just can't be afraid to give it a try. It's not unlike taking a foreign language in high school, such as Spanish. If you don't practice it, you will lose command of it, although you might be surprised by just how much your brain has retained if you try to use it when you can. There are many opportunities these days to practice your Spanish, a lot more than I have to practice signing. But I don't miss out on the opportunity when given the chance.

*

The following season would be a difficult one for Coach Hottle and his Bison. They'd win just two of their ten games in 2008, yielding more than 300 points to opposing offenses during the course of the season. But it was the team's lackluster offensive performance that drew most of Ed's ire, scoring just a little more than ten points per game. Fletch began the season as the incumbent quarterback, but over the course of the year ceded playing time to Jimmy. Ed later replaced Ryan as offensive coordinator at the end of the season. Ryan returned to his hometown of Findlay, Ohio where he's employed as a financial advisor.

The year 2009, though, was a year of big changes for the Gallaudet football program. The school joined seven other colleges and universities to form a single sport, NCAA Division III athletic conference. It was to be the inaugural season of play for the Eastern Collegiate Football Conference. Chuck Goldstein, the team's new offensive coordinator insisted upon running the *triple-option offense*, the same offensive system that Ed considered to be garbage. Ed resisted at first, but begrudgingly gave in and allowed Goldstein to install the new offense. And Jimmy became the team's starting quarterback. The offense flourished, scoring more than twenty-four points per game and helping the Bison to a six win season. After the 2009 campaign, Ed Hottle left Gallaudet to become the first ever, head football coach at Stevenson University, just outside of Baltimore. Goldstein took over the reigns as the head football coach at Gallaudet.

Most, if not all, of the players from the 2007 team have either graduated or moved on from the school by now, though several remain on the campus as either teachers or employees of the university. Like all graduates of Gallaudet University, the boys from that team, who went on to earn a degree, received a very unique diploma. Because the university is a federally chartered institution, the President of the United States is the patron of the university, and every sitting president has signed the diplomas of Gallaudet graduates since Ulysses S. Grant in 1869. Since 2008 was an election year, some of the boys from that team received a diploma signed by George W. Bush, while others later received diplomas signed by Barack H. Obama.

The only coaches from the 2007 staff who remain with the program as of 2013 are Brian Tingley and Chris Burke. Brian continues to pursue a Master's Degree in School Counseling at Gallaudet. He also coaches the team's linebackers. Chris, also a linebacker coach, still works on campus as a technology advisor. Kerry Phalen still teaches Phys Ed down in Calvert County, and Ron Cheek remains a member of the university's grounds maintenance crew. Harold Catron is no longer associated with either Gallaudet or MSSD, but is a personal trainer in Northern Virginia. And I don't know exactly what became of Ron Luczak, the defensive line coach who worked as a risk management consultant for the housing lender, FREDDIE MAC. After the collapse of the nation's housing markets in 2008, it's possible, perhaps, that Ron simply got onto his motorcycle and headed off into the sunset.

As for some of the players, they took many divergent courses:

--Jason Coleman was the Gallaudet Male Athlete of the Year in 2007. He moved to the west coast and became the head football coach at the California School for the Deaf in Riverside, California. He married his long time girlfriend, Tamijo, who was the Gallaudet Female Athlete of the Year in 2007. They have two children, both deaf, and now live in Frederick, Maryland where JC is a physical education teacher at The Maryland School for the Deaf.

--Kevin Alley was the Gallaudet Male Athlete of the Year in 2008, an All-Conference level player in both football and baseball. He currently works as a fitness consultant and personal trainer in Northern Virginia. Kevin and his wife, Erica, who is a staff interpreter at Gallaudet, had a baby girl in 2012. She hears quite well.

--Justin Lathus, became a certified distributor of medicinal marijuana in the State of California. He later sold his two distributorships to become the Chief Operating Officer of THC Labs, a Cannibis Analysis Laboratory in Denver, Colorado.

--Josh Ofiu, still living in Anchorage, Alaska, continues to pursue a career in Mixed Marshal Arts, and has become known throughout the MMA circuit as "The Silent Monster."

--Rusty Nawrocki remains a world class Taekwondo artist, competing in both the 2009 and 2013 Deaflympics, held in Taiwan and Bulgaria, respectively. He and his girlfriend, Eleasha, were married in 2012 and together continue to have a steadfast love for The Lord. They reside in Washington, D.C. where Rusty teaches at The Model Secondary School for the Deaf.

--Jimmy Gardner eventually became the team's starting quarterback, despite the fact that Ed Hottle remained the head coach for the next two seasons. In 2009, he led the team's *triple-option offense* in both passing and rushing. He currently teaches at the Model Secondary School for the Deaf in Washington, D.C. and is the school's head football coach.

--Fletcher Kuehne returned to Austin, Texas where by most accounts, he is busy simply being "Fletch."

*

In the fall of 2009, I would spend an enormous amount of time on the football field. From two o'clock in the afternoon until six o'clock in the evening, I was on the practice field with the Severna Park High School football team. Thirty minutes later, I was at Cardinal Field in Crofton where I was also the head coach of Mark's twelve-year-old football team. We usually practiced until about 8:30 p.m. And, I also helped to coach Tyler's ninety-pound team. We had games on Friday nights, Saturdays, and often times, Sunday afternoons. We were a football crazy family, for sure, much to the chagrin of my wife, of course. But she enjoyed cheering on her boys, all of us. And for a change, football brought us all together, instead of sending us our separate ways.

2007 Gallaudet Bison Football Team Roster

1	Carey Heisey	LB	Fr	5'10"	186	Frederick, MD
2	Fletcher Kuehne	QB	Jr	6'1"	195	Austin, TX
3	Robin Shannon	DB	Sr	5'9"	165	Honey Creek, IA
4	Shawn Shannon	WR	Sr	5'7"	150	Honey Creek, IA
5	Jason Coleman	QB	Sr	6'3"	205	Frederick, MD
6	Andrew Zernovoj	WR	Jr	6'0"	210	Woodside, CA
7	Cole Johnson	WR	So	6'0"	175	Edina, MN
8	Martin Blomquist	DB	Jr	5'10"	170	Neptune, NJ
9	Jimmy Gardner	QB	So	6'0"	170	St. Augustine, FL
10	Chester Kuschmider	WR	Jr	5'9"	175	Olathe, KS
11	O'Dell Armwood	WR	Jr	5'8"	165	Bronx, NY
12	Rantz Teeters	LB	Jr	5'11"	245	Medina, OH
14	Paul Donets	DB	Jr	5'9"	177	Glenview, IL
15	Derrick Williams	WR	Jr	5'10"	150	Frederick, MD
17	Vladislav Yusupov	LB	Jr	5'9"	180	Rego Park, NY
18	Kevin Alley	WR	Jr	6'0"	185	Lebanon, OR
19	Allan Williams	WR	Fr	5'9"	185	Albuquerque, NM
20	John Hurlburt	RB	So	5'10"	185	Elgin, IL
21	Camillus Santiful	DB	Fr	5'10"	133	Annapolis, MD
22	Justin Wilson	DB	So	5'9"	175	Carmichael, CA
23	Willis Cook	DB	So	6'2"	195	London, OH
24	Chris Green	DB	Jr	5'6"	140	El Paso, TX
25	Daniel Alexander	WR	So	5'11"	190	Phoenix, AZ
27	Justin Grigsby	DB	Jr	6'0"	195	Phoenix, AZ
28	Scott Lehman	RB	Fr	6'0"	184	Frederick, MD
32	Michael Daze	DL	So	6'3"	210	Frederick, MD
33	Dima Rossoshansk	RB	So	5'10"	195	Chicago, IL
34	Pierre Price	RB	Fr	5'11"	180	Normal, IL
35	Gary Sidansky	DB	So	5'9"	150	Thousand Oaks, CA
38	Ben Taylor	DL	So	6'0"	200	Indianapolis, IN

40	Richard Bailey	LB	Fr	6'1"	240	Willingboro, NJ
41	Shannon Callahan	LB	Fr	5'9"	165	Shadyside, MD
47	Matthew Hamm	LB	Fr	5'11"	210	Irvine, CA
48	Calvin Doudt	LB	Jr	5'10"	220	Medina, OH
49	Joseph Scroggins	LB	Fr	5'11"	195	Little Rock, AR
50	Mike Harper	LB	Fr	5'9"	175	Wichita, KS
51	Eric Jindra	OL	Jr	6'0"	280	San Mateo, CA
52	David Morgan	OL	So	6'1"	250	Roanoke, VA
53	Josh Ofiu	DL	Fr	6'2"	235	Anchorage, AK
54	Richard Bauman	OL	Fr	5'6"	193	Hollywood, FL
55	Dominick Leto	OL	Sr	5'5"	230	Elmwood Park, NJ
57	Adam Tygart	LB	Sr	5'7"	175	Wayne, WV
58	Adam Brimmer	OL	Sr	5'10"	255	Indianapolis, IN
59	Justin Lathus	OL	Jr	5'11"	215	Chicago, IL
60	Ryan Barlongo	DL	So	6'0"	266	Hilo, HI
62	Phillip Endicott	OL	Sr	6'2"	250	Philadelphia, PA
63	David Uzell	OL	Fr	6'0"	205	Evanston, IL
64	Benjamin Bottoms	DL	Jr	5'10"	245	Chesterfield, VA
66	Bill Jacobs	OL	Jr	6'0"	235	Austin, TX
69	Brady Humphrey	OL	Fr	6'3"	210	Portland, OR
71	Nathaniel Eubanks	DL	Fr	6'2"	240	Cincinnati, OH
73	Tyler Kerger	OL	Jr	6'0"	250	Council Bluffs, IA
83	Roman Nawrocki	DL	Jr	6'2"	185	St. Augustine, FL
88	Charlie Palmer	OL	Fr	6'1"	200	Unadilla, NY
92	Daniel Dosemagen	DL	Fr	6'1"	326	Kenosha, WI
99	Javier Goodwin	DL	So	6'0"	205	St. Christian, U.S. VI

Jim Overmier is a native of Annapolis, Maryland. A former junior college quarterback, Jim began coaching high school football in 1996, after resigning his commission as an officer in the U.S. Air Force. In the summer of 2003, he launched Jim Overmier's Quarterback Academy, a private, quarterback training program for student-athletes who aspired to play the position at the high school level and beyond. He continued to coach high school football, at both public and private schools, until 2013, with the exception of one year: in 2007, Jim ventured into coaching collegiate football when he accepted the position of quarterbacks coach at Gallaudet University. It would become the most unique experience of his coaching career.

CPSIA information can be obtained
at www.ICGtesting.com
Printed in the USA
BVHW07s2052120918
527339BV00001B/4/P